SYDNEY ANGLICANISM
WORLD ANGLICANISM

Ashgate Contemporary Ecclesiology

Series Editors
Martyn Percy, Ripon College Cuddesdon, Oxford, UK
D. Thomas Hughson, Marquette University, USA
Bruce Kaye, Charles Sturt University, Australia

Series Advisory Board
James Nieman; Sathi Clarke; Gemma Simmonds CJ; Gerald West;
Philip Vickeri; Helen Cameron; Tina Beattie; Nigel Wright; Simon Coleman

The field of ecclesiology has grown remarkably in the last decade, and most especially in relation to the study of the contemporary church. Recently, theological attention has turned once more to the nature of the church, its practices and proclivities, and to interpretative readings and understandings on its role, function and ethos in contemporary society.

This new series draws from a range of disciplines and established scholars to further the study of contemporary ecclesiology and publish an important cluster of landmark titles in this field. The Series Editors represent a range of Christian traditions and disciplines, and this reflects the breadth and depth of books developing in the Series. This Ashgate series presents a clear focus on the contemporary situation of churches worldwide, offering an invaluable resource for students, researchers, ministers and other interested readers around the world working or interested in the diverse areas of contemporary ecclesiology and the important changing shape of the church worldwide.

Sydney Anglicans and the Threat to World Anglicanism
The Sydney Experiment

MURIEL PORTER
University of Melbourne School of Historical and Philosophical Studies, Australia

ASHGATE

© Muriel Porter 2011

All rights reserved. No part of this publication may be reproduced, stored in a retrieval system or transmitted in any form or by any means, electronic, mechanical, photocopying, recording or otherwise without the prior permission of the publisher.

Muriel Porter has asserted her right under the Copyright, Designs and Patents Act, 1988, to be identified as the author of this work.

Published by
Ashgate Publishing Limited
Wey Court East
Union Road
Farnham
Surrey, GU9 7PT
England

Ashgate Publishing Company
Suite 420
101 Cherry Street
Burlington
VT 05401-4405
USA

www.ashgate.com

British Library Cataloguing in Publication Data
Porter, Muriel.
 Sydney Anglicans and the threat to world Anglicanism : the
Sydney experiment. -- (Ashgate contemporary ecclesiology)
 1. Anglican Church of Australia. Diocese of Sydney--
History. 2. Anglican Church of Australia. Diocese of
Sydney--Influence. 3. Anglicans--Australia--Sydney
(N.S.W) 4. Women in the Anglican Communion--Australia--
Sydney (N.S.W.) 5. Sydney (N.S.W.)--Church history.
 I. Title II. Series
 283.9'441-dc22

Library of Congress Cataloging-in-Publication Data
Porter, Muriel.
 Sydney Anglicans and the threat to world Anglicanism : the Sydney experiment / Muriel Porter.
  p. cm. -- (Ashgate contemporary ecclesiology)
 Includes bibliographical references and index.
 ISBN 978-1-4094-2028-6 (hardcover) -- ISBN 978-1-4094-2027-9 (pbk.) -- ISBN 978-1-4094-2029-3 (ebook) 1. Anglican Church of Australia. Diocese of Sydney. 2. Conservatism--Religious aspects--Anglican Communion. I. Title.
 BX5712.S93P67 2011
 262'.039441--dc22

2011015691

ISBN 9781409420286 (hbk)
ISBN 9781409420279 (pbk)
ISBN 9781409420293 (ebk)

Printed and bound in Great Britain by the
MPG Books Group, UK

Contents

Foreword		*vii*
Preface		*xiii*
1	Introduction	1
2	Anglicanism in Sydney Today	9
3	Sydney Anglicans: How It Came to This	29
4	Tensions: Sydney and the Anglican Communion	51
5	Tensions: Sydney and the Australian Church	77
6	Women: Equal but Different	113
7	Current Challenges	135
	Conclusion: The End of the Experiment?	163
Select Bibliography		*165*
Index		*169*

Foreword

It is easy to mock fundamentalism. Just consider the humour that surrounds the phenomenon. For example, a fundamentalist pastor goes on a cruise of the South Seas. In the course of the voyage, a storm brews up, the ship sinks and all hands are lost – except the pastor. When a passing ship spots him years later, the rescue party are surprised to discover he has built two churches. Naturally curious, they ask why. 'Easy', he replies, 'here's the one I go to, and there's the other one I most certainly don't.' In a variant of the joke, two fundamentalist pastors later get washed up on the same island, and when they are rescued, two churches have also been built, each pastor having founded their very own international outreach ministry. Or consider the apocryphal story of the liberal Episcopalian church in the USA that puts up a sign outside their church proclaiming 'there ain't no hell'. The Southern Baptist church replies with their own poster: 'the hell there ain't'.

But what has any of this to do with Sydney Evangelicals, which is the subject of Muriel Porter's perceptive analysis in this book? The first thing to say, perhaps, is that the term, 'fundamentalism' is arguably so broad and pejorative as to be almost useless; it has become a term that can be applied too loosely, and generally unflatteringly. Nevertheless, in connection with religion, the word still carries weight as a signifier of attitude, temperament, doctrine and ideology. True, the use of the term is diverse and fissiparous. It can be linked to religious extremism within nationalist movements in almost any world faith. The second thing to say is that Muriel Porter writes with a purpose that connects with this first observation. Her intention in this volume is to alert the Anglican Communion to the risks that the Diocese of Sydney might pose to worldwide Anglicanism. Such risks include an explicit agenda to convert the world, and starting with Sydney, to a fundamentalistic-Puritanical style of Anglicanism. This is, of course, not just a movement with a fundamentalistic theological agenda. It is a cultural movement too, that seeks to set a certain type of tone in ecclesial life, and in wider society.

Historically, and in terms of Christianity, fundamentalism is a recent movement, opposed to 'the mixed offerings of modernity'. It takes its name from *The Fundamentals*, a series of pamphlets issued in the USA between 1909 and 1916, which sought to argue for and reassert conservative views on doctrine. A world conference on fundamentals was subsequently convened in Philadelphia in 1919, in reaction to liberally inclined theology. In part, this precipitated the formation of the Southern Baptist Convention. But fundamentalism has also spawned countless seminaries, ministries and new denominations. In one sense, each of these might be said to be linked by a single strand of DNA; one composed of fear (of the polluting culture of the world, and its power to corrupt true or revealed religion) and aggression (that without resistance and fighting, real religion will be overwhelmed). The fear-aggression dynamic is at the heart of even the most innocent ecclesial spats on, say, gender or sexuality.

As Muriel Porter shows, such concerns are to be found amongst Sydney Anglicans: flight, fright and fight combine to produce a powerful faith. But how can one portray and analyse Sydney Anglicans? An obvious observation, perhaps, is that characterization might have some weight; but caricature should be avoided. Porter's study is careful to avoid the latter, and seeks to narrate the Sydney Anglican movement as a complex phenomenon, with patterns of behaviour and forms of belief that show it to be *fundamentalistic* without actually being an obvious and identifiable form of fundamentalism. The difference is crucial. The sheer breadth of fundamentalism makes it a difficult movement to characterize. Indeed, because it is not one movement, but rather a term that describes diverse forms of behaviour, belief and practice that are widespread, extreme caution should be observed in using the word at all.

Nevertheless, the attributes of fundamentalistic behaviour and belief do have character and form. Martin Marty and Scott Appleby have suggested that there are nine such characteristics.[1] Five of these are ideological in outlook: a reaction to the perceived marginalization of religion; selectivity of religious essentials and issues; moral dualism; a commitment to an inerrant scripture and a tendency towards absolutism; millennialism and 'messianic' interests. The remaining four characteristics are organizational: an 'elect' membership (i.e. an elite, whose identity is clear); sharp delineation of boundaries (e.g. 'saved' and 'unsaved', 'church' and 'world', etc.); authoritarian and charismatic leadership (i.e. anointed leader, guru, etc.); and behavioural requirements (e.g. abstinence, etc.). The vast majority of the expressions of fundamentalism from within the 'Abrahamic' faiths exhibit these characteristics. Many expressions of fundamentalism that fall outside this category also share most if not all of these characteristics. In a slightly different vein, Martin Marty sees fundamentalism almost entirely as a matter of 'fighting'. He also notes how the mindset is reliant on control and authority. Somewhere in this characterization, Sydney Evangelicals can be located.

We can summarize these characteristics in the following way. First, fundamentalism is a movement that engages in 'backward-looking legitimation': the answer to present crisis, whatever it may be, is deemed to have been revealed in the past. Second, fundamentalism is always dialectical: it must exist in opposition to something. (Take liberalism away, and fundamentalism has no *raison d'être*.) Third, fundamentalism is a tendency: a habit of the heart or mind more than it is necessarily a specific creed. Fourth, fundamentalism is trans-denominational, trans-religious as well as being sectarian: it is a widely disseminated and pervasive outlook. Fifth, fundamentalism is cultural-linguistic: believers are offered a 'sacred canopy' under which to shelter from the threats of modernity, pluralism, and other movements or issues that are held to be deleterious and detrimental towards the

---

[1] Martin Marty and Scott Appleby (eds), *Fundamentalisms Observed* (Chicago, IL: University of Chicago Press, 1991).

purity of the faith. Fundamentalism offers to its adherents a near-complete 'world' that can be developed to take on other world-views.

That said, a common misconception about fundamentalism is that it is simplistic. On the contrary, and as Porter shows in this study of Sydney Anglicans, the structure of fundamentalistic thinking is, far from being simple and clear, in fact highly complex, differentiated, accommodating and fluid. Exegesis (i.e. reading meaning 'out of' a text), eisegesis (i.e. reading meaning 'in to' a text), interpretation and exposition abound. The Bible can function almost totemically in Sydney Anglican churches.

But bearing in mind that for such communities, authority flows *from* the inerrancy of scripture (which is to say that ecclesial and ministerial authority is regarded as being *under* the Word), the patterns of authority and teaching in such communities will vary widely. Where there are similarities between them, they may be morphological rather than doctrinal (in other words a matter of style, not substance). The role of women in faiths and society is an arena where fundamentalistic views can be tested and studied comparatively. In Protestant Christian fundamentalism, or forms of ecclesial polity such as Sydney Anglicanism, members will not regard women holding spiritual authority or office to be either appropriate or biblical. A fundamentalistic outlook tends to assign an apparently 'traditional' role to women – as wife, mother and homemaker. Invariably, the roles assigned to women are traced back to (apparent) scriptural norms, but this can lead to some peculiar anomalies. Some will go further, and argue that the maleness of Christ reveals an absolute truth about appropriate representation in leadership. Amongst Sydney Anglicans, women will have limited roles in leading churches, and few opportunities to exercise any kind of ordained ministry.

Yet at the same time, it cannot be said that all forms of fundamentalism absolutely and necessarily resist modernity. Fundamentalists – in all their manifest variety – are remarkably adept at accommodating the world in order to achieve their higher religious, political and social purposes. Thus, whilst some may decry the influence of the media or the internet, it is precisely in such arenas that fundamentalists are also to be found at their most active. Fundamentalism, in other words, does not simply resist modernity; it also engages with it – radically – in order to achieve the restoration of a 'purer' form of faith that will provide a credible alternative to secularity. Fundamentalism therefore continues to be a diverse but pervasive spiritual force within most societies at the beginning of the twenty-first century.

So at this point, and before concluding, let me offer three remarks on the politics of fear, fundamentalism and the life of the Anglican Communion, and Muriel Porter's prescient study of Sydney Anglicans. Clearly, Christian tradition and the scriptures hold important keys to resolving the disputes that currently wrack the church. But I would expect the wider Anglican Church to take account of three issues at this point.

First, the Bible (or Holy Scriptures – and yes, note the plural) is a consequence of Christianity, not its cause. Whilst all orthodox Anglicans are entirely committed to upholding the authority of the Bible, it has to be read with care and discretion, and, crucially, interpreted. Christians do not disagree about what the Bible says so much as what it means, and what kind of weight to attach to the different passages, and their many nuances. Sydney Anglicans have, as Porter shows, found a way of reading and interpreting scripture that is particular to their cultural logic, and the challenges they believe they face, yet is unmistakably a tight form of hermeneutical control that shapes and delimits the polity of the movement. The scope for breadth and diversity is severely limited, because a variety of interpretations of scripture would lead to a dilution of the concentrated power of that polity.

Second, it is true that some Christians believe that scripture has come from heaven to earth in an unimpaired, totally unambiguous form. In such a view, there is no room for doubt; knowledge replaces faith. Scripture is utterly authoritative: to question the Bible is tantamount to questioning God. But to those who believe that scripture is a more complex nexus of writings, the authority of scripture lies in the totality of its testament. Thus, the Bible does indeed contain many things that God may want to say to humanity (and these are to be heeded and followed). But it also contains opinions about God (even one or two moans and complaints); it contains allegory, parables, humour, histories and debates. In other words, the very nature of the Bible invites us to contemplate the very many ways in which God speaks to us, which are open to a variety of interpretations. The Bible is not one message spoken by one voice. It is, rather, symphonic in character – a restless and inspiring chorus of testaments, whose authority rests upon its very plurality.

Third, the Bible is not necessarily clear on matters such as homosexuality (or, by the way, the grammar and rules for heterosexuality). True, we have translations that seem to suggest the very opposite of this, but such translations are themselves (in part) 'culturally produced'. We also have to bear in mind that there are many forms of observance that the New Testament urges upon us, to which we now pay little attention. Many Christians do not think twice about taking out a mortgage (collusion with usury). For Anglicans, including those from Sydney, the key question in relation to the use of the Bible is this: is scripture, assuming it can be established that its meaning is plain and clear (two different things), always right about all things moral and cultural? If the answer to this question is 'yes', then there is very little scope for any debate to be had about same-sex relationships and other areas of fierce moral contention. But working on the assumption that most agree that scripture is not always obviously 'plain' – that is to say, Anglicans need to focus less on what the Bible says, and more on what it means – Anglicans have an obligation (and indeed vocation) to look together for the common purposes of God as they are revealed in scripture, tradition and the world today.

Paula Nesbitt (an American sociologist of religion), in her reflections on the Lambeth Conference of 1998, has sketched how the Anglican Communion has been largely unable to avoid being gradually bifurcated: caught between increasing cultural diversity on the one hand, and the need to provide coherence and identity on the other. She notes how successive Lambeth conferences have moved sequentially from being grounded on traditional authority (i.e. the establishment of churches and provinces during the colonial era), to rational authority (which presupposes negotiation through representative constituencies for dominance over meeting outcomes), to (finally) negotiated authority (but which normally lacks the power to stem the momentum of change).

Nesbitt notes that these kinds of authority, when pursued through the four 'instruments' of unity in the Anglican Communion, are usually capable of resolving deep disputes. They enable complex inter-action and conversation, but they do not lead to clear and firm resolutions. Correspondingly, Nesbitt argues that a new, fourth authoritative form has emerged within the Anglican Communion, which has in some senses been present from the very beginning, and is now tied up with the identity of scripture. She writes of this authority:

> [it] could be used to countervail the relativism of cross-cultural alliances without affecting their strategic utility: symbolic authority. The symbol, as a locus of authority, has a tangible and timeless nature. Where the symbol is an authoritative part of the institutional milieu, either traditional or rational authority must acknowledge its legitimacy ... scripture is an authoritative symbol ....[2]

Nesbitt points out that the symbolic authority of sacraments may create shared bonds and enhance communal cohesion, but they are normally unable to regulate or negotiate conflict. But in contrast,

> Scripture, when canonized as complete or absolute, becomes symbolic of a particular era or set of teachings and beliefs.[3]

She continues:

> However, unlike sacraments, the use of scripture as symbolic authority can be constructed and constituted according to selecting those aspects or passages that address an issue at hand. Furthermore, scripture as symbolic authority can be objectified or absolutized, which transcends cultural boundaries in a way that other forms of authority can less easily do. The appeal of scriptural literalism provides an objectification of authority that is independent of the influence or control of dominant perspectives, social locations, and circumstances. As symbolic authority, it can be leveraged against cultural dominance as well as provide common ground for cross-cultural alliances ....[4]

In other words, with scripture raised almost to the level of apotheosis, a cross-cultural foundation for authority exists that can challenge the dominance of

---

[2] Paula Nesbitt, *Religion and Social Policy* (Lanham, MD: AltaMira Press, 2001), p. 257.
[3] Ibid., p. 257.
[4] Ibid., p. 257.

rational authority, which is normally associated with highly-educated elite groups from the West or First World. Scripture, given symbolic authority, becomes an important tool in the hands of Southern (non-elite) Christians who are seeking to counter-legitimate more Conservative perspectives.

As Nesbitt notes, 'scriptural literalism as symbolic authority represents the easiest and most accessible form of counter-legitimisation across educational or cross-cultural divides'.[5] And as Lambeth Conferences, like the Anglican Communion itself, have become increasingly diverse in their cultural expression, symbolic authority has risen to the fore. So at present, the only contender for being a focus of symbolic authority is the Bible, since cross-cultural negotiation only leads to sterile relativism: and so long as this situation continues, the dominance of groups like Reform within the Church of England looks set to continue.

We should note that the only other alternative to the Bible – the Communion itself becoming or attaining the status of symbolic authority – has so far failed, mainly because the very resourcing of that requires a looser, more elastic view of truth-claims, and a necessary tolerance towards competing convictions. Typically, those who press for the Communion as a natural focus for symbolic authority tend to be Liberal Catholic.

But the apparent lack of clarity that this aspect of the Anglican tradition embodies is largely unacceptable to Conservative Evangelicals (and certainly to fundamentalists), and as Porter shows, to most Sydney Anglicans. So could it be, then, that a scripturally-based polity is set to triumph over one that configures itself through a theological trilateral (i.e. scripture, tradition, reason) or quadrilateral (i.e. scripture, tradition, reason and culture/experience), or through the actual Communion itself? At present it is hard to make easy predictions.

The Bible, not unlike a sophisticated computer, can only give an answer that is proportionate to the nuance and sophistication of the question it is asked. The current problem in the sexuality debate is that Anglicans have yet to learn to be more deeply demanding of the scriptures. The present moment of crisis in the Communion lies not so much with the answers Anglicans have found as with the questions we have yet to ask. So, Porter's prescient study poses questions of Sydney Anglicans that must be asked in all parts of the Anglican Communion. How shall we read the scriptures as a body? And as we read, mark and learn together – and fumble for those elusive forms of coherence, complementarity and communion – how shall we continue to live together?

Revd. Canon Professor Martyn Percy
Ripon College Cuddesdon, Oxford

---

[5] Ibid., p. 257.

Preface

This book is written at a time of crisis in the relationship between Sydney Diocese and the rest of the Anglican Church in Australia and elsewhere. Sydney Synod has very recently defied the Anglican Church of Australia's highest court, the Appellate Tribunal, over its decision that an earlier Sydney Synod resolution allowing deacons to preside at Holy Communion is unconstitutional.[1] In response, the Synod has repeated its claim that deacons may indeed preside, arguing that the Tribunal's decision, technically an opinion, is merely 'advisory' and thus able to be ignored. In defying the Tribunal in this way, it can be claimed that the diocese is effectively turning its back on the national church constitution which, it has been argued at the highest level, treats Tribunal opinions as binding on members of the church.[2] How this stand-off can be resolved is pressing hard on the national church leadership. How Sydney's position on such a controversial matter as diaconal (and lay) presidency will be viewed in the wider Anglican Communion is also troubling some of those leaders, who fear it might tarnish the national church's status. Will the Australian church now be treated as a renegade church, in the way that the Anglican churches in North America are currently being shunned by conservatives for their acceptance of gay bishops and same-sex unions? This unprecedented stance by Sydney Synod is the culmination of the diocese's steady movement away from mainstream Anglicanism into a radical conservative Protestant congregationalism over the past half century. A study of Sydney Diocese in the context of its national and international relationships, and how the current situation has come to pass, is both timely and important.

Writing a critique of the Anglican Diocese of Sydney gives me no pleasure. Though I have lived outside Sydney since the mid-1970s, I am a child of the diocese, baptized and confirmed in one of its parish churches and married in another. I have fond memories of my Sydney Anglican childhood, teen and young adult years, but I am pained by what my first diocese has now become. It is not the diocese I knew in the 1950s and 1960s.

---

[1] Sydney Synod Resolutions 16 of 2010 and 27 of 2008; Appellate Tribunal 'Report to Primate on Reference on the Legality of the Administration of Holy Communion by Deacons or Lay Persons', 10 August 2010. In Anglican polity, only persons ordained as priests may preside at the central Christian service of Holy Communion. Allowing deacons or lay people to take this role is highly controversial.

[2] Justice Keith Mason AC, 'Believers in Court: Sydney Anglicans Going to Law', The Cable Lecture 2005, delivered at St James' Church, King Street, Sydney, 9 September 2005, p. 14. Mason, a member of the Appellate Tribunal and formerly a member of Sydney Synod, was, until his recent retirement, President of the New South Wales Court of Appeal.

My first parish was a fairly typical low-church Sydney suburban parish of the time. I attended Sunday school, sang in the choir, was a member of the youth group, and spent much of my childhood with the Rector's children, who were my friends. For the current Archbishop of Sydney, Peter Jensen, the Anglicanism that flourished in 1950s Sydney was 'lowest common denominator Christianity', a religion concerned with behaviour rather than belief. 'The ranks of church-goers were swollen with the unsaved', he has said.[3] That was not my experience nor, I suggest, that of most other Anglicans in that time and place.

In the 1950s and '60s, the parish I attended was a place of excellent preaching and teaching, dignified liturgy, high-quality music, energetic children's and youth ministry, generous pastoral care, and loving engagement with the wider community. Attendance was strong and diverse. My parish was not unusual. Anglican parishes in the surrounding middle-to-working class suburbs were very similar. Were these parishes filled with the 'unsaved', led by clergy concerned to inculcate appropriate patterns of behaviour rather than to preach the Gospel? Not in my experience. As a cradle Anglican now on the wrong side of middle-age, having spent my entire life as a regular worshipper in a number of parishes in various parts of Australia and in England, and having been closely involved in church life at diocesan and national levels for more than 25 years, I can confidently assert that Sydney parishes of the 1950s were exceptionally good. Their clergy and congregations were as committed to the Gospel, and to being a part of mainstream Anglicanism, as any I have known.

Archbishop Jensen's very different perception of the Sydney Anglicanism of half a century ago is a striking indicator of the enormous changes that have occurred in Australia's largest Anglican diocese over that time. In short, Sydney Diocese no longer reflects mainstream Anglicanism in terms of its parish life, worship or leadership because it now wears the (modern) face of sixteenth-century English Puritanism. Now at the heart of the diocese is an extremely narrow understanding of Christian belief, a version of the Gospel so limited that it no longer accords with the understanding of most other mainstream Christians or indeed with the Gospel I heard preached in my Sydney childhood. Like its Puritan forebears, Sydney is in no doubt that its version is the only right one. Further, Sydney Diocese is now so certain that everyone else's views are wrong that it believes its God-given mission is to impose its version of the truth on others, in the rest of Australia and in the worldwide Anglican Communion. This is what makes the changes that have occurred in Sydney over the past half century, and the current crisis in particular, so serious.

This book is an expanded, revised and updated version of my earlier publication, *The New Puritans: The Rise of Fundamentalism in the Anglican Church* (Melbourne: Melbourne University Publishing, 2006). I am grateful to Melbourne University Publishing for reverting to me full volume rights in *The*

---

[3] Peter Jensen, 'Build on the Past, Seize this Moment, Create the Future', address to the Anglican Church League annual synod dinner, 9 October 2000.

New Puritans, allowing me to revisit this subject and to reproduce some parts of the earlier book here, in particular the historical overview of Sydney Diocese and portions of chapters on the diocese's attitudes to women in ministry, lay presidency and homosexuality. There is, however, much that has been updated, for a great deal has happened since 2006. Sydney has become a powerful player in what has been called a conservative alternative Anglican Communion; Australia has two women bishops following a constitutional interpretation that angered Sydney Diocese; deacons have been allowed to celebrate Holy Communion, a highly-controversial practice; and the diocese has suffered catastrophic financial losses that will have a big impact on its future operations. I believe I have to write this updated critique of Sydney Diocese because the events of the past few years have persuaded me of the importance of alerting the wider Anglican world to the danger to mainstream Anglicanism that the diocese's ideology poses.

As with the earlier book, I am obviously not able to report on Sydney objectively and even-handedly. Impartiality would be impossible for me, given my participation in national church affairs and in particular, some of the key issues that involve Sydney, such as the ordination of women debate. The debate around these issues has often been highly polemical on both sides, given that they involve deeply important convictions. I have sought to set out the issues and arguments as clearly and fairly as possible so they will be readily accessible to a wider international audience, grounding my commentary in diligent research and careful analysis. My analysis is informed by my own close involvement in national church life for more than two decades, including my presence at a range of national and other meetings, and my collection of unpublished documents and notes.

I write from the perspective of a Sydney-born Anglican insider, who nevertheless looks in on Sydney Diocese from the outside. As an Anglican laywoman, I have been closely involved in the operations of the national church for more than two decades, as noted, and most particularly and publicly as an advocate of the full equality of women in the church. None of those experiences gives me insider knowledge about the deep internal workings of this complex diocese, however, though they have given me the journalistic tools of good contacts and a sound working knowledge of the sources and issues concerned. But I cannot write from the perspective of someone physically (or spiritually) inside Sydney Diocese, nor am I privy to much of the internal political machinations that led directly to the triumph there of ultra-conservative forces. I have not employed the techniques of investigative reporting to attempt to remedy that lack. My aim, in summary, is to hold up a lens to Sydney Diocese, to show what the more-or-less public face of Sydney looks like to those who examine it closely from outside.

But who are 'Sydney Anglicans'? It is not easy to write about an amorphous collective. It would be far simpler to concentrate on one man, say Peter Jensen, the current archbishop and former principal of Sydney's Moore Theological College. But that would be neither fair nor accurate. Dioceses have cultures, like cities or political parties, parishes or schools. The cultures predate the current leaders and generally survive them. In the long term, the culture must bear some responsibility for the appointment/election of the leaders and the behaviour they manifest in office. Peter Jensen, who in so many ways seems to embody his diocese, would be a fascinating study in himself, but that is not what I am attempting here.

Of course not every member of Sydney Diocese, clergy or laity, shares in the views and mindset this book will explore; a minority of people who regard themselves nevertheless as loyal Sydney Anglicans are deeply saddened by their diocese's current stance. But the term 'Sydney' is convenient shorthand to describe Sydney Diocese in its official decision-making capacities. By the diocese's leaders, I mean not just the archbishop and assistant bishops, but the dominant ethos of its synod and the synod standing committee, as well as the theological heavyweights – generally teachers at Moore Theological College – who together define and refine the party line, its rationale and the tactics used to impose its ideology. Taken together they are a remarkably homogenous group. Nevertheless, I am not referring to specific individuals unless I actually name them. Though much of the subject matter in this book is obviously of special interest to worshipping Anglicans across the world, I hope it will also be of interest to a wider audience of people concerned about the growth of religious conservatism generally.

* * *

I owe much to many people – too many to name – within the Diocese of Sydney and in the wider Australian church for insights and reflections that have assisted my understanding greatly. In particular I pay tribute to those loyal Sydney Anglicans who love their church and their diocese, patiently serving it and praying for it, even as they agonize over what the diocese has become in recent times. Most of all, as always, I thank my husband Brian, a fine Anglican priest dedicated to the best in our church's tradition, who supports me unstintingly in my roles as laywoman, committee member, commentator and author.

Muriel Porter
Hon. Research Fellow
University of Melbourne School of Historical and Philosophical Studies
30 November 2010

Chapter 1
Introduction

Sydney Diocese is the largest and, until recently, the richest Anglican diocese in Australia. Beginning with the first white settlement in 1788 and created as a separate diocese in 1847, it currently has more than 715 active licensed clergy[1] and 267 parishes. In 2006, the year of the last national census and National Church Life Survey, Sydney had a weekly attendance of 56,996[2] in a city where 738,000[3] call themselves Anglican. Recent figures, based on parish returns which are not always reliable, suggest there are more than 76,000 'regular members' of Sydney parishes.[4] If this is correct, Sydney has up to three times the attendance rate of the second largest Australian diocese, Melbourne. It also has a third more clergy than Melbourne. So conservative in doctrine and ethos that it is sometimes described as fundamentalist, Sydney Diocese promotes its stance in the Australian national church with a missionary zeal and determination that other dioceses find hard to counter. So on the Australian Anglican scene, on any measure, Sydney Diocese must be regarded as highly significant.

But in the context of the worldwide Anglican Communion, this would normally count for little. Australia, with a population of about 22.5 million, is not a first-world power. It is a minor player on the global stage and is a long way from the northern hemisphere's centres of influence. The Anglican Church of Australia, with 3.7 million adherents (19 per cent of the population), the same number as those Australians who claimed no religion at the last census in 2006, is not even any longer the main Christian denomination in Australia. It was overtaken by the Catholic Church in 1986 and the gap between the two churches has widened since. The 2006 census recorded the Catholic Church with 5.1 million adherents, or 26 per cent of the population. So it is hard to imagine that any Australian diocese would be worthy of international notice.

---

[1] *The Australian Anglican Directory 2010* (Melbourne: Angela Grutzner, 2010). Archbishop Peter Jensen, in answer to a question during Sydney Synod on 13 October 2010, said that there were currently 588 clergy in 'ministry positions' in the diocese. Sydney's clergy are overwhelmingly male, with just 45 women licensed as deacons. Sydney does not recognize women as priests or bishops, having refused to adopt the 1992 General Synod legislation for women priests. The Anglican Church of Australia is effectively a federation of autonomous dioceses, leaving considerable leeway for dioceses to go their own way on many issues.
[2] National Church Life Survey 2006.
[3] Census 2006.
[4] *Southern Cross*, November 2010.

Yet in the first decade of the twenty-first century, under the leadership of Archbishop Peter Jensen, Sydney Diocese has become a force to be reckoned with in the Anglican Communion. As a leader of the alternative international Anglican movement focused in the Global Anglican Future (GAFCON) project, it has become what can only be described as a destabilizing influence. This is just the public face of its international influence, however, an influence that has been steadily and quietly expanding below the radar for several decades through the leadership of key Sydney people in a range of global ministry programmes.

Previously, the diocese had attracted the interest, even fascination, of well-informed Anglicans in different parts of the world because of its unique reputation as an extremely conservative, hard-line monolithic Evangelical centre. It was not viewed with concern, however, because it seemed to inhabit an isolated, inward-looking world of its own. Not any longer. Sydney diocesan leaders seriously began their public involvement with the wider Anglican world in the lead-up to the 1998 Lambeth Conference, as will be discussed more fully in Chapter 4. At that time, they joined forces with conservative American Episcopalians (Anglicans) to draw African and Asian conservatives into a coalition designed to defeat what they saw as liberalizing tendencies in the Anglican Church, particularly in North America. Their first major victory was the controversial decision of the 1998 Lambeth Conference to oppose the ordination of homosexual people and the blessing of gay partnerships. That decision, and its rejection by both the US Episcopal Church and the Anglican Church of Canada, has in recent years provoked the development of the alternative GAFCON movement, in which Sydney has taken a leadership role disproportionate to its size and status. Peter Jensen, though not one of the Anglican Communion's 38 Primates (national leading bishops), is honorary secretary of the GAFCON Primates' Council, while his diocese provides the secretariat for the GAFCON offshoot, the Fellowship of Confessing Anglicans (FCA). On his webpage, Archbishop Jensen claims he is 'recognized as a key leader in the worldwide Anglican Church' and notes that he 'was one of the organizers of the Anglican Future conference in Jerusalem in 2008'.[5] Plans for a second GAFCON meeting in 2012, announced recently, included approval for an expansion of the secretariat.[6]

Sydney's role is not just secretarial. Its diocesan budget funds provision of training programmes to GAFCON-aligned national churches in Africa and Asia sourced from the diocesan training college, Moore Theological College, among other things. Until the diocesan finances were hit by the 2008 global financial crisis, the total provision for the diocese's work outside Australia was of the order of $A345,000 a year. In the 2010 budget, that figure had been halved to $154,000, of which $40,000 was directed to GAFCON specifically. The further reduction in the diocese's income, announced at the 2010 Synod as the result of poor financial management, will no doubt reduce that figure even further.

---

[5] http://www.sydneyanglicans.net/ministry/seniorclergy/archbishop_jensen/profile.

[6] 'Oxford Statement of the Primates' Council November 2010 AD', www.gafcon.org.

Though the total amount allocated for work outside Australia has reduced, Sydney Diocese has had until very recently a level of discretionary spending that other Australian dioceses could only dream of. And this from a diocese that has for some years now refused to meet funding requests from the national church, and lately, issued veiled threats about its obligatory diocesan financial contribution. Sydney Diocese has for the past 15 years stopped giving any financial support to the Anglican Communion through the Anglican Consultative Council, the body through which funding is provided for the Lambeth Conference and the regular meetings of the Primates of the 38 autonomous national churches that make up the Anglican Communion.[7]

Its international influence reaches beyond the churches assisted through the GAFCON/FCA network. For some time it has moved into the heartland of the Church of England through its close ties with the conservative Evangelical movement, Reform. Similarly, there are links with conservative movements in the Church of Ireland, in the New Zealand church, in South Africa, and in the United States and Canada. A former Sydney priest, David Short – son of a retired Sydney assistant bishop – is a leader among dissident Canadian Anglicans. He has received strong overt support from his old diocese, and some look to him as a possible successor to Jensen. Sydney Diocese has also been closely involved in the formation of the breakaway Anglican Church of North America, with a leading lawyer from Sydney Diocese assisting in the drafting of the ACNA constitution.

The Ministry Training Strategy programme (MTS)[8] developed in the late 1970s by Archbishop Jensen's brother Phillip – now Dean of St Andrew's Cathedral, Sydney – when he was chaplain to the University of New South Wales, has spread across the globe. It boasts that it has been 'developed, copied, refined and implemented in many parts of Australia and the world'. It claims it has reached into Britain, France, Canada, Ireland (both north and south), Singapore, New Zealand, Taiwan, Japan and South Africa.[9] Effectively, over almost 20 years, it has exported a programme to recruit and train ultra-conservative Protestant ministers around the world.

MTS claims to be non-denominational, but the reality is that its current director, Ben Pfahlert, and its previous director, Colin Marshall, both studied at Moore College. Marshall, who retired from MTS in 2007, worked with Phillip Jensen at the University of New South Wales in developing the original programme. Its

---

[7] 'Synod Appropriations and Allocations Ordinance 2009', *Report of Standing Committee and Other Reports and Papers 2009*, p. 301; Archbishop Jensen response to question 21 asked at Sydney Synod, 19 October 2009.

[8] The Ministry Training Strategy (MTS) is a form of apprenticeship for potential clergy, whereby they spend two years as trainees under supervision in selected parishes and student ministries before moving into formal theological training. See Colin Marshall, *Passing the Baton: A Handbook for Ministry Apprenticeship* (Kingsford: Matthias Media, 2007).

[9] Ibid., back cover.

Anglican genesis and close continuing Anglican ties make the non-denominational claim technical rather than substantial. Certainly MTS has been the primary recruiting ground for all Sydney clergy, a pathway strengthened by Phillip Jensen's 2003 appointment as director of Ministry, Training and Development, the diocese's department for the training of clergy. For the past 20 years, Phillip Jensen has had considerable influence in the selection of Sydney clergy. Through these roles and his church-planting activities, his role is arguably more significant than his brother's more public role. Together, the brothers have had a disproportionate influence on Australian and world Anglicanism for close to two decades.

The influence of Sydney Diocese and its leaders is felt in various parts of the Australian church in a number of ways. Until the diocese's recent financial debacle, funding was directed to certain Sydney-friendly dioceses. There is close contact with clergy and lay leaders in the orbit of Ridley Melbourne, one of the two theological colleges in the Diocese of Melbourne. To the distress of the bishops of yet other, mostly Anglo-Catholic, dioceses Sydney has offered a process of 'affiliation' to so-called independent Evangelical churches in their territories, sometimes so placed as to be in direct competition with a bona fide parish of the diocese. Although the diocese has not formally 'planted' these churches outside its diocesan boundaries, they have often been seeded by individual Sydney parishes in a wave of cross-border incursions dating from the 1990s. Five of the seven affiliates are headed by clergy ordained in Sydney, while a sixth was ordained in the Sydney satellite diocese of Armidale in rural New South Wales. There are also independent church plants in other parts of Australia, not so far formally affiliated with Sydney Diocese, that nevertheless have close links to Sydney Diocese, again with their 'senior pastors' mostly drawn from the ranks of men trained and ordained in Sydney. The websites of these churches, all of whom claim no denominational affiliation, nevertheless present remarkably similar conservative doctrinal positions, consistent with the position of Sydney Diocese. Naturally, these church plants have caused tension with the dioceses and bishops concerned, who are disturbed by this 'missionary' spread into their territory.

Phillip Jensen has actively promoted church planting in other dioceses. In 2001, he devoted a major public address to the topic of church planting. Arguing that the Bible did not mandate that the world must be divided into parishes and dioceses, Jensen claimed that 'restricting our ministries to one side of a road or a river or some other such artificial barrier and boundary can only make sense when we have confidence that the people on the other side of the boundary are being offered the same gospel'. When the gospel was being denied to people on the other side of the boundary, 'our obligation as Evangelicals to all people will not allow us to remain silent', he said.[10] Behind this church-planting project lies the outrageous claim that the dioceses into which Sydney Anglicans have infiltrated

---

[10] Phillip Jensen, 'An Evangelical Agenda', address to the Anglican Church League dinner, Sydney, 26 October 2001.

are not preaching the gospel. This is deeply offensive, and hardly conducive to good relationships within the Anglican Church of Australia.

Perhaps even more troubling is the close Sydney link with the Australian Fellowship of Evangelical Students (AFES), now the predominant student Christian organization across Australian universities since the demise of the once-dominant Student Christian Movement and the decline of diocesan-funded university chaplaincies. AFES claims to employ more than 100 people in campus ministries in every Australian state and territory. Linked with the International Fellowship of Evangelical Students, it is supposedly independent of denominational affiliation. However, it would seem to be an outreach of Sydney Diocese in all but name.

Its headquarters are in the same building complex as Matthias Media, the publishing arm of Phillip Jensen's former parish, St Matthias', Centennial Park. The current AFES director, Richard Chin, is a graduate of Moore College; his immediate predecessors were Sydney Anglican clergy. Online teaching resources that AFES provides are almost entirely the work of a range of Moore College graduates, with numbers of resources provided by Phillip Jensen. There are close links with the Phillip Jensen creation, MTS, with both organizations sharing the same doctrinal statement. AFES also runs conferences for what it describes as 'outside organizations', predominantly 'Equip' conferences, according to its website. These conferences, including conferences designed to train women in subordinate ministries, have speakers drawn from both Moore College and St Matthias', Centennial Park. Not that Equip seems to be truly 'outside' AFES; they share the same postal address. This Anglican link is not surprising, given that the first president of AFES's predecessor, the Inter-Varsity Fellowship, was the then Archbishop of Sydney, Howard Mowll. However, observers outside the Sydney-Evangelical orbit are only now beginning to recognize that AFES seems to have become, in many respects, a Trojan horse for Sydney Anglican teaching around the country.

There is some evidence of increasing Sydney influence on the question of the ordination of women infiltrating dioceses which support women in church leadership, most notably Melbourne Diocese, and AFES is part of that.[11] AFES has also been named recently as a key factor in the spread of Sydney-style opposition to women in church leadership in other parts of the country, and not only in the Anglican Church but in Protestant churches such as the Churches of Christ. Parishes near university campuses are, according to anecdotal reports, particularly vulnerable to influxes of students converted by AFES who bring their newly-acquired conservative stance into parish life.

Tension levels, historically always simmering between the oldest Australian diocese and the rest of the national church, have recently increased markedly for reasons other than the Sydney church-planting and infiltration activities, as we shall discuss in Chapter 5. The ordination of women to the priesthood in the early

---

[11] Bishop Barbara Darling (Melbourne), 'Opportunities and Challenges Facing Women in Practical Ministry', an address given to Melbourne curates on 15 June 2010.

1990s in the vast majority of Australian dioceses, but not Sydney, caused inevitable strains, but the consecration of women bishops in Perth and Melbourne in 2008 ramped up the tension significantly. This is mainly because of the means by which women bishops became possible. The previous year, the highest Anglican church court, the Appellate Tribunal, cleared the way for women bishops through an interpretation of the church's constitution. The constitution's basic qualifications for bishops ('canonical fitness') applied equally to women priests as to male priests, the Tribunal said. Sydney Diocese strongly resisted this interpretation, and complained bitterly when the Tribunal decision was announced. Its leaders, it seems, are still smarting.

More serious has been Sydney Diocese's recent introduction of diaconal presidency, and its Synod's overt support – some say, permission – for lay presidency.[12] The decision by the 2008 Sydney Synod to claim legitimacy for diaconal presidency – the culmination of many years of promotion of diaconal and lay presidency by the Synod – created considerable concern among the Australian House of Bishops, as well as internationally. The Archbishop of Canterbury expressed his disapproval in strong terms. This move was of such concern that it prompted a challenge to the Appellate Tribunal, which declared diaconal and lay presidency under the terms of the 2008 motion to be unconstitutional. The 2010 decision by Sydney Synod to defy the Tribunal on the matter is unprecedented, indeed provocative, and has created consternation around the national church. No one from Sydney Diocese has denied that the intention is to continue allowing deacons to preside at Holy Communion despite the Tribunal decision. On the contrary, the heading on the report of the debate at Sydney Synod in the diocesan newspaper was 'Deacons can keep celebrating'.[13]

As news of this decision by Sydney Synod filters through the national church, there is both shock and disbelief. Senior bishops and lay leaders around the country are deeply disturbed and troubled. Some fear it may cause problems for the Anglican Church of Australia within the Anglican Communion. With heightened concern about national churches that step outside the normal boundaries of Anglicanism, will the Australian church be threatened with sanctions for allowing a diocese to go its own way on such an important matter? Will the Australian church be asked not to send its Primate to the annual Primates' meeting, in the same way as the American Primate's presence is regularly challenged? In other words, will we become international pariahs, as The Episcopal Church in the United States or the Anglican Church of Canada have become in some quarters?

---

[12] Longstanding church law and tradition in the Anglican Church, as in the Catholic and Orthodox churches, authorizes priests and bishops only to preside at the central Christian rite of Holy Communion. In defiance of this position, diaconal presidency allows clergy in deacon's orders, a preliminary order to priesthood, to preside. Lay presidency allows non-ordained persons to preside.

[13] *Southern Cross*, November 2010.

Of greater concern is the notion that a diocese would publicly declare that the opinion of the Appellate Tribunal is merely 'advisory' and able to be ignored. This undermines the church constitution and such goodwill as continues to exist between the dioceses. The Tribunal is the body that interprets the constitution; it is the final arbiter. If it is to be ignored, then the constitution itself is being ignored. It is a throwing down of the gauntlet that cannot be ignored. The Australian church is facing a real crisis that may yet prove to be the 'bridge too far'. How the national church will be able to handle this situation and prevent possible repercussions both nationally and internationally is as yet unclear. Sydney's pursuit of lay and diaconal presidency is fully discussed in Chapter 5.

For all these reasons, Sydney Diocese can be seen to pose a threat to the stability of the Anglican Communion, to the cohesion of the Australian Anglican Church, and also to other Anglican churches such as those in the United Kingdom, in the United States, in Canada, and New Zealand. It is also potentially a danger to those third world Anglican churches that are part of the GAFCON organization, because it claims its involvement is in response to Gospel truth. Sydney and its friends are the true believers. Churches not aligned with it, taking a different view principally on the issue of homosexuality but also on women in ordained ministry, are portrayed as deniers of the Gospel. These claims, from determined, persuasive, well-resourced church leaders bearing gifts of support for, and assistance to, emerging churches, are hard to resist. Overall, Sydney's influence is of real concern for the future of world Anglicanism.

But is the tide turning? Some informed observers suggest that what they describe as the 'Sydney experiment' may have run its course. The 'experiment' – to impose with authoritarian zeal a strict, narrow and ideologically pure form of Anglicanism on an entire diocese and from there, further afield – began effectively with the appointment of a radical conservative theologian, Broughton Knox, as Principal of Moore Theological College in 1959. His tenure was long – 26 years as principal, more than 40 years at the college in all – and deeply influential. The experiment reached its fulfilment with the election of his faithful disciple Peter Jensen as Archbishop of Sydney in 2001, and for a few years following that high point, the tide seemed unstoppable. It was feared by some in the diocese and many outside as a tidal wave, even a tsunami, which would in a relatively short space of time overcome more reasonable, authentic and central expressions of Anglicanism in Australia generally.

But in the very years of its giddy success, the seeds of its possible failure were sown. Surely this was not unexpected. Both history and psychology teach us that hubris is its own undoing. In the heady early years of Peter Jensen's leadership, when presumably it seemed apparent that God was on the side of the new dispensation, nothing seemed impossible. Jensen's ambitious project to win, within a decade, 10 per cent of Sydneysiders into 'Bible-believing' churches, principally his own, was clear evidence of that mentality. While there have been modest gains since the Mission's formal launch in 2002, it has had nothing like the success that seemed so inevitable when it began. This could only lead to significant levels of disillusionment.

And such an extraordinary expansionary programme would cost a great deal of money, so a radical re-prioritizing of the diocese's financial resources was underway before the 2008 global financial crisis hit. Some initial estimates suggested the initial Mission programme might cost as much as $500 million over ten years.[14] The diocese was rich but not that rich. It needed more, so risks were taken to borrow substantial amounts to invest in pursuit of swift gains. The global financial crisis not only brought that strategy undone; the decision to sell out at the bottom of the market left the diocese's budget severely constrained by the loss of close to $200 million from the diocese's financial corpus, as will be discussed in Chapter 7. Worse, in 2010 it was revealed that poor management over some years had further seriously weakened income flow. And in the backwash to these startling revelations to a diocese long used to a comfortable financial position, the Synod itself began to question its leadership. It asked hard questions of its leaders, and then turned down a proposal to sell the Archbishop's residence as a means of releasing cash flow, despite the proposal's unqualified support from the diocesan establishment, not least the Archbishop himself. The significance of that vote will take time to assess, particularly in what it reveals of the corporate psychological processes of a Synod digesting the reality that their leaders were fallible. Some saw it as a vote of no confidence in the ruling junta, perhaps even in the Archbishop himself; others as an unspoken reluctance to shed a powerful symbol of the diocese's more stable, more 'Anglican', past.

Our examination of the Sydney story and its implications for the Australian church and the Anglican Communion will begin in the next chapter with an overview of what Anglicanism looks like in Sydney in the twenty-first century. We will then explore the diocese's history, which sheds light on how it has come to this point. Next, this study will examine in detail Sydney Diocese's involvement in the controversies at present wracking the Anglican Communion, before turning to the current tensions in the Anglican Church of Australia. Because the diocese's opposition to women as priests and bishops is so indicative of, and integral to, its ideology, we will then look in some depth at the Sydney claims that women are 'equal but different'. Finally the focus will shift to the challenges the diocese is grappling with at present, challenges that include uncertainty about who might follow Jensen when he retires in 2013 – and when the diocesan leaders who worked hard and long to bring him to power are also on their way out. These challenges signal that the Sydney experiment might be beginning to unravel.

---

[14] Chris McGillion, *The Chosen Ones: The Politics of Salvation in the Anglican Church* (Sydney: Allen & Unwin, 2004), p. xiv.

Chapter 2
Anglicanism in Sydney Today

In the twenty-first century, Sydney Diocese is a closed entity operating by its own increasingly idiosyncratic rules and codes, and displaying many of the characteristics of a sect instead of the openness characteristic of historic Anglicanism. This is not how it used to be in Sydney. The diocese has always been predominantly low-church Anglican with a strong conservative Evangelical commitment. It has historically eschewed the rituals of high-church or Anglo-Catholic forms of worship, along with their associated theological perspectives. Small 'l' liberal and relativist views, such as those espoused in extreme form by the American bishop and prolific author Jack Spong, have always been anathema to them. It has always guarded its borders, making it difficult for most other clergy from other parts of Australia to find employment in the diocese. But the diocese was until recently undeniably part of the Anglican mainstream both in Australia and worldwide, genuinely valuing the devotional tradition of the 1662 *Book of Common Prayer*, the worship standard of Anglicanism. Nevertheless, with the benefit of hindsight, it is now clear that the seeds of what Sydney Anglicanism has become were planted decades ago, principally through the radical conservative teaching provided to Sydney's trainee clergy through Moore Theological College from the late 1950s.

These days, Anglican visitors from most other dioceses around Australia and the rest of the worldwide Anglican Communion are puzzled, if not shocked, by what passes for worship in most Sydney parishes. As in those so-called independent Evangelical community churches aligned with Sydney, almost all the formalities of traditional Anglican liturgy have now disappeared. Instead of distinctive robes, clergy usually wear street dress, and sometimes the street dress is so casual that it has recently earned a public rebuke from one of Sydney's regional bishops.[1] The sermon is so all-important to church services that the Sydney website 'Better Gatherings', devoted to equipping 'service leaders to craft meetings', has felt the need to note that 'Christian gatherings are not just a sermon'.[2] There are usually no prayer books or organ music, and few conventional hymn books. Where prayer books are used, they rarely include *A Prayer Book for Australia*, approved by the Australian General Synod in 1995 and now the main standard of worship in the majority of Australian dioceses. This is an ongoing low-key tension in the Australian church.

---

[1] Bishop Robert Forsyth, 'Giving Clergy a Dressing Down', 4 January 2010, http://www.sydneyanglicans.net/ministry/critique/giving_clergy_a_dressing_down/.

[2] http://bettergatherings.com/.

The 1995 General Synod fully expected it would approve a new prayer book for the whole of the national church. The 1978 *An Australian Prayer Book* had been one of the first revisions of Anglican liturgy across the Communion and had necessarily been quite conservative. It rendered liturgy in more contemporary language and in particular made structural changes in the service of Holy Communion to bring it into line with scholarly ecumenical liturgical thinking. While it caused controversy among those who could not countenance anything but the 1662 *Book of Common Prayer*, it was well-received by the 1977 General Synod that adopted it almost unanimously. Bishop Donald Robinson of Sydney, later the archbishop, had worked hard to see the book adopted so readily.

After the significant success of the 1978 book, the General Synod Liturgical Commission continued to develop and refine prayer book services and related material. Following consultations and the trialling of various formats, *A Prayer Book for Australia* was presented to General Synod in 1995. There was to be no easy passage for the new book, however. It took days of protracted debate and on-the-floor revision as representatives from Sydney in particular took issue with anything that seemed too catholic. Material was jettisoned in the hope that they would finally accept it, allowing it to pass the Synod. After a great deal of compromise, however, it emerged that the Sydney representatives would pass it only if it was described as 'liturgical resources authorised by the General Synod'. And the canon authorizing it, unlike the canon that had authorized its predecessor, was designated the kind that could only come into force in a diocese if its synod adopted it. Unsurprisingly, Sydney Synod did not adopt it, though until he retired as archbishop in 2001, Harry Goodhew gave the few parishes that requested it permission to use the new book. By contrast, *A Prayer Book for Australia* was rapidly adopted in the rest of the country.

So there is now no real 'prayer book for Australia'. While the 1995 book is in use in most dioceses, even the *Book of Common Prayer* and *An Australian Prayer Book* are not much used in Sydney. Sydney has developed its own liturgical resources, including the 'Better Gatherings' website just noted. ('Gatherings' and 'meetings', the older-style terminology of sects, are the current Sydney names for church services.) These new Sydney resources are designed to be flexible and used in more extemporary kinds of services, in direct contravention of longstanding Anglican principles. The Communion table (altar) is sometimes pushed out of sight. In St Andrew's Cathedral – the mother church of Sydney Diocese and of the wider Australian Anglican Church – the table has been put on wheels and relegated to a side aisle until it is wheeled out for Communion services. The Cathedral has become the heartland of the Sydney revolution since the appointment of Phillip Jensen as the Dean of the Cathedral in 2002.[3] Phillip Jensen had been a candidate

---

[3] The appointment of Phillip Jensen as Dean stirred considerable controversy in the Sydney media, with accusations of nepotism levelled against Archbishop Peter Jensen for the appointment of his younger brother to such a central diocesan position. The diocese's media officer insisted that the Archbishop had left the room when the Cathedral's governing

for election as archbishop of Sydney in 1993,[4] but his platform of radical diocesan and liturgical reorganization had then been too controversial. At the Cathedral, he has full rein in transforming traditional Anglican worship. He preaches in a Geneva gown, a garment usually worn by non-Anglican Protestant ministers, and under his leadership, the Cathedral's traditional choir has had its role severely curtailed. Cathedral worship services are also called 'meetings' or 'gatherings'. And he uses the Cathedral as a base for church-planting activities in the city of Sydney.

Parishes that retain conventional ordered prayer book Evangelical forms of worship, until very recently the norm in Sydney, are now fast becoming as isolated as the few longstanding Anglo-Catholic shrines, such as two major city churches, St James', King Street, and Christ Church St Laurence, Railway Square, and a few more central mainstream parishes. One recent estimate has suggested there might be as few as 14 to 20 such parishes left out of a total of 267.[5] And through the diocese's growing inroads into other dioceses, the same stripped bare forms of worship are emerging in increasing numbers of parishes outside Sydney.

Church buildings are becoming less conventional as well. Of course the ubiquitous overhead screen is firmly in place, along with the paraphernalia of the resident music group. But the central symbol of the cross is missing in many places, because the symbol is deemed to be idolatrous. This is ironic, given that the whole thrust of preaching in Sydney Diocese is centred around the atonement wrought by Jesus in his death on the cross. By contrast, the cross remains proudly in view in those parishes that maintain Anglican worship norms. These parishes are informally known as 'stole' parishes after the long coloured liturgical scarf worn by non-Evangelical priests and deacons as part of their clergy dress for services such as Holy Communion and Holy Baptism. The stole has become the symbol of a mainstream approach to Anglican worship.

Terminology has changed as well. The word 'priest', used in the *Book of Common Prayer* and subsequent Australian prayer books, has been changed to 'presbyter' in all diocesan documents, a move designed to remove any lingering suggestion of

---

body, the Chapter, debated whether to agree with the Archbishop's nomination of his brother, allowing Chapter members 'to discuss the matter freely and without constraint': Kelly Burke, 'Archbishop Offers Key Church Job to Brother', *The Sydney Morning Herald*, 21 October 2002; 'Rector of St Matthias Offered Post of Dean of Sydney', 18 October 2002, www.anglicanmediasydney.asn.au/2002/396.htm.

[4] A Sydney assistant bishop, Harry Goodhew, was elected as a compromise candidate in 1993.

[5] Douglas Golding, 'Endangered Species? "Mainstream" Anglicans in the Diocese of Sydney', paper delivered at the conference *From Augustine to Anglicanism: Anglicans in Australia and Beyond*, St Francis College, Brisbane, 14 February 2010. Just 13 parishes are publicly identified with Anglicans Together, the lobby group of disenfranchised mainstream Sydney Anglicans. However, other informed observers have suggested that Dr Golding's estimate is too low, and that there could be up to 40 'mainstream' parishes left in Sydney.

sacerdotalism. Parish rectors are now generally called 'senior ministers' or 'senior pastors' (except in stole parishes). A recent change in ordination policy reserves priestly ordination only for those (male) deacons approved for appointment as rectors of parishes. This clearly identifies priestly ordination as linked solely to leadership of a church, not to sacramental ministry, which will be discussed more fully in Chapter 5. Other clergy – parish curates, school chaplains and the like, who once would have proceeded to priestly ordination almost automatically, and women of course – remain deacons, one of the factors behind the 2008 decision to implement diaconal presidency at the Eucharist. Increasingly, there are also reports of a loss of the traditional pastoral dimension in parish ministry, at least as far as the clergy are concerned. Pastoral care of parishioners tends to be mediated through other lay people. In some places, the very word 'pastoral' is deemed unacceptable, the emphasis on caring for people being regarded as a denial of the imperative to evangelize the lost.

Underlying these significant changes in style is an even more significant ramping up of the diocese's conservative theological stance. Sydney Diocese is now in several key respects so conservative as to verge on the fundamentalist, though this is a badge it detests. In his first major address after his election as Sydney's archbishop in 2001, Peter Jensen insisted that he and his diocese were Evangelical Christians, not fundamentalists.[6] The very word, he said, was 'ugly', with fundamentalism today implying 'an anti-intellectual, backward-looking and ugly zeal in the cause of religion'. The key difference between the Evangelical and fundamentalist position for Jensen is that while he reads the bible literally – 'that is, on its own terms' – he does not read it 'literalistically', he said. It is a highly nuanced distinction, so nuanced that its meaning is not immediately clear; I assume he means that his 'literal' meaning does not require him to believe 'literalistically' that creation happened in just six 24-hour days, for example.[7] Australia needs, Jensen argued, 'a Christianity which is classical but not fundamentalist'. In contrast to fundamentalist literalistic reading of the Bible, 'classical Christianity', while giving the scriptures full priority and authority, nevertheless made full use of both traditional interpretation and 'the genuine advances of the more recent historical approach' in interpreting the Bible. It was also prepared to learn from contemporary thought, he said.

---

[6] Peter Jensen, Presidential Address to the 2001 Sydney Synod, 26 October 2001.

[7] Peter Jensen's son, Michael – also a Sydney clergyman – has explained the distinction in a blog posted on the Sydney website: 'Literal or Literalistic? What Is the Difference?', 28 September 2010, http://www.sydneyanglicans.net/life/culture/literal_or_literalistic_whats_the_difference/. He writes, 'The "literal" – or better "plain" – reading is an attempt to read the text in terms of its original context and genre and so on, and by recognizing metaphor, symbolism and other literary devices in the text ... On the other hand, a "literalistic" reader reads without (or with a deficient) awareness of metaphor, symbolism, genre, literary style, inexact numbers, and so on, and in fact may deny the presence of these things entirely.'

There is nothing there that most mainstream Anglican leaders would not agree with. But there is more to fundamentalism than a 'literalistic' reading of the Bible, and indeed more to a fundamentalist approach to the Bible than Jensen's explanation suggests. Australian theologian and Anglican priest Kevin Giles has argued that since the 1970s, the term 'fundamentalism' has broadened to mean an 'absolutist hermeneutic'. The true fundamentalist, he says, 'claims that what I am saying is what my holy book is saying and this is what God is saying'. In other words, the contemporary fundamentalist is making an absolutist claim to be speaking for God. (It is hard not to see this 'absolutist hermeneutic' at work in Sydney Diocese. There is anecdotal evidence that on occasion parishioners who have questioned a preacher's interpretation of Scripture have been told that to question, is to question God.) Giles continues that it is not recognized that in arguing this way Evangelical fundamentalists adopt the same hermeneutic as the Catholic Church where the Pope tells the faithful what the Bible says.[8]

As well as this hardline approach to Scriptural interpretation, a 'fundamentalist mentality' has also been identified in conservative Evangelicals of the kind who now characterize Sydney Anglicanism.[9] There is a vast academic literature on this topic, and considerable debate swirls around it, but in short, there are some key markers of a fundamentalist mentality: a rationalist mindset, a 'Calvinistic zeal to root out error and preserve doctrinal purity',[10] charismatic and authoritarian leadership, behavioural requirements,[11] and a tendency to separatism. I would add that a commitment to male 'headship' is another important marker of Christian Protestant/Pentecostal fundamentalism. Giles has noted that Evangelical fundamentalism in the modern sense 'is characterised by a rejection of the recent insights into hermeneutics and by opposition to women's emancipation in the church and in the home'. All expressions of fundamentalism in all the great world religions oppose the emancipation of women, he writes.[12] This aspect of the Sydney viewpoint will be discussed in Chapter 6.

A rationalist mindset was a key component of sixteenth century Puritanism. It is a strong element in all forms of Protestantism in varying degrees. Critics have sometimes suggested that strict Protestants substituted a 'paper pope' – the Bible – for the Pope in Rome, and swapped external rituals for cerebral forms. In other words, though their religious observance took outwardly different markers, it still had more in common with the forms that had been rejected than its proponents were prepared to recognize. Sydney Diocese, as with Puritanism, has taken religious rationalism to the extreme, and in particular in its adherence to what is called

---

[8] Kevin Giles, 'What Is Theology and What Is Evangelical Theology?', lecture notes supplied to author.

[9] Harriet A. Harris, *Fundamentalism and Evangelicals* (Oxford: Clarendon, 1998), p. 11.

[10] Ibid., p. 4.

[11] Ibid., p. 327.

[12] Giles, 'What Is Theology and What Is Evangelical Theology?'

'propositional revelation'. (I will explore the origins of propositional revelation, an important element in the background to contemporary Sydney Anglicanism, in the next chapter.) At the risk of being accused of caricaturing a theory propounded with considerable nuance and sophistication by Sydney protagonists,[13] I would summarize propositional revelation as the theory that God is revealed solely through propositions presented in the Bible, that is, through the written words of Scripture in which the fundamental proposition is that 'Jesus is the Christ, the Lord'. This is not merely information, but information that provokes an existential response; that response can only be absolute obedience.[14]

The theory refers to revelation imparted through rational thought processes alone, without any subsidiary, complementary or external revelatory processes, such as through sensuous experiences mediated through liturgy, music, nature, or Eucharistic participation. The role of all worship, in this view, is to facilitate the hearing and expounding of this verbal revelation, not to provide alternative opportunities for revelation. The guidance of the Holy Spirit is thus seen by purists as mediated always and only 'through Scripture'. This last is a claim that has taken many Anglicans outside Sydney by surprise, given the more general view that the Holy Spirit – the 'third person' of God the Holy Trinity – while undoubtedly speaking through the Bible, is not restricted to that one location. The Holy Spirit is often claimed to inspire people through a variety of contexts and places, not by any means confined to the church. I argue, for instance, that aspects of the feminist movement in secular society, leading to the recognition and establishment of full female equality, were inspired by the Holy Spirit.

Theologians outside Sydney claim biblical warrant for this wider interpretation from Jesus' words to his disciples before his death: 'When the Spirit of truth comes, he will guide you into all the truth; for he will not speak on his own, but will speak whatever he hears, and he will declare to you the things that are to come' (John 16:13). Peter Jensen has dismissed this interpretation: it is a 'common belief of popular piety that we need a continuous revelation of God, contemporary words of God', he has said. He continues: 'for example, developments in ecclesiastical life that occur in spite of what the Bible teaches are sometimes justified on the

---

[13] See paper by Michael Jensen: 'Rethinking the Term "Propositional Revelation" or, *What Broughton Knox Really Said*', Matthias Media website, http://mpjensen.blogspot.com/2006/03/re-thinking-term-propositional.html. Michael Jensen makes the point that the term 'propositional' here should not be taken to mean a reductionist interpretation of the words of Scripture, in the sense of the 'logical positivism' of the mid-twentieth-century philosophical debate on language and meaning.

[14] I am indebted here to the discussion on this topic provided by Melbourne Anglican priest Dr Duncan Reid in his paper, 'Anglican Diversity and Conflict: A Case Study on God, Gender and Authority', in Bruce Kaye (ed.), *'Wonderful and Confessedly Strange': Australian Essays in Anglican Ecclesiology* (Adelaide: ATF Press, 2006). The most recent authoritative discussion from inside Sydney is Peter Jensen's *The Revelation of God: Contours in Christian Theology* (Leicester: InterVarsity Press, 2002).

ground of the ongoing revelatory work of the Spirit'.[15] He has claimed too that by 'guidance into all the truth', Jesus meant only that the Holy Spirit would guide the apostles as they wrote the gospels, epistles and other documents that would in time constitute the New Testament.

This 'prophecy', then, Jensen has argued, was limited to the immediate apostles, and ended with the completion of their written work. For later generations, the Holy Spirit would guide their reading of those materials, but not reveal 'new' truths not contained there. Dr Jensen has justified this stance on the grounds of the brief New Testament letter of Jude, in which the little-known apostle speaks of 'the faith that was once for all entrusted to the saints' (Jude v.3).[16] Dr Jensen has written: 'Even at that early stage in the history of the church, Jude was able to think of the faith as a body of truths, as "the faith" on which faith is based ... It was a faith, furthermore, that had been passed on entire, "once for all".'[17]

Regardless of contrary views on this aspect of revelation, the real crux of dispute over revelation among Anglicans is in the issue of interpretation of the Scriptures, the way Scripture is believed to work. Sydney Anglicans seem unwilling to accept that for numerous scholars and general readers, the Holy Spirit inspires quite different interpretations of the given words of Scripture than they propound. This is a topic which could and has occupied entire books, but in brief, Sydney's claim that they adhere to the 'plain' reading of Scripture rather disingenuously suggests that there is one straightforward, obvious meaning in the Bible, the one to which they faithfully hold, and a highly uniform message in the Scriptures. This suggests that other Christians subvert or twist Scriptural meanings to get a different set of interpretations, so that they can then claim biblical support for the ordination of women or gay people, or other 'innovations'. This support for a 'plain' meaning is a hallmark of the fundamentalist approach to Scripture.

Many commentators have demonstrated that no 'plain' reading is actually possible, given the nature of the Hebrew and Christian Scriptures, which are thousands of years old. They reflect entirely different thought-worlds to that of the twenty-first century, and inevitably are imbued with the ancient cultural patterns, norms and expectations from which they were written. More than one hundred years of scholarly criticism has revealed the complexity of interpreting the meaning of the Bible for contemporary Christians. Similarly, many scholars have pointed out clear examples of the Christian Church changing its mind as over the centuries it has read the Scriptures with fresh insight.

The classic example is slavery, which until the eighteenth century was almost universally condoned as having a biblical warrant. Until then, Christians routinely accepted that New Testament strictures to slaves to obey their masters were

---

[15] Peter Jensen, *The Revelation of God*, p. 275.

[16] All Bible quotations come from the New Revised Standard Version (NRSV), by the Division of Christian Education of the National Council of Churches in the USA (1989, 1995).

[17] Peter Jensen, *The Revelation of God*, p. 279.

evidence that the practice of slavery was acceptable to God.[18] English Quakers were the first to denounce it as a 'hellish' practice, and call for its abolition, a call later taken up by John Wesley, the founder of the Evangelical revival that became Methodism. William Wilberforce, an Evangelical, spear-headed the move for its outlawing by the British Parliament, despite determined opposition by mainstream theologians who called on the Bible as their chief witness. Similarly in the United States, leading Protestant theologians resisted the abolition of slavery on the grounds that it was supported by Scripture.

Abolitionists however, in re-reading Scripture, saw beyond the cultural reality of the implicit first-century acceptance of the institution of slavery, and recognized instead that far more significant was the great New Testament trajectory of freedom from all forms of bondage, and the equality of all people in Christ 'in whom there is no longer Jew or Greek ... slave or free ... male and female' (Galatians 3:28).[19] Today, few Christians would seriously argue that slavery is biblical, though a Sydney regional bishop, Dr Glenn Davies, has tried to make a case for imprisonment as a form of slavery still acceptable in modern society.[20]

The church's change of mind over the issue of slavery is particularly relevant to the debate about women clergy, as there are some obvious parallels. Proponents of women clergy have argued that the biblical texts quoted against women in leadership – that they should keep silent in church and obey their husbands, for example – arose from the implicit cultural norms of the first century, when women were restricted to domesticity as a matter of course. Over-riding those norms, however, was the dynamic claim of full equality in Christ, where there was no longer male and female. As I will discuss in more detail in a later chapter, the first Christian women who, in the nineteenth century, began to assert their claim to full equality in church and state, did so on the basis of that biblical statement of their equality in Christ. Like the abolitionists before them, they re-read Scripture and saw what it contained in a new light. The 'plain' reading of female subservience, as pronounced by four Bible verses, was turned around to affirm true male/female equality. I would claim that fresh interpretations, arising from the New Testament itself, are an instance of the guidance of the Holy Spirit revealing God's will for the contemporary church and world, in the same way that the Holy Spirit guided the reading of the abolitionists. And I believe these interpretations to be faithful, valid and intellectually coherent readings of Scripture, not the wilful denial of biblical truth of which I and my friends are often accused.

---

[18] For instance, 1 Peter 2:18 'Slaves, accept the authority of your masters with all deference, not only those who are kind and gentle, but also those who are harsh' (NRSV).

[19] A useful brief summary of the slavery debate can be found in Kevin Giles, *The Trinity and Subordinationism: The Doctrine of God and the Contemporary Gender Debate* (Downers Grove, IL: InterVarsity Press, 2002), pp. 215–50.

[20] Glenn Davies, 'Have You Not Read ...?', in Scott Cowdell and Muriel Porter (eds), *Lost in Translation? Anglicans, Controversy and the Bible, Perspectives from the Doctrine Commission of the Anglican Church of Australia* (Melbourne: Desbooks, 2004), p. 93.

Sydney Anglicans also demonstrate a classic fundamentalist 'zeal to root out error and doctrinal impurity' in numerous ways, too many to discuss in detail here. Some examples will demonstrate the pattern. Virtually alone in the worldwide Anglican Communion, Sydney Diocese enforces a symbolic restriction on the use of a ceremonial garment called a chasuble. The chasuble is the outer vestment worn by Catholic clergy when they celebrate Mass, and was re-introduced into Anglican practice during the late nineteenth-century Anglo-Catholic revival, finally becoming officially acceptable in the Church of England in 1965. As its use had been abolished as 'popish' during the English Reformation, its nineteenth-century re-introduction was highly controversial, and led to cases in the civil courts. The debate only served to make the garment very popular. Wearing the chasuble was a sure marker of clergy committed to more 'catholic' understandings of Anglican liturgy, though it has become so widely adopted it has now lost its earlier symbolism. Everywhere but Sydney, that is. In 1910, Sydney Diocese began to require all clergy to sign an undertaking that they would not wear Eucharistic vestments, a requirement subsequently entrenched by a 1949 Sydney Synod ordinance that is still in force.[21] Not that there are many clergy or parishes left in Sydney where chasubles, or indeed any traditional liturgical garments, even those required by the *Book of Common Prayer*, would even be an option, as I have said. Another example of 'zeal to root out doctrinal impurity' is refusal by many Sydney clergy to allow lay women to play any significant part in the main Sunday services – even reading lessons from the Bible – as a means of keeping faith with their claim that women must not exercise any leadership in mixed (that is, male and female) congregations.

You do not have far to look to identify Sydney's dependence on 'charismatic and authoritarian leadership', another marker of fundamentalism. It is a truism of Sydney Anglicanism that its archbishops have been almost universally caste in that mould, to a greater or lesser extent. Some have been more charismatic than others, but all have had at least the bearing of a certain authoritarianism, except perhaps Peter Jensen's predecessor Harry Goodhew, who found it hard to lead the diocese in the face of the political machinations of others, as religion commentator Chris McGillion has demonstrated.[22] More telling, though, is the authoritarian masculinity of the overall diocesan establishment, which exercises a corporate male dominance.

Ironically, Sydney lays claim to having a grass-roots rather than hierarchical polity. Congregationalism, or the supremacy of the local congregation, rides high in its teachings about the nature of the church. Like its Puritan predecessors, it takes a low view of the role of bishops in general. As Peter Jensen said in his

---

[21] The 1949 ordinance forbad clergy celebrating Holy Communion from wearing 'the alb the chasuble the dalmatic the tunicle', so in Anglo-Catholic parishes in Sydney the cope is usually worn instead.

[22] Chris McGillion, *The Chosen Ones: The Politics of Salvation in the Anglican Church* (Sydney: Allen & Unwin, 2005).

2002 Presidential Address to Synod, 'we are a fellowship of churches, not an army with an episcopal general, and you must feel free to choose your own path of obedience to Christ'.[23] This supports the Sydney ecclesiology that the heart of the church is the individual parish, not the overarching diocesan structure, including the archbishop. In practice, as the experience of the few remaining parishes that follow a more traditional and moderate form of Anglicanism attests, their parochial freedom is in fact severely constrained by restrictive diocesan regulations and expectations that favour the dominant conservative mindset. The minority parishes do not find it easy to follow the forms of worship they prefer, for example, and they sometimes find it hard to obtain the rector of their choice, given diocesan opposition to clergy outside the prevailing Sydney mould. Some of the stole parishes have been without rectors for years at a time, as every potential appointment they suggest is declined. Instead, they feel pressured to accept clergy who they know would not respect their parish traditions. Clearly only parishes that accept the ethos of the diocese enjoy the full freedom suggested by the claims that Sydney regards congregations as the supreme manifestation of the church.

The term 'charismatic' (using its general meaning of influential and attractive, rather than the religious meaning associated with Pentecostal worship) came into its own in Sydney with the election of its current archbishop. Peter Jensen is, at first glance, an unexpected candidate for charismatic leadership. He is in many ways a reserved, retiring man, very much the intellectual at heart. His professional life has been spent in the world of academe, as student, scholar, teacher and writer. He has never been a parish rector and was only briefly a parish curate. He loves nothing more than to immerse himself in a library. His personal appearance is unremarkable; his clothing style is conventional for a man of his age (he was born in 1943) and interests. He eschews the usual street wear of most Anglican bishops, including his immediate predecessors as archbishop, appearing usually in collar and tie rather than a purple or deep blue clerical shirt. In conformity with long-standing Sydney practice, he and his assistant bishops do not wear pectoral crosses.

Since his election as Archbishop of Sydney in 2001, however, this bookish man has launched himself onto the Sydney scene, and indeed the international scene, in unprecedented fashion. He has revealed himself to be a shrewd, confident media player, contributing to all manner of public debates and conversations with great personal charm and a level of accessibility both admirable and rare in church leaders. His webpage describes him accurately as 'an outspoken figure on the Australian religious scene'.

Within the diocese, there is little sign of the kind of power struggles and turmoil that marked Harry Goodhew's time in office, which suggests – at least to the external observer – that Peter Jensen's authority is unchallenged and his personal influence considerable. Whether this equates with authoritarianism I do not know, but I suspect this archbishop does not need to be authoritarian. It seems

---

[23] Peter Jensen, Presidential Address 2002.

to outsiders at least that his diocese has been, until very recently, eating out of his hands. Sydney insiders have suggested that when he was elected archbishop, the culmination of the radical conservative project, it was seen as akin to the Second Coming. He is the ultimate benign 'father figure'. Almost a decade later, with the Mission faltering and the diocesan finances in chaos, disillusionment is however setting in in some quarters.

There is also every indication that Jensen's leadership charisma was initially magnified by an astonishingly effective public relations exercise, casting him as something of a celebrity. His profile in all Sydney Anglican Media products has, until recently, been consistently high, although since the diocese's financial crisis he has retreated considerably. His earlier high-profile stance was demonstrated by the break with precedent for the opening of the 2005 Sydney Synod. The Synod met initially in the Sydney Town Hall, specifically to allow a large number of Sydney faithful to hear the archbishop's annual synod charge (a kind of 'state of the nation' address). Usually only keen synod members are expected to show that level of interest. While this event was principally designed to encourage support for the Diocese's Mission to Sydney – which will be discussed in more detail later – the by-product was inevitably a significant lifting of the profile of the leader.

As to behavioural requirements, Sydney has long exercised a harsher set of rules concerning personal morality than most other Anglican dioceses. Remarriage after divorce remains problematic. As Peter Jensen's predecessor Archbishop Harry Goodhew reminded Sydney Synod in 2000, the Sydney position remains unchanged from what it was in 1918: 'a member of the clergy may conduct the marriage of a divorced person (whose spouse is living) only where the former marriage is dissolved due to the infidelity of the other partner ....'[24] This situation is significantly different from other parts of Australia. Divorce is totally unacceptable among the Sydney clergy and they must not be married to divorcees, again differing from the protocols operative in other places. The diocese is strict on matters of heterosexual morality, opposing all sex outside marriage more stridently than other parts of the Anglican Church. Clergy should be married, and rectors in particular are required to be married men, ostensibly perhaps to meet the biblical expectation expressed in 1 Timothy 3 that clergy should be married only once, and show evidence of managing a household well. There is also possibly an underlying fear that singleness might mask an unacceptable sexual identity or that a man might fall prey to sexual temptation.

Separatism: this is a charge which Sydney Anglicans would reject on the basis that they have no intention of withdrawing from the modern world, as classical fundamentalists do. They would point to their Mission, which inevitably involves high-level interaction with the secular world. It is important to note that this involvement is on their terms, however. In Jensen's own words, he is 'impelled' by his understanding of the death of Jesus Christ 'to enter the world as

---

[24] Sydney Synod Proceedings – Ordinary Session 2000. It must be said that in 1918, this was an open position in terms of prevailing world Anglican practice.

a missionary'.[25] The express purpose, then, is not to serve the needs of the wider community primarily, but to convert those outside the 'Bible-believing churches', and thus make them 'insiders'. (Jensen would argue, however, that as from his perspective people's most urgent need is salvation, which involves drawing them into acceptable congregations, then the Mission does serve the needs of the wider community.)

Sydney Diocese keeps itself safe from outside influence by imposing stringent conditions on clergy appointments, particularly for those who want to come to Sydney from outside. This has always been the case, but has become much more severe in recent times. The formal, public processes for appointing rectors are demanding, but even more daunting is what is colloquially referred to as the vetting by the 'visa committee' or 'border protection committee'. This additional process comprises a grilling on doctrinal stance, conducted by three people from a pool handpicked by the Archbishop. Even clergy seeking permission simply to conduct occasional church services are subject to this process. Clergy can be questioned, sometimes quite aggressively, about their views on homosexuality, same-sex marriage, the ordination of women, their attitude to ecumenical and inter-faith activities, and similar issues. If they are denied a licence, no reasons are given.

Sydney Anglicans are, however, proud to be 'counter-cultural' at many levels, which itself indicates a predisposition towards separatism. They see their opposition to many contemporary cultural trends as evidence of their Gospel commitment, rather like their Puritan forebears who railed against secular entertainments. So they feel no embarrassment in swimming against the tide in opposing gay sexuality, gay marriage or gay families, in insisting on a strict conventional heterosexual morality, and in denying women priestly ordination. On the contrary, going against the secular world is the sign for them that they are true believers. Hardly surprising, when their assessment of 'the world' is that it is a godless, sinful place, where the Spirit of God is not to be found. Their fervent opposition to women's ordination is also clear evidence of their commitment to male 'headship', a key teaching of fundamentalism that will be explored in a subsequent chapter.

Both internationally and nationally, Sydney Diocese promotes its own version of Gospel truth, one that it claims is the only truth, the faith 'once delivered to the saints'. In many ways it is a truth close to the 'truth' proclaimed by fundamentalists, though as I have said, that is a tag it repudiates. Its grand Mission to the city of Sydney, launched by Peter Jensen shortly after his election in 2001 and designed to capture the allegiance of 10 per cent of the city's population within a decade, is based on the fundamentalist premise that it alone has the truth. The Mission will be discussed in more detail later, but at this point, we should note that the Mission's underlying rationale is that those who do not conform to Sydney's truth are, quite simply, 'lost' and on the road to hell. Outlining in detail the rationale for

---

[25] Peter Jensen, Presidential Address 2001.

the Mission in 2002, Jensen referred to those outside Bible-believing churches as being condemned to a 'miserable' fate. He said that nothing was more important for these people than 'their need to know Christ and be saved from the wrath to come'. That was why the diocese needed to focus on the programme at all costs and above all other priorities, because it was focused on what he proclaimed to be the number one human priority. Other churches which did not accept this priority and the theological position driving it, were plainly wrong, according to Jensen. 'Many in the church now believe that salvation comes to all automatically, without exception and without need for faith in Jesus', he continued:

> I can only respond that they do not understand the cross of Christ and its absolutely central significance for the history of the world and the redemption of sinners. Nor do they understand the witness of the Bible to the sinfulness of our race, and the hopelessness of our saving panaceas, religious or secular.[26]

It seems clear that he was implying that the vast bulk of the world's Christian churches, including the largest of all, the Catholic Church, were in serious error, leading their people not just astray but to eternal damnation.

If other Christian churches are in error, how much more are other major world faiths – Islam, Judaism, and Hinduism? Most Christians, even conservative Evangelicals, avoid direct confrontations over the issue, and seek opportunities for sensitive dialogue. Not so Sydney. In his first sermon as Dean of Sydney in March 2003, Phillip Jensen created controversy when he declared that the religions of Hindus, Muslims and Jews 'cannot all be right'. That might of course be true, but his further comments shocked many: 'Some, or all of them, are wrong, and if wrong are the monstrous lies and deceits of Satan, devised to destroy the life of the believers, to capture them into the cosmic rebellion against God and to destroy the freedom they should have in Christ,' he said. Stretching social tolerance into religious or philosophical relativism was 'stupid'.[27]

Nor was he alone in his views. As the media reported the understandably angry reactions of leaders of other religions, as well as of more moderate Christians, a Sydney assistant bishop defended the Dean. Bishop Robert Forsyth, who is often used as the diocese's official spokesperson, backed Jensen's comments unreservedly. His views were not new, he said, in a tacit acknowledgement that they were the long-held views of the diocese. They were consistent with the New Testament, he said: 'outside of Christ people are enslaved to sin or to spiritual forces'. He added: 'If all people have a terrible disease and you believe that God has provided a particular cure for everybody that worked – but others were hawking cures that didn't work – you can't just say it doesn't matter. It's false and

---

[26] Jensen, Presidential Address 2002.
[27] Phillip Jensen, 'Pray that I May Declare It Fearlessly', sermon at Commencement Service as Dean of Sydney, 7 March 2003.

it's dangerously false in a spiritual sense.'[28] Media analysis of the furore noted that in the past, Phillip Jensen had been critical of one other Christian tradition as not being a 'true religion' as well. *The Sydney Morning Herald*'s Kelly Burke reported that Jensen had previously described Catholicism as 'sub-Christian' in both its doctrine and practice, and called it an 'unrepentant persecutor of the gospel'.[29]

The 'uniqueness of Jesus' is something that Sydney Anglicans – along with other conservative Christians – are passionate about. Jesus' redemptive death on the Cross, they maintain, only redeems those who explicitly and consciously make a faith commitment to him. The classical Christian position is rather more nuanced: Redemption is only through Jesus, yes, but that does not require explicit faith in him, but rather is effective wherever God's love evokes a response. Some theologians also claim that St Paul was suggesting universal salvation when he proclaimed that 'for as all die in Adam, so all will be made alive in Christ' (NRSV). The issue, in terms of their own understanding, however, has become one of the hallmarks of the 'true believer' for Sydney. It provided an excellent opportunity for Sydney Anglican leaders to criticize a former Primate of the Australian church, Archbishop Peter Carnley of Perth, at the time of his election and installation as Primate in April 2000. He was accused of denying the uniqueness of Jesus as the only path to human salvation in an article he had written for the now defunct Australian news magazine, *The Bulletin*.[30]

In the article, Carnley discussed Christian salvation in terms of divine forgiveness, pointing out that the risen Jesus had returned in loving forgiveness to the very people who had crucified him. This made Jesus 'uniquely significant as the bearer of salvation for those who had mistreated him', Carnley explained subsequently.[31] This uniqueness of Jesus was not just a matter of contrast with other world religions, which had either not existed at the time or not been known to the New Testament writers, his article argued. A range of Sydney Anglican commentators blasted the original *Bulletin* article on a number of grounds, including what they claimed was Carnley's denial of salvation through Jesus alone. The then Archbishop of Sydney, Harry Goodhew, said the article appeared to overturn traditional Anglican teaching.[32]

---

[28] Quoted in Kelly Burke, 'Outrage over Dean's Hostility to Other Faiths', *The Sydney Morning Herald*, 11 March 2003.

[29] Kelly Burke, 'Will the Real God Please Give Us a Sign', *The Sydney Morning Herald*, 15 March 2003. She quotes Jensen's comments on Catholicism from his 1991 publication *Have Evangelicals Lost Their Way?*, co-authored by Tony Payne (Sydney: St Matthias Press).

[30] Peter Carnley, 'The Rising of the Son', *The Bulletin*, 25 April 2000.

[31] Peter Carnley, *Reflections in Glass: Trends and Tensions in the Contemporary Anglican Church* (Sydney: HarperCollins, 2004) p. 7.

[32] 'Background for Overseas Readers', 26 April 2000, www.anglicanmediasydney.asn.au/bulletin_summary.htm.

A number of Sydney clergy used the *Bulletin* article as the springboard to call for a boycott of Carnley's installation as Primate, which was to take place in Sydney on 30 April. This was an extraordinarily rude and aggressive response to the archbishop of another metropolitan diocese, properly elected as Primate. One of the clergy calling for boycott was Phillip Jensen, then rector of a Sydney parish, St Matthias', Centennial Park. In a long and detailed article published on the Sydney Anglican Media website, he first took issue with Carnley's theology before declaring that a boycott would be 'a small symbolic part to play ... in a long fight that we must now clearly engage in. The alternative is to withdraw wholly from a largely apostate denomination.'[33] In the event, though most Sydney regional bishops did not attend the installation, St Andrew's Cathedral was packed to the doors, as more moderate Sydney Anglicans, sparked by the boycott calls, made a concerted effort to attend, along with visiting bishops, clergy and laity from other dioceses. In his later apologia, Carnley wisely avoided a full-scale discussion on the topic of salvation through Christ alone, instead cryptically pointing out that the 'prerogative of separating the sheep from the goats belongs to God alone. We humans need to use a little caution before presuming to exercise the judgement that belongs to God.'[34]

In the furore against Carnley's views, Sydney Anglicans regularly asserted that he was denying Anglican teaching, and in particular the Thirty-nine Articles of Religion. Increasingly in Sydney, commitment to the Articles is used as a yardstick of orthodoxy. The Thirty-nine Articles are the product of compromise, arising from a politically-fraught sixteenth-century process whereby the Church of England, under Queen Elizabeth I, set down its view in relation to the theological controversies of the time. Finalized in 1571 and unchanged since then, the Articles are a set of 'short summaries of dogmatic tenets'.[35] It must be remembered that the Articles are, except in minor detail, the same as the Forty-two Articles defined in 1553, during the reign of King Edward VI, England's first Protestant monarch. His reign – which we will explore in more detail – represents the purity of true Protestant Anglicanism to the Sydney mindset, which explains the symbolism of adherence to the Articles. Anglican lay people are not required to subscribe to the Thirty-nine Articles, and in general clergy have not had to subscribe to them in full since 1865.[36]

---

[33] 'Phillip Jensen's Response to the Primate's Easter Article', 28 April 2000, www.anglicanmediasydney.asn.au/bulletin_jensen.htm.
[34] Peter Carnley, *Reflections in Glass*, pp. 7–8.
[35] F.L. Cross and E.A. Livingstone (eds), *The Oxford Dictionary of the Christian Church*, third edition (Oxford: Oxford University Press, 1997), p. 1611.
[36] Since 1975 in the Church of England, clergy have been required only to acknowledge the Articles as one of the historic formularies 'which bear witness to the faith revealed in Scripture and set forth in the catholic creeds' (ibid., p. 1611). According to its constitution, the Australian Anglican Church retains and approves the doctrine and principles of the Church of England embodied in the Articles of Religion, among other

To my mind the Articles are a quaintly-worded, seriously limited summary of Anglican understandings of faith and doctrine, scarcely relevant to modern Australian life. In some areas, they are now directly contradictory to current Christian teaching. For instance, Article Thirty-seven declares that 'the laws of the realm may punish Christian men with death, for heinous and grievous offences'. This is hardly a teaching to attract support these days among most Australian Anglicans in a country where capital punishment has long been abolished. They also reflect the strong anti-Catholicism of sixteenth-century England: Article Nineteen says that 'the Church of Rome hath erred, not only in their living and manner of ceremonies, but also in matters of faith', while Article Twelve weighs in against certain 'Romish doctrines' which it describes as being 'a fond thing vainly invented … repugnant to the Word of God'. I acknowledge that theologians who have studied them closely take a more positive view. Dr Charles Sherlock, an Australian theologian of note, regards the Articles of Religion highly. They 'speak to what matters and use pastoral criteria for truth', he writes.[37] However, without recourse to scholarly analysis, the majority of modern-day Anglicans, if they have even heard of them, regard the Articles as an interesting but dated historical record.

In elevating the Articles to a position just below holy writ, on the other hand, Sydney Anglicans deliberately link themselves to the struggles of the English Protestant Reformation. It has been said of a former Sydney archbishop, the late Marcus Loane (archbishop from 1966 to 1982), that for him, 'the sixteenth century was not so long ago',[38] and the same could be said of his successors. At one level, Sydney Anglicans are still fighting Reformation battles, though this time against 'apostate' Anglicans more than the Church of Rome. They believe they represent real Anglicanism as it was established in the Reformation under Edward VI, and that other kinds of Anglicans – high-church and Anglo-Catholic Anglicans, liberal and progressive Anglicans, moderate Evangelical Anglicans and even 'broad church' middle-of-the-road everyday Anglicans such as would represent the vast majority of the church's members in the Western world – are aberrations. Certainly, Sydney Anglicans see themselves as the direct heirs of the Elizabethan

---

things (*The Constitution of the Anglican Church of Australia* with alterations as at 16 June 2003, p. 3). Largely on the insistence of Sydney diocese, but with significant support from the relevant General Synod meetings, the Articles were required to be printed in Australia's two recent prayer books, *An Australian Prayer Book* (1978) and *A Prayer Book for Australia* (1995). Traditionally, they had been appended to the Anglican standard of public worship, *The Book of Common Prayer* of 1662. Australian clergy subscribe to the Articles more specifically than their English counterparts. In Melbourne, for instance, they must assent to the doctrine of the Anglican Church of Australia 'as expressed in the Book of Common Prayer and the Ordering of Bishops, Priests and Deacons and the Articles of Religion …' (Declaration and Assent to Doctrine and Formularies of the Diocese of Melbourne).

[37] Personal communication with author.
[38] J.R. Reid, *Marcus L. Loane: A Biography* (Melbourne: Acorn Press, 2004), p. 103.

Puritans, those English Protestants who were dismayed that, to their minds, the final form of the Protestant Reformation in England was half-baked.

Protestantism first gained a serious foothold in England during the brief reign of the sickly boy-king, Edward VI, who reigned from 1547 to 1553. Under Edward's father, Henry VIII, the Reformation had been a political, dynastic exercise rather than a religious reform. Henry had broken with Rome so his marriage to Catherine of Aragon could be annulled – a plan expressly forbidden by the Pope – allowing him to marry Anne Boleyn in a vain attempt to father a male heir. In the event, his only surviving legitimate son was born not to the ill-fated Anne, mother of Queen Elizabeth I, but to his third wife, Jane Seymour, who died shortly after the birth. Edward ascended to the throne aged just ten, and came under the influence of Protestant protectors. During his reign, the first Church of England prayer book was formulated, and then significantly revised, doing away with the Mass and other 'popish' superstitions. By the end of his reign, the Forty-two Articles of Religion had been formulated. The pure Reformation to which Sydney Anglicans continue to aspire had been established when the young king died.

But with his death, the Protestant Reformation almost died too. Edward was succeeded by Catherine of Aragon's only surviving child, the Catholic Mary who, as Queen Mary I, swiftly returned England to Roman allegiance. During her five-year reign, some 300 Protestants were burned at the stake as heretics. They included Thomas Cranmer, author of the prayer books of the previous reign when he had been Archbishop of Canterbury, and two other bishops. This savage retribution was monumentally counter-productive, leading some historians to argue that England was far more sympathetic to Protestantism at the end of Mary's reign than it had been at the beginning.

On Mary's death in 1558, Elizabeth I came to the throne of a deeply-divided and traumatized country, gripped by internal religious controversy and confronted by external threats, principally from Catholic Spain. She re-established a Protestant Church of England – arguably the only viable path open to her, given her half-sister's legacy – but largely through her influence, England's official form of Protestantism in the sixteenth century never went as far as it did on the European Continent. Elizabeth personally retained a strong affection for many of the symbols and forms of the old religion. She liked the kind of religious images the Puritans wanted to smash, for instance, and to the end of her reign, remained deeply opposed to married clergy, though she refrained from actually outlawing clerical marriage as Mary had done. Nor did she like the Protestant emphasis on preaching, sometimes chiding clergymen who attempted overlong sermons in her presence.

So the Church of England followed a *via media* approach, evolving as a church that was both catholic and reformed. Its worship was formal and ordered, using only the officially-sanctioned prayer book, and its ordained ministry retained the traditional orders of bishops, priests and deacons, unlike the more thorough-going Protestantism of continental Europe. This 'Elizabethan Settlement' of the Church of England has been described by Patrick Collinson, the pre-eminent scholar of

English Puritanism in an earlier generation, as a 'compromise in the lively political sense that it was the outcome of manoeuvres in which both the Queen and the Protestants were forced to yield some ground'. It must have seemed 'precarious and provisional, not a settlement to last four hundred years', he has written.[39] But apart from the brief period of the Puritan-controlled English Commonwealth in the mid-seventeenth century, this middle-ground approach became in time firmly established, and has been much celebrated as the 'genius' of Anglicanism.

Significant numbers of 'hot Protestants' were deeply opposed to the Elizabethan compromise, however, and continued to campaign for a 'further Reformation'. Their campaign would eventually – briefly – triumph under the leadership of Oliver Cromwell in the following century, when the Puritans, as their detractors called them, would implement their harsh, intolerant agenda in church and society. Collinson has defined Puritanism as being, at its heart, a 'strenuous search for salvation according to Calvinist understandings'.[40] During Elizabeth's reign, the Puritans resented the enforcement of the compromised religion, imposed through hefty fines and even imprisonment. Many regarded the prayer book worship services they were compelled to attend as 'popish', and abolition of the prayer book was high on the campaign list for them. They wanted an end to ceremonial clergy dress, religious images, symbolic gestures such as the sign of the cross, and many other aspects of Church of England worship they regarded as ungodly. They demanded express Scriptural warrant for all the details of public worship; everything else was superstitious or idolatrous.[41] Most also wanted to abolish bishops, agitating for a Presbyterian form of congregationalism, where power was centred in the local congregation, not in an over-arching hierarchy. They also had a wider societal reformation in mind, wanting to reform popular culture by abolishing long-standing 'pagan' rituals such as the maypole, as well as plays, pubs, public games, and even the celebration of Christmas. Further, they wanted to impose strict codes of dress and speech, and to enforce the observance of Sunday as a day restricted to sober religious activity.[42]

Why did religious ceremonial in all its forms so antagonize the Puritan mindset? Adam Nicolson, the author of an important study of this seminal period in English history, has answered that 'two entirely different and opposing worldviews, and two views of the nature of human beings', lie at the heart of these historical disputes. For the strict reformers, 'only the naked intellectual engagement with the complexities of a rational God would do. All else was confusion and obfuscation.' He continues: 'The word [that is, the Bible] was the route to understanding: everything else was mud in the water.' Puritans saw all forms of ceremonial, all bodily gestures such

---

[39] Patrick Collinson, *The Elizabethan Puritan Movement* (London: Jonathan Cape, 1967), p. 35.
[40] Patrick Collinson, *The Reformation* (London: Weidenfeld & Nicolson, 2003), p. 117.
[41] Cross and Livingstone, *The Oxford Dictionary of the Christian Church*, p. 1351.
[42] Collinson, *The Reformation*, pp. 116–17.

as bowing the head at the name of Jesus or using the sign of the cross, as distorting a purified religion of the word. On the other hand, those who wished to maintain a degree of religious symbolism saw God 'not as an intellectual system but as a mystery', and mystery could not be confined to the intellect. Ceremonial, for them, assisted in the human approach to the divine mystery, whereas for the Puritans, 'prayer was as serious and technical as a law lecture'.[43]

Professor Michael Horsburgh, a former Sydney Anglican lay leader who for many years struggled against the prevalent diocesan mindset, has commented that 'in terms of their "frame of mind", the current Sydney scene is redolent of the Puritans, their rationalism and objectivism'.[44] I would go further, and say that Sydney Anglicans are the direct heirs of the sixteenth- and seventeenth-century English Puritans, and like their forebears, they too seek a 'further Reformation' of the Anglican Church. They are not on their own; a growing minority among English Evangelicals, much influenced by Sydney, has a similar agenda. This mindset has developed to its current extent over the past half-century.

Like the Puritans, Sydney Anglicans want to remove everything they believe distracts from the pure knowledge of God through God's Word, whether it is religious ceremonial, liturgical dress, religious images, or anything that appeals primarily to the senses. They have succeeded almost entirely in Sydney, where now only a small number of parishes still maintain traditional Anglican forms. This is not a mere matter of taste or aesthetics, such as might create debate or controversy between other Anglicans or other Christians, in terms of preferences for church music, hymns, church decoration or the like. It is also far more than simply being 'low-church' or 'high-church'. It is in fact a form of dualism, a separation of the cerebral and the spiritual from the bodily and the material. In its intense rationalism it is also highly anti-intuitive.

This is where Sydney Anglicans part company with Pentecostal churches such as the Assemblies of God and its best-known manifestation in Australia, Hillsong church in Sydney. Though Pentecostalists share many of Sydney's conservative views and beliefs, their worship style is primarily experiential and often charismatic in the religious meaning of the word, 'speaking in tongues' under the supposed direct intervention of the Holy Spirit. Whether technically charismatic or not, Pentecostal worship focuses on feelings and the creation of a mood of excitement and well-being. Sydney Diocese's worship is most certainly not based on emotion; the diocese is extremely suspicious of charismatic phenomena and of Pentecostalism generally. Sydney Anglican parishes make full use of youth-oriented contemporary music as a means of attracting young congregations, but at the heart of the worship is an expository style of preaching aimed at locking in intellectual commitment to a set of rationalist propositions.

---

[43] Adam Nicolson, *God's Secretaries* (New York: HarperCollins, 2003), pp. 36–8.

[44] Michael Horsburgh, *Understanding the Diocese of Sydney*, address to a forum held in Melbourne on 20 February 2005 by Melbourne Anglicans Together Inc.

Conservative, even fundamentalist, yes. But by any measure, Sydney Diocese has been, until recently, a dynamic, pace-setting enterprise. It is led by an internationally-recognized, energetic leader who came to power as the result of decades of planning by conservative powerbrokers. Its tentacles reach around the globe and throughout the Australian church. It has record numbers of ordination candidates each year, strong church attendance figures and, despite recent losses, still-significant financial resources. It has well-established specialist ministries, particularly to young people, and a theological college that spreads the Sydney gospel far and wide. But in the twenty-first century there are nevertheless significant challenges, to which we will turn in Chapter 7.

Chapter 3
Sydney Anglicans: How It Came to This

White settlement in Australia began in Sydney, and Sydney began as a prison. The city's inauspicious beginnings are an important aspect in the evolution of contemporary Sydney Anglicanism. Unlike the United States of America, where the first English settlers, deeply devout men and women, sought a godly life free from the constraints of their (Anglican) homeland, Australia was colonized in January 1788 as a dumping ground for convicts. Australians have not yet really grasped the significance of this beginning, let alone its possible ramifications for the contemporary Australian character. Nor have they fully realized how perilous was the situation of the convicts, the sailors, the marines and the few free settlers who arrived in the 11 ships of the First Fleet. They were all effectively dumped on the other side of the world with few resources and an alarming paucity of people experienced in even basic food production, building techniques, or other essential survival skills. The colonists, convicts and gaolers alike, were on the verge of starvation by the time the Second Fleet, carrying much-needed provisions, arrived in Sydney Harbour in June 1790. It was a grindingly harsh beginning for a new nation.

When transportation of convicts to the Australian colonies ceased in 1868, 160,000 convicts had been shipped there. Just 25,000 of them were female, ensuring that European Australia began as a heavily male-dominated society. Particularly in the first decades of Sydney town, before significant numbers of free settlers arrived, the imbalance meant that convict women had little choice but to become the mistresses or de facto wives of both convict and free men. Some early commentators complained that the whole colony operated as a brothel, with sexual favours openly traded and most colonists increasingly addicted to rum, the local currency in the colony's first years. An early stereotype of convict women as degraded whores was implanted on the colony's psyche, leading to an inevitable exaggeration of the traditional dichotomy of women as either virgins or whores: 'damned whores and God's police', as Anne Summers' landmark 1975 book of the same name categorized them.[1]

The convicts, drawn mainly from the urban working (and criminal) classes of Britain, generally reflected the contempt for established religion that was common to their class. Historians agree that most were nominally Anglicans, with a significant minority of Irish Catholics. But in the late eighteenth and early nineteenth centuries, the Church of England was a church for the gentry

---

[1] Anne Summers, *Damned Whores and God's Police: The Colonization of Women in Australia* (Ringwood: Penguin, 1975).

and middle classes, certainly in the teeming cities that were a by-product of the Industrial Revolution. Where there was contact between Church of England clergy and city dwellers in the home country, it was most likely to be in the clergy's role as agents of the state as magistrates, or as moralistic preachers attempting to uphold law and order.

In Sydney's early days, this was precisely the relationship that existed between the convicts and the church. Richard Johnson, an Evangelical clergyman, was sent with the First Fleet as chaplain. By all accounts a decent and caring man who attempted to offer some genuine pastoral care to his motley flock, Johnson's first duty nevertheless was to assist the Governor, Arthur Phillip, to 'enforce a due observance of religion and good order among the inhabitants of the new settlement'. The two went hand-in-hand – established religion and orderly behaviour. He was inevitably 'part of the disciplinary apparatus of a prison settlement'.[2] Given the 'gross immoralities, depredations, drunkenness, riots and even murders, daily committed' in the colony, of which Johnson complained, it is no wonder his concern and his preaching focused on issues of personal morality first and foremost.[3] As an Evangelical, reform of individual convicts was a high priority for him in any case.

This clash between the realities of convict life and the expectations of the established church was magnified under Johnson's successor, the 'flogging parson', Samuel Marsden. Another Evangelical committed to the cause of reform, Marsden was a more energetic and forceful character than Johnson. An extremely able man, he was also very much a man of his age. As two historians of Sydney Diocese have put it, given the revolutionary era in Continental Europe and social unrest in Britain and Ireland, Marsden's primary concern was maintaining order – order was 'God's will for the world and an urgent necessity for New South Wales'. It was 'the prime motive in his pulpit denunciations of sin … (and) his severity on the bench as a magistrate'.[4] And severe he was. From the Governor, Lachlan Macquarie, down, he was regarded as the most severe magistrate in the colony. A popular saying concerning Marsden was that 'he sentences the prisoner on the Saturday, admonishes him on Sunday, and flogs him on Monday'.[5]

He was particularly harsh in his response to Irish convicts (of whom there was a significant number), particularly after the 1798 Irish Rising. By 1803, Catholics

---

[2] Michael Hogan, *The Sectarian Strand: Religion in Australian History* (Ringwood: Penguin, 1987), p. 12. Hogan provides a useful overview of the relationship between convicts and clergy, and the development of religious pluralism and practice in early Sydney.

[3] Ibid., p. 11.

[4] Stephen Judd and Kenneth Cable, *Sydney Anglicans: A History of the Diocese* (Sydney: Anglican Information Office, 2000), p. 4.

[5] Allan M. Grocott, *Convicts, Clergymen and Churches: Attitudes of Convicts and Ex-Convicts towards the Churches and Clergy in New South Wales from 1788 to 1851* (Sydney: Sydney University Press, 1980), pp. 233–4.

comprised about one quarter of the convicts, but their calls for priests to minister to them were denied until 1820, though that was earlier than Catholic emancipation was enacted in England. The involvement of Irish convicts in the 1804 armed rebellion at Vinegar Hill, west of Parramatta, only intensified sectarian feeling in the colony. These strands of convict 'immorality' and religious indifference, together with Irish rebellion, all confronted by unyielding and often punitive Anglican clergy (the practice of appointing Anglican clergy as magistrates did not cease until 1827), created a legacy of 'us and them' between the first white Australians and the Anglican Church. Though much has changed in Australian society, particularly in the post-World War II era of immigration from countries other than Great Britain and of religious and cultural pluriformity, the vestiges of the legacy remain, particularly in Sydney.

The Anglican Church and the other mainstream Protestant churches which established themselves early in the colony, maintained generally good relationships. These were strengthened by their united opposition to the substantially Irish Catholic Church. In turn, the Catholics, embittered by the years of discrimination and the long memory of English domination of their homeland, had little sympathy for the Protestants. This sense of competition and distrust between Anglicans and Catholics still flares from time to time, particularly in Sydney. Archbishop Loane's refusal to meet Pope Paul VI on his Sydney visit in 1970 is a case in point. It was a cause of great embarrassment to more ecumenically-minded Anglicans around Australia. Peter Jensen's enormous admiration for the late Pope John Paul II, coupled with his ongoing friendship with his Catholic counterpart, Cardinal George Pell, seems to signal an end to the bad old days of sectarian rivalry in Sydney. This does not suggest, however, that Sydney Anglican leaders are any more comfortable today with Catholic teaching and worship than their predecessors have been. Rather, they have sensed a useful conservative alliance.

At the time of Pope John Paul II's death, Australian Anglicans were taken aback to discover how significant he had been to their conservative leadership. Archbishop Peter Jensen surprised many when he proclaimed the Pope one of the 'great men of history'. Jensen, in company with numerous other astute conservative Protestants around the world, has recognized the enormous support that the moral conservatism of Rome offers their particular causes. Pope John Paul II was a 'radical conservative', Jensen said, a description he could well apply to himself. The late Pope had encouraged him 'to be willing to be strong even if the culture is moving in a different direction'. The Pope's opposition to the ordination of women and to homosexuality were areas in which Jensen and John Paul II, for all their doctrinal differences, were of one mind. Pope John Paul II had 'stood against the forces which folk Protestantism capitulated to: the relativism, libertarianism, individualism and materialism of western culture', Jensen said.[6]

---

[6] Peter Jensen, 'The Protestant Conscience', the Bernard G. Judd Memorial Lecture to the NSW Council of Churches, 5 April 2005.

Jensen also shares a 'radical conservatism' with Cardinal Pell. As well as moral conservativism, the two men have much in common. Both DPhil graduates of the University of Oxford, they took up office in Sydney in the same year, 2001. Both are vehemently opposed to the very notion of women or gay clergy. And they are both defiantly counter-cultural, fiercely proud that the orthodoxy they claim to represent is often at odds with 'the culture of the day'.[7] Both regard liberals in their churches as the enemy within. So it is not really surprising that they claim a friendship, clearly demonstrated by the invitation to Jensen to launch a biography of Pell in 2002, an invitation Jensen accepted. They are also obviously both astute political operators, and realize that in secular twenty-first century Sydney, it makes eminent sense for the leaders of the two largest Christian churches to make common cause wherever possible.

The conservative Evangelical drive to preach reform to an irreligious, immoral, disordered society so evident in the early days of the colony is still very much part of the Sydney mentality, as has been made explicit so recently in Peter Jensen's Mission programme. All the Protestant churches share this propensity in Sydney though, often seeing themselves in open confrontation with the wider community. It is no accident that the Festival of Light campaign against 'moral pollution', though initially launched in Adelaide, swiftly based itself in Sydney. Nor is it a coincidence that the annual Gay and Lesbian Mardi Gras is a Sydney institution. The more the churches and para-religious organizations position themselves in opposition to secular culture, the more they seem to trigger the very phenomena they abhor. While there are similar processes at work in other parts of Australia and elsewhere, the Sydney manifestations have a peculiarly harsh, conservative edge to them.

Sydney as a city retains, too, a more overtly hedonistic air than the other Australian capitals. Its nicknames – 'sin city', 'the emerald city' – say it all. The pursuit of pleasure, money and fame, and the ostentatious display of all three, are symbolized in the sweep of multi-million dollar homes and apartments around the harbour, and the rich men's yachts on the water. Flamboyance is a way of life, carrying with it a touch of the arrogant nose-thumbing at all forms of establishment, including formal religion, which is not far removed from the legendary cheekiness of the convict.

Nor should it be overlooked in passing that the flavour of male domination has continued more strongly in Sydney's mainstream churches than elsewhere. It is significant that the first women ordained in the Methodist, Congregational and Presbyterian churches were in Adelaide, Melbourne and Perth, while the first women ordained in the Anglican Church were ordained in Melbourne.[8] Is there a

---

[7] Peter Jensen's speech launching Tess Livingstone's biography, *George Pell* (Sydney: Duffy & Snellgrove, 2002), 29 October 2002.

[8] The first woman ordained in Australia, Winifred Kiek, was ordained for the Congregational Church in Adelaide in 1927, followed by the Revd Isabelle Merry in Melbourne in 1937. The first Methodist ordained woman, Margaret Sanders, was

lingering correlation between the early assessment of Sydney's convict women as 'damned whores' and the reluctance to allow women into church leadership in that city?

Mainstream church leaders in the rest of Australia have long recognized the conservative leanings of their Sydney counterparts. In fact, some claim that Sydney religion in general is growing ever more conservative, complicating national internal church relationships. The very different patterns of colonization in the other states, apart from Tasmania, go a long way to explaining these differences. The free settlement of Melbourne, for instance, where industrious, sober, churchgoing Presbyterians were predominant, created a very different religious climate. Church and society were partners there in the joint enterprise of building a prosperous community. There were few grounds for confrontation. As a consequence, the mainstream churches in that city have rarely promoted large-scale moral reform programmes, though Melbourne Protestant churches too have strong Evangelical roots.

This might be a good place to reflect briefly on Evangelicalism as a subset of Christianity. Strictly speaking, all Christian churches are, or should be, 'evangelical' because 'to evangelize' means to preach the Gospel of Jesus Christ, which is the fundamental duty of the Christian community. Evangelicalism, in the sense that it is used in this book, relates to an eighteenth-century movement that developed in the Church of England at a time when the church was at a low ebb. Church life was largely moribund, with many clergy described as being negligent and worldly. The Wesley brothers John and Charles who, like their father, were Anglican clergymen, were the main leaders at the beginning of the movement, which subsequently was forced out of the established church to become the Society of Methodists. However an ongoing Evangelical 'school' remained within the Church of England influenced, in contrast to the Methodist Church, by the Calvinist ethos of the Thirty-nine Articles, the *Book of Common Prayer*, and the teachings of the influential preacher George Whitefield (1714–70).

Evangelicalism increasingly became a force in England, particularly at the University of Cambridge. Its proponents raised funds for the training of sympathetic clergy and laity to work both in England and in overseas missions, and by the early nineteenth century, Evangelical Anglicans were becoming bishops, and thus more influential in the Church of England. Prominent lay Evangelicals are household names for their zealous humanitarian work: William Wilberforce (1759–1833) led the group that campaigned for the abolition of the slave trade, while Lord Shaftesbury (1801–85) effected factory reform, including the protection of child workers, through the various Factory Acts passed by the British Parliament. A

---

ordained in Western Australia in 1969, closely followed by Coralie Ling in Melbourne in the same year. The first Presbyterian woman to be ordained in Australia was Marlene 'Polly' Thalheimer, ordained in Melbourne in 1974. The first Anglican women deacons were ordained in Melbourne in 1986. See Muriel Porter, *Women in the Church: The Great Ordination Debate in Australia* (Ringwood: Penguin, 1989).

deep concern for social justice issues has traditionally been a hallmark of classical Evangelicalism.

As with all church 'parties', however, Evangelicalism has been subject to internal disputes and divisions, with some groups espousing extreme and sometimes idiosyncratic views. In the late nineteenth and early twentieth centuries, some American Evangelicals, in reaction to Darwin's theory of evolution and the development of biblical criticism, developed what is now known as Christian fundamentalism. While English and Australian Evangelicals did not go so far down the track of what we might call formal fundamentalism, they nevertheless divided into 'liberal' and 'conservative' wings. Put succinctly, liberal Evangelicals accept the findings of biblical criticism, that is, that the Bible contains far more sophisticated literature than had previously been imagined. Conservatives, on the other hand, hold to the verbal inspiration of Scripture. But all Evangelicals nevertheless place 'special stress on conversion and salvation by faith in the atoning death of Christ'.[9] Because of this stress, Evangelicalism has an inbuilt bias towards preaching for conversion and therefore for missionary activity. It has traditionally also had a concern for personal holiness of life, which at times has developed extreme forms, such as the promotion of 'sinless perfection', as will be discussed later. Evangelicalism also tends to be centred in home and family rather than in the church; 'early rising and family prayers have been at the heart of Evangelical piety'.[10] In public worship, Anglican Evangelicals were until recently traditionally categorized as 'low-church', maintaining ordered, dignified prayer book services that conform to the rubrics (rules) of the old prayer book. They avoid the ceremonial trappings associated with 'high-church' or Anglo-Catholic worship, though there is a vast spectrum of symbol and ceremony that is encompassed in that term. Under the influence of both Sydney and American Protestantism, old-style low-church worship is now less common in liberal Evangelical churches, which are more likely now to favour more extempore forms of worship.

Evangelicalism, as we have seen, came to Sydney right at the beginning, with its first two chaplains. Both Johnson and Marsden had been promoted for their posts by key Evangelical backers, concerned both for the reformation of the convicts and a possible mission to Australia's Indigenous people. There is not space here, in one short chapter, to describe Sydney's development as an Evangelical diocese in the detail it deserves. There have been some limited attempts to provide the historical framework, but they have generally been either too circumspect[11] or too

---

[9] F.L. Cross and E.A. Livingstone (eds), *The Oxford Dictionary of the Christian Church*, third edition (Oxford: Oxford University Press, 1997), p. 580.

[10] Ibid.

[11] The most comprehensive attempt to date is Judd and Cable, *Sydney Anglicans* but this volume was prepared and published at the behest of Sydney Diocese's Standing Committee, which inevitably seems to have bred a degree of caution in the work.

polemical.[12] The best study to date is that of Stuart Piggin. His is a perceptive and erudite work, but it is limited by the inclusion of Sydney within the broader scope of a survey of Evangelicalism in Australia generally.[13] Sydney really requires a full-scale, no-holds-barred examination of its historical development. Here, I will confine myself to providing some broad brushstrokes of the main events and personalities that have brought Sydney Anglicanism to its current form of extreme, conservative Evangelicalism.

A century after the arrival of the First Fleet, Sydney churchgoing was still predominantly Evangelical in character, but was markedly different from its earliest colonial forms. No longer a pioneer settlement perched perilously on the edge of the known world, Sydney town was now a flourishing city, with commuter suburbs developing rapidly. The old male/female imbalance was a thing of the past, though it was still a reality in far-flung rural areas. In the churches, women now often outnumbered men two to one, setting up a pattern that has only begun to change in recent years, as increasing numbers of younger women have abandoned regular worship. But in the 1880s, women were coming into their own, in the sense that much of suburban parish life now depended on them. Sunday schools, choirs, fund-raising activities, pastoral visitations to the sick and poor, were becoming the preserve of women, and as Judd and Cable have pointed out, there was a marked feminization of church buildings as well. Floral arrangements became a regular feature of church decoration, for instance, and there was an increase in the use of stained glass. Men, however, still led all aspects of church life, from bishops to priests to churchwardens and the like, with women – specially middle-class wives and unmarried daughters – comprising the willing parish workforce.[14]

But low-church though Sydney resolutely remained, it was nevertheless challenged before the end of the century by some outbreaks of what was termed 'ritualism', and an attempt to moderate its intellectual conservatism. They came together during the short five-year episcopacy of Sydney's third bishop, Alfred Barry, bishop from 1884 to 1889. In his new diocese, Barry attempted to promote a greater respect for the new biblical criticism and scientific knowledge gaining attention in Europe by appointing a sympathetic principal to Moore Theological College, and engaging Anglicans in a more liberal discussion of their faith. Neither gained him friends in influential church circles. It was feared he was trying to introduce Anglo-Catholic principles, particularly given what was happening in the mother country.

---

[12] The various writings by the former Archbishop of Sydney, the late Marcus Loane, come into this category. He wrote a series of valuable but rather hagiographical biographies of key Sydney leaders.

[13] Stuart Piggin, *Evangelical Christianity in Australia: Spirit, Word and World* (Melbourne: Oxford University Press, 1996), second edition, *Spirit of a Nation: The Story of Australia's Christian Heritage* (Sydney: Strand Publishing, 2004).

[14] Judd and Cable, *Sydney Anglicans*, pp. 115–16.

In England, controversies had erupted over the development of Anglo-Catholicism, that is, forms of Anglican belief, worship and practice influenced by Roman Catholicism. To Anglicans of a staunch Evangelical and low-church mind, this was a highly dangerous move, and smacked of a return to the 'popery' that had been expelled from the Church of England at great cost by their martyred spiritual ancestors in the sixteenth century. In England, Anglo-Catholicism was met by fierce opposition, resulting in controversial challenges to the courts (because the Church of England was and is, a state church), and the growth of church societies dedicated either to promoting the new practices, or opposing them.

In Sydney, Barry's attempts to change staffing and other arrangements at St Andrew's Cathedral looked ominous to his critics, who erupted at a proposal to include a traditional crucifixion scene in an alabaster sculptured panel behind the main altar. Ironically, though Evangelicals are focused on the death of Jesus, and sing heartily about the cross of Jesus, they reject pictorial depictions of it for fear that they are a form of 'popish idolatry'. The critics of the panel won, and it was replaced. But some parish churches, nevertheless, were introducing ritualist elements, with altar lights and crosses, robed choirs and Eucharistic vestments appearing in places such as Christ Church St Laurence, Railway Square. Branches of the polemical English church societies sprang up in Sydney from 1880 on, dedicated to the same aims as their distant mentors. The Evangelical societies came together in 1909 to form the Anglican Church League, initially established as a 'centre unity' Evangelical party. In time, though, it was to become a hardline conservative Evangelical organization, and the engine house of Sydney's current extreme form of Evangelicalism.[15]

On the wider church front, Sydney was also becoming increasingly alienated from the other dioceses in Australia, as many of them adopted the very Anglo-Catholic doctrines and practices Sydney was resisting. This alienation was not helped by a controversy over the disputed election in 1889 of Bishop William Saumarez Smith. Because at the time Sydney's bishop was also *ex officio* the Primate, the other Australian diocesan bishops had the deciding vote in who became bishop of Sydney. An unfortunate muddle over Smith's election led to a serious misunderstanding between Sydney and the rest of the church, which ended with a General Synod decision to divorce the Primacy from Sydney. Sydney was now free to choose its own bishops, and the Australian bishops were free to choose a Primate who might not necessarily be from Sydney.[16]

At the same time as Sydney Evangelicals were uniting against high-church elements, they were also, according to Judd and Cable, withdrawing from wider society. The influence of a mission in Australia led by an Irish clergyman, George G. Grubb, was a key factor in this. Grubb represented a new wave of Evangelicalism, then sweeping England, devoted to the pursuit of personal holiness. Grubb's

---

[15] For this section, I am indebted to Judd and Cable, and to Ruth Frappell, 'Party Politics', published in *Anglicans Together Newsletter*, 20, April 2003.

[16] Judd and Cable, *Sydney Anglicans*, pp. 139ff.

was an emotional style of revivalism, and one that sprang from an introspective theology. But though his mission had little effect in Sydney's wider community, it led to regular revivalist practices, such as calls to make 'decisions for Christ', in Sydney parishes. And he had some notable converts, some of whom became leading Sydney clergymen. Though still keen to evangelize secular Sydney, many Sydney Anglicans also retreated into the pursuit of personal holiness within the community of the faithful. In the parishes, church organizations which duplicated secular activities – church football, cricket, and tennis clubs, scout and guide clubs and the like – kept parishioners closely tied to church life, and effectively separate from the outside world.[17]

With the 1910 introduction of the requirement that all clergy in Sydney must undertake not to wear Eucharistic vestments, the advance of ritualism was effectively stalled in the diocese. Strongly committed Anglo-Catholics not prepared to give up vestments and all that they symbolized, were now less likely to accept appointment in Sydney. Still, there remained significant numbers of high-church clergymen, ensuring that the diocese did not become monochrome. The Anglican Church League, seemingly confident that the battle against ritualism had been won, was politically astute enough to include some high-church representatives in its informal voting advice in relation to synod elections to various church bodies. Up to a quarter of the available places were made available to them, though not key strategic places. For one thing, the practice kept the high churchmen content and unlikely to initiate separate campaigns. But such a reasonable compact was not to last.[18]

By the 1930s, the Anglican Church League was becoming more hardline, even as it tasted the fruits of its first major victory. It orchestrated the 1933 election of Howard Mowll, a conservative Evangelical and former missionary, as Archbishop of Sydney, despite opposition from its own president and vice-president, both liberal Evangelicals. They resigned from the League over the tactics used to secure the election. The writing was on the wall not only for high church sympathizers, but liberal Evangelicals as well. Mowll was a vigorous, imposing, youthful man, whose authoritarian tendencies had been confirmed by his first ministry as a bishop in the mission field of China. He was immensely popular, and was served devotedly by his League backers. His 24-year reign as Archbishop of Sydney was to set the seal on the conservative Evangelical tenor of the diocese. Two events during his time as Archbishop ensured the future: first, his appointment of a conservative Irishman to lead Moore Theological College; and second, his refusal to give any quarter to a significant group of disaffected clergy.

The Revd T.C. Hammond was appointed Principal of Moore College in 1935. From Cork, he had been head of the Irish Church Missions in Dublin, a Protestant organization striving to convert Catholic Ireland. As Judd and Cable note, 'he came from a polarised religious environment in which controversy and polemics

---

[17] Ibid., pp. 150, 151, 155.
[18] Ibid., pp. 168, 169.

were the order of the day'. He was already known in Sydney from a mission he had conducted some years earlier for the Anglican Church League. He encouraged Evangelicals to adopt a position of no compromise and like him, to defend Scripture and the Elizabethan Reformation Settlement. His influence, particularly through the training of clergy for the diocese, could only intensify the conservative Evangelicalism already dominant there.[19]

The disaffected clergy came from the liberal Evangelical and high-church wings of the diocese. It has been estimated that together they formed about 40 per cent of the diocesan decision-makers in the mid-1920s, a figure that had dropped to about 20 per cent a decade later.[20] Concerned about the increasingly monochrome nature of the diocese, 50 of them – comprising more than a quarter of Sydney rectors – wrote to Archbishop Mowll in 1938. The letter became known as 'The Memorial' and its authors as 'The Memorialists'. They asked to see the Archbishop to discuss their concern to see diversity respected in the diocese. The signatories were in the main ordinary Sydney clergy, 'not agitators who had come into the Sydney diocese in order to undermine its Evangelical character'.[21]

Mowll handled the petition extremely badly. He required each signatory to give him detailed answers to 14 questions on the issues they had raised. The questionnaire, and the accompanying uncompromising letter, had been prepared by T.C. Hammond, and carried the stamp of the Irish controversialist. Mowll refused to meet the Memorialists without individual responses to the questionnaire; they in turn would only substantiate their claims in a private meeting with him. The result was a stalemate, followed by a full airing of the issues in the secular press, which ended any hope of reconciliation. It was a heavy-handed and graceless response to senior men airing genuine grievances. In time, the treatment of the 'Memorialists' became a byword outside Sydney for the diocese's intransigence. It marked the end of any hope of genuine respect for diversity in Sydney.[22] By the time of Mowll's death in 1958, the Memorialists had waned – there were just 14 of them still engaged in active ministry in Sydney – and the influence of Hammond's empire, Moore College, had grown apace.

Only a few years after the Memorialist controversy, Sydney Diocese had the opportunity to demonstrate how far it would go to limit diversity not only in its own territory, but beyond. In 1942, the Anglo-Catholic Bishop of Bathurst, Arnold Wylde, authorized the use in his diocese of an order for Holy Communion that was more 'catholic' than the only formulary authorized in Australia, the *Book of Common Prayer*. Nicknamed the 'Red Book' (because of the colour of its cover), the book was introduced into Bathurst churches, where it was quickly denounced by some lay people. When their complaints were not acted on, they applied to Archbishop Mowll, asking him to intervene as Metropolitan of New South Wales.

---

[19] Ibid., p. 233.
[20] Ibid., p. 237.
[21] Ibid., p. 238.
[22] Ibid., pp. 238f.

(Capital city archbishops have certain limited rights in the regional dioceses in their state.) Mowll referred the complainants to T.C. Hammond, his usual political adviser, as in the case of the Memorialists. Hammond engaged sympathetic legal counsel for the complainants. Wylde refused to compromise his authority by withdrawing the book, so in 1944, a number of laymen from Bathurst parishes took their bishop to court. There, directed by Hammond, they claimed that the Red Book was illegal as it contained practices not lawful in the Church of England. This made the use of the book a 'breach of the trust in which the church buildings were vested'.

The Equity Division of the Supreme Court upheld the laymen's challenge, and Wylde's subsequent appeal to the High Court was dismissed. The High Court, however, varied the previous injunction, limiting the banning of the Red Book to the 20 churches whose trusts had been proved by the earlier ruling. As Judd and Cable have commented, 'there were few victors'. The book disappeared from about 40 per cent of Bathurst parishes, but it remained in use in others. More significantly, the High Court decision 'made it unlikely that a general ruling against liturgical innovation could ever be obtained'.[23]

The Red Book case became a by-word among other Australian Anglicans for the lengths to which some Sydney Evangelicals would go to uphold their convictions – while denying others *their* convictions – even to the extent of interfering in the affairs of other dioceses. A similar case would occur many years later, in February 1992, over the projected ordination of women priests, when a Sydney layman would play a leading role in a challenge to the Supreme Court of New South Wales to stop the then Bishop of Canberra and Goulburn, Owen Dowling, from a planned ordination. Once again, the civil court would decline to do the church's work. The New South Wales Court of Appeal dismissed the case brought against Dowling, as the Supreme Court of Western Australia had earlier dismissed a similar challenge brought by the same plaintiffs in a failed attempt to prevent the March 1992 ordination of women priests in Perth. From both judgements, it seems that unless a breach of a trust is involved, the courts will not intervene in internal church machinations. That had been the inescapable lesson of the Red Book case, to which the 1992 plaintiffs perhaps paid too little heed.

Archbishop Mowll died unexpectedly in October 1958. The following year was to be a crucial one for Sydney: a milestone for Moore College, for conservative Evangelicalism, for the diocese's financial resources, and for its overall future. This was despite the fact that Mowll's successor, who took up his post in 1959, was not cast in the same mould as Mowll at all, and whose episcopate was something of an embarrassment. Though clearly an Evangelical, Hugh Rowlands Gough turned out to be a more liberal Evangelical than his new diocese had expected. He insisted that although he was a devoted Evangelical, he regarded himself as an Anglican first, unlike some members of his diocese, for whom the situation was reversed. An aloof and patrician Englishman, he won few hearts during his seven-year

---

[23] Ibid., pp. 253ff.

sojourn in Sydney, and left the diocese under the cloud of rumours of an extra-marital affair.[24] The diocese's power-brokers, who had been caught unprepared by Mowll's death, would ensure they were in control of his successor's election. So Gough's replacement was a man firmly in the conservative mould. Nevertheless, three significant events with long-term repercussions occurred during Gough's episcopate, two of them dating from 1959: Broughton Knox took over as principal of Moore College; the first Sydney Billy Graham crusade was held; and Sydney Diocese's financial structures were reorganized. Broughton Knox's appointment, given his role in shaping Sydney Diocese as it is today, is probably the most important of the three.

Knox, the son of an influential Sydney priest and brother-in-law of Gough's successor as archbishop, Marcus Loane, was vice-principal of Moore College when he was appointed principal by Mowll shortly before his death. Knox had tutored at Moore from 1947, and been vice-principal from 1954. He was to be principal for 26 years – the longest-serving principal in the college's 129-year history when he retired in 1985.[25] He and the new Archbishop Gough, whose terms of office virtually began together, clashed significantly, causing Knox to ensure that the archbishop was kept at arm's length from the college. He became one of Gough's fiercest critics. More important, however, was his theological perspective, which has so powerfully influenced contemporary Sydney.

Where T.C. Hammond had been a conservative Evangelical theologian in a more traditional mode, Knox was a conservative Evangelical in a radical form who changed the college's focus to Calvin's theology. In particular, assisted by his deputy, Donald Robinson, a future Archbishop of Sydney, Knox concentrated on teaching a radical (for Anglicans) view of the nature of the church. They taught trainee clergy that the church, in the New Testament sense, was the 'actual meeting of believers', rather than an 'ongoing society of believers'.[26] (This change of emphasis also explains the significance of the term 'meeting', now used in many Sydney parishes to designate worship services.) The essence of the church was found in the local congregation, nowhere else. Moore College was now conforming to the ideas of the Congregationalists or Plymouth Brethren, rather than to traditional Anglican views.

Marcus Loane and members of the college's own council feared it was losing its Anglican moorings. Its congregationalism, however, fitted the mood of the 1960s and 1970s, ensuring that the students lapped it up. Loane later commented that he tried in various ways to modify the new teaching at Moore, without success,

---

[24] See Ruth Frappell, 'A Barchester Chronicle: The Election to the Archbishopric in Sydney in November 1958', paper delivered to an Anglican historians' meeting, 1997.

[25] Donald W.B. Robinson, 'David Broughton Knox: An Appreciation', in Peter T. O'Brien and David G. Peterson (eds), *God Who is Rich in Mercy: Essays Presented to Dr D.B. Knox* (Sydney: Lancer Books, 1986) p. xi.

[26] Judd and Cable, *Sydney Anglicans*, pp. 289ff. The quotations in this section are taken from there.

though he managed to control some of its manifestations, such as instances of clergy trying to flout their ordination vows to uphold Anglican norms. When he retired as archbishop in 1982, however, 'the flood burst'.[27] His successor, Donald Robinson, also found his own teaching had created significant difficulties in dealing with some clergy and their congregations. As we shall see in Chapter 5, the Knox-Robinson teaching made the concept of a national Anglican church, let alone an international Anglican Communion, significantly less important, and in effect, gave permission for an even further loosening of the emotional ties between Sydney and the rest of the Australian church. It led directly to the assertion of some Sydney Diocesan leaders that Sydney and the rest of the Australian church inhabit parallel universes.

Peter Jensen is very much the product of the Knox-Robinson teaching about the nature of the church. In what some have seen as his 'election manifesto', his address to the Anglican Church League's annual synod dinner held the year before he was elected archbishop, Jensen described the church as the local congregation: 'However important the diocese, the episcopacy [leadership by bishops] and the liturgy (and all are important), they exist to serve the congregation and not the other way around', he said. Significantly, he added: 'We [Sydney Diocese] have not waited for permission [from the national church] to change what happens in church; we have done what needs to be done to nurture Christians of all ages.' This he described as a 'principled radicalism'.[28]

Broughton Knox also taught the intensely rational theological principles of biblical revelation known as 'propositional revelation', which we have discussed in the previous chapter. These principles, so fully elucidated in recent years by Peter Jensen, are Knox's second key contribution to the evolution of contemporary Sydney. Peter Jensen, who succeeded Knox as principal of Moore College from 1985, is evidently a keen disciple of Knox's teaching in this regard, as well as in his understanding of 'church'. Melbourne theologian Dr Duncan Reid has helpfully summarized Jensen's argument as presented in his book, *The Revelation of God: Contours of Christian Theology*, published in 2002. Reid writes that there are two basic themes in Jensen's presentation: 'Revelation is fundamentally propositional, and the proper attitude of the Christian believer is obedience to revelation.' Reid is quick to add, however, that 'neither of these themes is developed [by Jensen] in such an unsophisticated way as such a bald summary might suggest'.[29]

Reid takes issue with what he identifies as Jensen's rejection of the Enlightenment and the problem he believes that has been created by the

---

[27] J.R. Reid, *Marcus L. Loane: A Biography* (Melbourne: Acorn Press, 2004), pp. 108–9.

[28] Peter Jensen, 'Build on the Past, Seize This Moment, Create the Future', address to the Anglican Church League annual synod dinner, 9 October 2000.

[29] Duncan Reid, 'Anglican Diversity and Conflict: A Case Study on God, Gender and Authority', in Bruce Kaye (ed.), *'Wonderful and Confessedly Strange': Australian Essays in Anglican Ecclesiology* (Adelaide: ATF Press, 2006), pp. 254–5.

Enlightenment's liberation theme 'entering the Christian soul'. 'Jensen seems to want to return to the pre-Enlightenment ... world', Reid comments. Analysing this particular approach to the Bible, Reid continues: 'There is no post-modern or post-colonial hearkening here to the dissonances, the spaces between the words, or the minority voices in the text.'[30] Further, Reid supports the contention that propositional revelation tends dangerously towards gnosticism, that is, secret revealed knowledge, given only once. This can lead to the 'arrogant assumption that one's knowledge is right and everyone else therefore must be wrong. Such a stance closes dialogue.' He quotes the former Australian Primate, Dr Peter Carnley, as discerning in Sydney's insistence on propositional revelation a 'retreat into protestant scholasticism'. Reid maintains that this stance is not faithful to mainstream Evangelicalism, which (in part) developed as a reaction against an eighteenth-century form of scholasticism.[31]

A revealing anecdote concerning Broughton Knox, quoted by both Carnley and Reid, demonstrates the implications of his 'propositional revelation' theory most dramatically. In 1956, Archbishop Mowll asked Knox to advise him how to respond to churches seeking permission to place large crosses on or above their altars. Such crosses were likely to be used for superstitious purposes, Knox replied, because idolatry is not the 'worship of a statue instead of God so much as the worship even of the true God by means of materialistic representations', as Carnley has paraphrased it. Knox had written: 'if we persistently worship God with the aid of material media, our religious life will be confined to the lowest element in our soul, the sensuous, and we will never truly know God'. True faith, for him, seemed to be a matter of intellectual understanding only. Carnley comments that 'there are indicators of an alarming dualism in Dr Knox's statements, insofar as he draws an unfortunate gnostic dichotomy between the spiritual and the material'.[32] In Knox's scenario, God cannot be truly worshipped with the senses, the emotions, the feelings, or any other bodily/sensory aspect. Religious art and symbols, colour, music and fragrance (such as incense), and bodily posture and movement, let alone the beauty of nature or any form of Christian meditation or mysticism, are at best irrelevant and at worst dangerous to true Christian worship. A moment's thought will confirm that such a theory effectively negates a great deal of Christian tradition and practice, and even much of the imagery that informs Scripture itself. The rationalist propositional revelation teaching is the direct opposite of holistic spirituality, and reflects nothing of feeling, imagination, intuition, or the place of silence in religious meditation.

Reid draws this opposition in doctrinal terms. If this dichotomy between the spiritual and the material is accepted, he argues, 'we deny the possibility of the spiritual revealing itself through matter. Christian discourse about the

---

[30] Ibid., pp. 256–7.
[31] Ibid., pp. 257–8.
[32] Ibid., p. 258; Peter Carnley, *Reflections in Glass: Trends and Tensions in the Contemporary Anglican Church* (Sydney: HarperCollins, 2004), pp. 69–70.

Word's becoming flesh, God's bodily participation in the world, would then be transformed from a radical claim into a pious myth, a mere manner of speech with no real content.' This connects directly with the Trinitarian subordination of the Son (Jesus) to the Father that has been discerned in the theological underpinnings of Sydney's objection to women in church leadership, Reid maintains.[33] This dualism in Sydney Anglicanism – so graphically illustrated in the anecdote about Knox – may be the crux of the matter, according to Reid:

> Such a dualism will see no fundamental problem in subordinating some people to others, nor in a cavalier approach to the sacraments, but will fear the power of sense experience, whether this be in the form of charismatic spiritual experience or the aesthetic experience of the creative arts. Such an outlook betrays an attitude that can only be described as fundamentally anti-incarnational, and therefore anti-trinitarian. This methodological tendency strikes me as closer to the heart of things than a particular stance on sexuality, or the ecclesiastical-political matter of the ordination of women ...[34]

Knox was so foundational to the current Sydney thinking on most theological and ecclesiological issues that he has become virtually a local saint whose ideas must always remain, unaltered, as the cornerstone of diocesan policies and ideologies. If Knox was against something – the ordination of women is a good example – then it is inconceivable that that position could ever change.

The next important event in 1959 was the Billy Graham crusade. Graham, an American Baptist who became a legendary figure in world Evangelism in the twentieth century, drew phenomenal crowd numbers during his first Australian crusades that year. He drew close to one million people – 983,000 to be precise – over the 26 Sydney crusade meetings. In the post-war world of the cold war, he preached the standard Evangelical message of personal repentance and commitment to Christ as the means of overcoming society's many ills. Commentators have noted that his crusade style, for all its superb organization, stirring hymns and mass appeal, was nevertheless low-key. It avoided excessive emotionalism, and offered a positive spin to the traditional Evangelical teaching. Graham – then a tall man with piercing blue eyes and film-star good looks – was undoubtedly a media star, the main factor to which Melbourne historian Judith Smart attributes his astonishing success in this country.[35]

Sydney Diocese threw its weight behind the crusade, and reaped some significant benefits. It has become a truism of contemporary Sydney Anglicanism that the crusade was instrumental in converting a large number of men who were to become leaders of the denomination. Among that number are key party organizers

---

[33] Reid, 'Anglican Diversity and Conflict', p. 258.
[34] Ibid., p. 259.
[35] Judith Smart, 'The Evangelist as Star: The Billy Graham Crusade in Australia, 1959', *Journal of Popular Culture*, 33(1) (Summer 1999), p. 167.

and Jensen backers such as the Revd Bruce Ballantine-Jones who was, like Peter Jensen, 15 when he attended the crusade. Moore College reported increased enrolments of potential clergy in the following two years,[36] while still more converts came in subsequent years. One later arrival at Moore (he began in 1966) was Graham convert Peter Jensen, who still speaks glowingly of his experience of the Graham crusade. In fact, he has nominated it as 'the critical moment' of his life. Under the influence of the Graham crusade, he became 'a definite, committed, evangelical Christian, living for the Lord Jesus Christ', and second, he was 'led to the ministry of God's word'. Previously, he had been a conventional churchgoer, from a conventional churchgoing family. He has subsequently poured scorn on conventional Christianity which was flourishing in 1950s Sydney, a time of large attendances at both churches and Sunday schools. For Jensen it was 'lowest common denominator' Christianity, a religion concerned with behaviour rather than belief: 'the ranks of church-goers were swollen with the unsaved', he has said.[37]

Jensen attended 17 of Graham's Sydney meetings and significantly, has described his conversion there as not a 'terrifically emotional experience'. Rather, it was a 'clarifying moment', when what he had learnt at Sunday school at last 'made sense'.[38] Even at 15, Jensen seems to have embodied the rationalism of propositional revelation. His younger brother Phillip, now Dean of Sydney, was also converted at the crusades. Chris McGillion has suggested Peter Jensen (and one might add, his brother) still displays the zeal of the convert.[39] The crusade undoubtedly gave an enormous fillip to Evangelicalism in many parts of Australia, not least Sydney, a boost that was not repeated in later Graham missions which were not even pale reflections of the earlier success story.

The third major 'event' of the Gough episcopacy, the reorganization of the diocesan finances, did not look nearly so significant at the time. Nevertheless, the diocese has, until its recent devastating losses, reaped the benefit of vast financial resources beyond the dreams of other dioceses. In 1959, Archbishop Gough established a commission to survey the diocese's administration and its finances. It took nearly five years to report, so complex were the issues involved. Its major recommendation was to appoint a central body to take over from the many different committees, trusts and boards that then had responsibility for diocesan resources. Reform was much-needed, as the diocese's assets were returning inadequate revenue from depreciating assets at a time when the city's suburban expansion needed a higher level of expenditure from the diocese if it were to provide ministry in the growth areas. The commission's recommendations, accepted by a special synod meeting in 1965, effectively brought diocesan administration into line with

---

[36] Piggin, *Evangelical Christianity in Australia*, p. 167.
[37] Jensen, 'Build on the Past ...'.
[38] Chris McGillion, *The Chosen Ones: The Politics of Salvation in the Anglican Church* (Sydney: Allen & Unwin, 2004), p. 88.
[39] Ibid.

modern financial and managerial methods. Because of the complex legal structures of the Anglican Church, it would take more than a decade for the full impact of the changes to be integrated into the life of the diocese.[40]

In 1959, the diocese's assets were tied up in glebe lands, lands given by the Crown to the earliest parishes and to the bishop as a means of support. This was a system well known in England, where glebe lands allowed the village parson to supplement the income he received from his parishioners' tithes. In Sydney, the glebes initially supplemented state stipends. During the first half of the twentieth century, when the state stipends had long gone, the parish glebes were gradually subsumed under diocesan control. Mostly the glebes – in parcels of about 40 acres – were leased for small-scale housing under 99-year leases with no provision for rent review. Consequently, they were returning very little income by the 1950s and 1960s, when the leases were expiring. It has been estimated that they were returning little more than 1 per cent of their value. Now the diocese had the opportunity to develop the land more productively.

The transition from local landlord to commercial enterprise was not easy for the diocese, which at times found itself embroiled in community disputes, union green bans, media antagonism and public criticism. But despite the setbacks, in time the strategy paid off. Over the 25 years between 1962 and 1987, the income available to the diocese from the Glebe Board multiplied 80 times. That was just from the combined parish glebe endowments; the glebe set aside for the bishop, which constituted the land now covered by the Sydney suburb of Glebe, funded the Endowment of the See fund, out of which the archbishop, regional bishops, archdeacons, dean, registrar and the central diocesan administration known as the Registry, are separately financed. Continued careful stewardship, until recently, meant that the diocese was the envy of other dioceses, from its central Sydney base in St Andrew's House, to its highly-professional media, public relations and internet establishment, to its well-resourced administration and programme arms. Much of that is now depleted and its future funding is under review.

Sydney's previous wealth meant that it was not just envied, but feared and resented. Feared, because it had the resources to exert considerable influence on the rest of the Australian church. Sydney Anglican leaders saw that influence as benign, as no doubt did beneficiaries in certain small rural dioceses, such as the Diocese of North West Australia, which would otherwise be in dire financial straits. Such assistance could however mean that recipients would be reluctant to oppose Sydney national initiatives or the introduction of Sydney-trained clergy, for instance. Resented, because on ideological grounds, Sydney has for years now refused to pay the voluntary 'special assessment' contribution levied by the national General Synod. Other dioceses, many of them strapped for cash, pay their contribution, even though it is often a struggle. But Sydney takes refuge in the strict legal position that the fund is voluntary.

---

[40] Judd and Cable, *Sydney Anglicans*, pp. 267ff.

Sydney's consistent posture of independence from the national church is not surprising, given the nature of the Anglican Church of Australia. Under its constitution, adopted in 1961 and implemented in 1962, real power in the Australian church remains in the hands of individual dioceses. In many ways, it is a federation of dioceses, not unlike the federation of states that is the Commonwealth of Australia. However, unlike Australia's federal government, the Anglican Church of Australia has very limited overall powers, with extremely high bars to achieve any national consensus. This is quite unlike the situation in other Anglican national churches, and is the direct result of the refusal of Sydney to agree to any form of national constitution that did not protect its ongoing autonomy.

The many attempts to create a national church in Australia were a sorry saga, bedevilled as they were by Sydney's intransigence. The first national constitution, agreed in 1872, established a General Synod, but its powers were even more limited than its 1961 successor. It was effectively no more than an advisory body. More importantly, legal opinion was that, despite the 1872 constitution, the Australian dioceses remained part of the Church of England in England. This suited Evangelical dioceses, and particularly Sydney, as they saw this situation as protecting their Reformation heritage from the inroads of the increasingly powerful Anglo-Catholic dioceses in Australia. To make matters worse, it was these dioceses which were making all the running for a genuinely independent Australian Church, and this spelt danger. In summary, to protect their allegiance to the past, Sydney would contemplate a new constitution only with watertight restrictions on any liturgical or doctrinal developments, while other dioceses wanted a structure with enough flexibility to meet new challenges.

After decades of thwarted attempts at developing a home-grown constitution, the Australian dioceses were faced by a debilitating stalemate when the then Archbishop of Canterbury, Geoffrey Fisher, attended the 1950 meeting of the General Synod. It is generally acknowledged that it was his decisive intervention that turned around plans to abandon the development of a constitution. He went even further; on the homeward voyage, he personally prepared a working draft, which became the basis of the constitution finally adopted in 1961.

It seems Fisher's intervention was successful for two main reasons: he recommended giving Sydney 'every safeguard', so that they would get behind the project, and perhaps more importantly, he hinted that the Australian church needed to establish its own autonomy because of forthcoming changes in English Canon Law. Those changes would, among other things, have disallowed significant Sydney stances, such as the requirement that clergy not wear Eucharistic vestments. As Broughton Knox is quoted as saying, 'the Church of England could not be relied upon to remain as Protestant as ... Sydney would wish'.[41] In the event, Sydney's minority conservative Evangelical position – in relation to the then

---

[41] John Davis, *Australian Anglicans and Their Constitution* (Melbourne: Acorn Press, 1993), p. 141.

Anglo-Catholic or liberal Evangelical tenor of the rest of the Australian Church – would be protected by two key elements in the constitution.

One was the hefty requirement of a two-thirds vote in each of the three 'houses' of the new General Synod – bishops, clergy, and laity – for canons (church laws) concerning ritual, ceremonial or discipline. Even then, the decision is merely provisional unless every one of the 23 Australian dioceses agrees with it or it is ratified by the same two-thirds level of support at a subsequent General Synod. The second was related: even when such a canon is duly passed, individual dioceses are not required to implement it within their own boundaries. Hence, Sydney Diocese has not had to introduce women priests, even though the measure received the necessary two-thirds votes (twice) when it was approved in 1992.[42] Further, the difficulties of changing the constitution itself are so demanding that any changes require almost complete consensus, giving an additional safeguard to conservative interests. The end result is a constitution where 'diocesanism is writ large'.[43]

Even so, despite the safeguards, many in Sydney were still not entirely sure about the proposed constitution, though the 1955 General Synod meeting had approved it 'without a dissentient voice'.[44] Dioceses had now to consider the agreed constitution, before the matter could finally go to state and federal parliaments for ratification. There was considerable opposition aired at the 1957 Sydney Synod, mainly on the grounds that there was insufficient protection for the overall status of the Reformation Settlement. But Archbishop Mowll, backed by T.C. Hammond, swung his support behind the constitution, and his synod agreed. An unfortunate last-minute attempt to get the New South Wales Parliament to delay its agreement in 1960, led significantly by Broughton Knox, then principal of Moore College, and the vice-principal, Donald Robinson, did not succeed.[45]

Since the constitution blueprint was agreed in 1955, much has changed in Australian and church life. The severe limitations of the compromise constitution have made it extremely difficult for the national church to keep pace with the changes, let alone offer real leadership. It is continually constrained by Sydney's relentless exercise of its constitutional rights. It is my assessment that the protection of their interests, which have flourished, has been at the expense of the interests of most other dioceses and members of the church, who have found the constraints frustrating and demeaning. Sydney's version of the Gospel is free to be preached relatively unhindered, while the version preferred by some other

---

[42] Because the issue of women's ordination had become so urgent by 1992, a special second meeting of General Synod was called six months after the first vote, rather than waiting the usual three-year interval for the next scheduled meeting.

[43] Ross Border, *Church and State in Australia 1788–1872: A Constitutional Story of the Church of England in Australia* (London: SPCK, 1962,) p. 283, cited in Davis, *Australian Anglicans and Their Constitution*, p. 157.

[44] Davis, *Australian Anglicans and Their Constitution*, p. 156.

[45] Ibid., pp. 161, 162.

dioceses, including those concerned to see the ordained ministry enhanced by the leadership of women or a greater emphasis on sacramental worship included in official formularies, has been thwarted.

In hindsight, the compromises of the 1950s have been debilitating for the national church. Would it have been wiser to create a national church that did not include Sydney, if it was not prepared to accept the will of the majority? I suspect it would have had little impact on Sydney's ongoing life and its relationship with the rest of the church if it had remained separate. Certainly in recent years it has substantially gone its own way regardless of the rest of the church, and been quick to warn that schism will result if national decisions are taken that it does not like. The threats are never specific, and do not necessarily imply that Sydney would formally leave the national church. Rather, they are suggestions that a different style of federation would be required when women became bishops, for instance. These threats have never materialized, even with the introduction of women bishops in 2008.

An Australian church without Sydney, I believe, would have released enormous energy for growth and renewal in the rest of the dioceses, freed from Sydney's relentless negative impact. I acknowledge that this is a minority view. Most Anglicans still fondly hope that one day, real national unity of purpose will be achieved with Sydney coming onboard without its current agenda. But as a member of General Synod since 1987 and of its Standing Committee since 1989, I know this is highly unlikely. I also know only too well the huge burden the church carries in trying to cope with the continual, determined and well-resourced opposition that emanates from Sydney. Sometimes families reluctantly have to agree to take separate paths for the good of everyone concerned. Perhaps this is what should have happened in 1955, though possibly the fathers of the constitution believed that if Sydney were adequately protected from any unwelcome intrusions into its territory, it would become more relaxed and cooperative in its relationships with the other dioceses. Sadly, this has not happened.

Alternatively, the constitution should not have provided two avenues of protection for minorities: either the high bar of a two-thirds vote on key decisions or the discretion for dioceses not to adopt specific canons, but not both. It is manifestly unfair that a minority can frustrate the will of the majority on an issue such as women priests or bishops, preventing other dioceses from introducing the measure, even though there is no way it can be adopted in their own diocese without their approval in any case. These protections mean that diocesanism works in one direction only: Sydney Diocese controls what it will allow within its jurisdiction, but effectively, because of the size of its membership of General Synod, also controls what other dioceses can and cannot do. Some kind of separation yet might need to happen. Given Sydney's much greater comparative strength now, any such division at this point would be far more damaging for everyone than it would have been in 1955.

Before leaving this overview of Sydney's evolution, it is important to glance briefly at a strange and largely forgotten aspect of Sydney's past that may offer an unexpected insight into recent events. In the late 1930s, a 'holiness' movement had an enormous impact on non-denominational Evangelical organizations in Sydney such as the Inter-Varsity Fellowship, the Sydney University Evangelical Union and the Crusader Union. Some leaders in these bodies began promoting 'sinless perfectionism'. Historian Stuart Piggin summarizes sinless perfectionism as meaning that 'by an instantaneous experience of the Holy Spirit, sin is eradicated in believers so that they are able not to sin anymore'.[46] This teaching split the organizations concerned, with the promoters of 'sinless perfection' eventually expelled. They later formed a commune – some have described it as a sect – of perfectionists in Sydney, known best by the name they gave one of their business ventures, 'Tinker Tailor'. It was a time of sad division among families and friendships that otherwise shared so much in their Evangelical heritage.

Perfectionism, known by a variety of names, has a long and persistent history in Christianity, connected to the longing of most Christians to live holy lives. In its contemporary manifestations, Piggin describes it rather colourfully as 'an aberration of the holiness movement of the nineteenth century, a caricature of Evangelicalism, and a bastard growth of revivalism'.[47] As with any form of perfectionism, it inevitably becomes elitist, and from there, can develop sectarian tendencies.

It seems that none of the Sydney perfectionists came directly from the Anglican Church, though Anglican leaders such as Marcus Loane and Broughton Knox had family connections to the group. Nevertheless, it was strongly resisted by key Sydney leaders. T.C. Hammond was one who counselled young Anglicans against involvement. He was also instrumental in developing strong arguments from Scripture against the perfectionists. Future archbishops Marcus Loane and Donald Robinson, keen and influential members of the various student bodies involved, were also at the forefront of the struggle against the aberrant teaching, as was Broughton Knox.

David Millikan, who has written the most comprehensive account of this saga, has linked this important Evangelical struggle with the subsequent development of contemporary Sydney Anglican theology. He notes the diocese's 'strong emphasis on rational theological thought and the rejection of "experience" as a way to truth', and the legalism of their approach to all matters doctrinal. It is possible, he has said, that 'the formation of this Sydney character was influenced by the need to protect the Evangelical cause from the influence of perfectionist thinking'.[48] Propositional revelation certainly rejects any experiential means of revelation; its very rationalism forms a firm bulwark against any experience-based theologies. Broughton Knox was developing his teaching of propositional revelation over the

---

[46] Piggin, *Evangelical Christianity in Australia*, p. 105.
[47] Ibid., p. 106.
[48] David Millikan, *Imperfect Company: Power and Control in an Australian Christian Cult* (Melbourne: William Heinemann Australia and ABC Books, 1991), p. 8.

same time period as the sect was exerting influence in Sydney Evangelical circles. Millikan's theory is worth further consideration.

So too is an intriguing element in this saga, that of the role of women in the perfectionist movement (and, it must be said, among its opponents). Three women from a wealthy Tasmanian family – Vera Agnew and her daughters Del and Nancy – were prominent leaders of the movement. Del Agnew became perhaps the most influential of the Sydney perfectionists. Piggin describes her as the 'high priestess'. There were other women as well in the movement's leadership, some of whom, by all accounts, promoted some highly idiosyncratic religious views.[49] This leads me to ponder: did the leadership of women in a movement that was regarded by many as unorthodox, unscriptural and divisive, have a subconscious impact on the conservative male Sydney Anglican leaders who opposed them? Is it significant that the major opponents of perfectionism included Broughton Knox, Marcus Loane and Donald Robinson, all of whom would be instrumental in developing and promoting Sydney Diocese's theological opposition to the ordination of women? Did some of the refinements of Scriptural disputation that they developed in the context of that debate, underscore their later refutation from the Bible of women as clergy? And did their rejection of revelation through experience also weigh heavily against their preparedness to listen to women who claimed that they were called by God to priesthood? Did this evoke dangerous memories of an earlier generation of women who claimed to be called by God, though to a very different, decidedly heterodox, form of spiritual leadership? Did the memory impact on the Sydney dismissal of feminism per se as a godless ideology?[50] It is an area that may well repay further examination.

---

[49] Piggin, *Evangelical Christianity in Australia*, pp. 109ff.

[50] In 'Build on the Past ...' Peter Jensen links 'the twin ideologies of the gay and feminist movements' as having had a detrimental effect in helping shape society away from the teaching of the Bible.

Chapter 4
Tensions:
Sydney and the Anglican Communion

Sydney's Archbishop Peter Jensen is the best known Anglican leader in Australia, and the best known Australian churchman internationally. Many assume he is the Primate of the Anglican Church of Australia. He is not, but that has not stopped him operating as a frequent national spokesman, and assuming the mantle of an international Anglican leader. As has been noted, on his webpage profile he describes himself as being 'recognized as a key leader in the worldwide Anglican Church' and an 'outspoken figure on the Australian religious scene'.[1]

He is not Primate, but early on some thought he might have been. In July 2005, four years after he became Archbishop of Sydney, he was a candidate for election as Primate following the retirement of Archbishop Peter Carnley of Perth. But the Board of Electors, a national body consisting of the diocesan bishops and 24 elected clergy and laity, went instead for the youthful Phillip Aspinall, the Archbishop of Brisbane. At 45, Aspinall was the youngest Primate in living memory. He had been in his Brisbane post for just three years. Outsiders might have expected Jensen, at 62, to have secured the top job, but though he received a surprisingly high number of votes from the diocesan bishops in three consecutive ballots, he did not do at all well among the elected members of the Board, receiving very few lay and clergy votes. Clearly these electors were wary of Jensen; his conservative views on key issues such as the consecration of women as bishops, and his advocacy of lay presidency, had been manifestly clear at the 2004 General Synod that had elected the clergy and lay representatives to the Board. Perhaps some of his supporters among the diocesan bishops hoped making him Primate would reign in any Sydney excesses. Aspinall, on the other hand, was known to favour women bishops, and was described at the time as a central, moderate churchman.

Aspinall was elected initially for just three years under a special provision to give the national church time to consider making fundamental changes to the role of Primate. Under the Australian church's constitution, the Primate has a minimalist position. Despite the vastly-increased workload – Primates retain their current role, that of a diocesan bishop or archbishop – there are only limited additional resources available to them. But by the time the three-year bridging appointment was concluded, the General Synod had been unable to offer much more support to the role, other than to change it to a limited tenure instead of lasting until retirement. When the next election was held in 2008, Aspinall was re-elected,

---

[1] http://www.sydneyanglicans.net/ministry/seniorclergy/archbishop_jensen/profile.

this time for six years. He had more than proved his worth in the three years, including his masterful chairing of the 2007 General Synod. Jensen was not in serious contention at the 2008 election, although there was an attempt engineered by some Sydney Board members to try to thwart the Aspinall re-election. They did not succeed. When Aspinall steps down in 2014, Jensen will have retired.

But not being Primate has not stayed Jensen's hand on either the local scene or the international stage. Locally, he was readily available for media appearances, public presentations, and for consultation with political leaders, until the diocese's 2009 financial crisis seemed to put a stop to his previous ready involvement with the media. He has kept a relatively low profile since. Until then he had been swift to take initiatives not taken by Aspinall, whose public presence has been limited. Not many Australians – including some Anglicans – would recognize Aspinall's national role, but most know who Jensen is. Nor has Aspinall taken an international role other than that required of him as Primate, though he has become an important figure in the internal workings of Anglican Communion deliberations as a member of the Primates' Standing Committee, usually as the Primates' media spokesman. That has not translated into a wider international profile.

From the time of his election as Archbishop of Sydney, however, Peter Jensen has fostered a prominent world role. So much so that some commentators have suggested that he has seen himself as an alternative Archbishop of Canterbury.[2] He has delivered lectures to large gatherings of conservative Anglicans and other Protestants in the United Kingdom, Ireland and New Zealand, among other countries, and worked assiduously with African and Asian church leaders to promote conservative issues. Visiting Dublin in 2005, Archbishop Jensen lectured to the Irish Church Missions on the legacy of Irish-born T.C. Hammond, Principal of Moore Theological College 1936 to 1953. The Irish Missions has strong ties with Sydney, offering a Moore College correspondence course. As well Sydney Diocese has been sending 'a growing number of missionaries and clergy to minister' in Ireland.[3] He has also promoted ties with Evangelicals from other faith communities in Europe; in the second half of 2005, he delivered the keynote address to the annual European Evangelical Leaders Forum in Hungary.

Returning to Australia, he said that European Evangelicals, in the old Communist bloc countries in particular, needed support from 'like-minded Christians in Australia'. Evangelicals were facing difficulties in the region, including harassment 'from some traditional churches', he said.[4] He said he would

---

[2] For example see Chris McGillion, 'Sydney Dreams of Being a New Canterbury', *The Sydney Morning Herald*, 26 October 2006. McGillion begins his article by claiming that 'Archbishop Peter Jensen says the world has shifted on its axis in ways that could see the Anglican Diocese of Sydney become the new centre of post-Reformation Christendom'.

[3] 'Eastern Bloc Evangelists Need Our Support: Archbishop', 5 August 2005, http://www.sydneyanglicans.net/news/stories/eastern_bloc_evangelists_need_our_support_says_archbishop1/media.

[4] Ibid.

be likely to accept more invitations to preach overseas, in what will obviously be a further extension of Sydney's influence.[5]

In 2006 he told Sydney Synod that (under his leadership presumably), it was well-placed to support and resource Evangelical churches in other first-world churches. These included 'embattled' Evangelicals in the UK, New Zealand, South Africa, Canada and the United States, he said. 'The fact that we exist and can speak up brings comfort to thousands of people around the world', he added. He predicted a 'giant shift in loyalties' that would affect the standing of the office of Archbishop of Canterbury.[6] In hindsight, he was probably preparing his Synod for the realignments soon to emerge under the GAFCON banner.

Jensen became Archbishop at an opportune time for an international role, given the tempest about to hit the worldwide Anglican Communion as The Episcopal [Anglican] Church (TEC) in the United States consecrated a bishop in an ongoing gay relationship. Nor did he have to start from scratch. He stepped into a role which had been laid out for him, rather surprisingly, by his mild-mannered predecessor Archbishop Harry Goodhew. And he took up the challenge with gusto, to the point where he is now a leader of the Global Anglican Future alliance that has set itself up as an alternative Anglican Communion in all but name.

The ongoing debate about homosexuality in the Anglican Church became electric in 1998, when the Lambeth Conference of bishops was effectively shanghaied by an astonishingly well-organized and vocal anti-gay lobby. As the end result of a particularly ugly public brawl, the Lambeth Bishops 'rejected homosexual practice as incompatible with Scripture' and rejected the blessing of same-sex unions and the ordaining of 'those involved in same gender unions'.[7] But this was more than the triumph of a particular theological point of view. It was the opening gambit in what would become a struggle for control of world Anglicanism, a struggle in which Sydney is playing a significant and leading role.

What became apparent for the first time at the 1998 Lambeth Conference was the alliance that had been formed between what might be termed first-world conservatives – from England, the United States and Australia – and third-world conservatives. While the first-world conservative Anglicans were clearly a minority within their national churches, their colleagues in Africa, Asia and South America represented a huge majority. Given that the Church of England – the Mother Church of the Anglican Communion – is the established or state church in England, Anglicans had until then thought of world Anglicanism as principally a genteel, respectable church with a generally broad position on doctrinal matters. Daughter churches around the world, though legally independent, were nevertheless looked on as still the children of Empire. In this imperialist scenario, African and Asian Anglicans were the grateful heirs of the established church. Their bishops, it was thought, would continue to follow meekly where the Communion's white leaders

---

[5] Ibid.
[6] Peter Jensen, statement to Sydney Synod, 23 October 2006.
[7] Lambeth Conference 1998 Resolution 1.10.

led. At the 1998 Lambeth Conference, it became painfully obvious that this was no longer the case. In a contemporary twist on anti-colonialism, it became apparent that these churches also harboured a resentment of the new world superpower, the United States, despite the substantial financial assistance TEC often gave them. It was the bishops from the newer Anglican national churches in the old Empire countries who gave the conservatives' demands the numerical backing they needed. The so-called third-world churches gladly demonstrated their new-found self-confidence, particularly as they recognized their own startling numerical advantage.

Is it possible that backroom deals were also done to forge the winning alliance between conservative first-world leaders and their third-world friends? One deal might have been: 'Don't hassle us about polygamy, and we will back you on homosexuality.' It seems entirely possible, in the light of the surprisingly generous, culturally-conditioned response conservatives have taken on that issue. At the 1988 Lambeth Conference – where homosexuality was not even discussed – a decision was made that Muslims with more than one wife would not be compelled to 'put away' any of their wives if they converted to Christianity, because of the social deprivation they would suffer. They would not be allowed to take another wife once they converted unless all their previous wives had died. This decision was made despite the Conference's recognition that monogamy was 'God's plan', and despite a tougher line taken in the Lambeth Conference held 30 years earlier.[8] The African bishops had argued for this more lenient position, though it did not accord with the conservative claim that the Bible upheld monogamy, because of the cultural reality of their local contexts. The continued acceptance of this sensible compromise by conservative hardliners who usually insist on rigid adherence to 'God's Word written', no matter what the cost, indicates their seriousness about their alliance with the African bishops.

Certainly American conservatives had channelled enormous energy, finances and planning into wooing the Africans' votes at Lambeth 1998. Many believe that the American right remains the main source of funding of initiatives designed to fragment the Anglican Communion. British journalist Stephen Bates, in his account of the Anglican war over homosexuality, has documented how they did it.[9] Initially, they held a tactical planning meeting in September 1997 in Dallas – heartland of US Episcopalian conservatism – a meeting attended by some 50 bishops, mainly from Africa. At the Lambeth Conference the following year, they established a centre close to the Conference location, using it to provide the bishops from the developing world with every kind of assistance and encouragement. Food, mobile phones, free telephone links home, strategy talks, crib sheets, were all readily available to them. Some observers have likened the centre to a high-tech

---

[8] Lambeth Conference 1988 Resolution 26; Lambeth Conference 1958 Resolution 120.

[9] Stephen Bates, *A Church at War: Anglicans and Homosexuality* (London: I.B. Tauris, 2004), pp. 126ff.

US political campaign office. One of the speakers at the centre's various events was Peter Jensen's predecessor, Archbishop Harry Goodhew. And young Sydney graduates were to be found among the troops running the day-to-day operations of the centre. Not a great deal was written at the time about Sydney's involvement behind the scenes at Lambeth 1998, and not much is known outside Sydney to this day. Their involvement has assumed importance only in hindsight.

Not that most of the developing world bishops needed any encouragement to support resolutions hostile to homosexuality, but what was needed was to weld together a determined politically-effective power bloc to ensure that any liberal agenda was defeated. It worked, and took many in the Anglican world by surprise. One additional gain of the triumphant conservative bloc was that conservative Nigeria was able to grab the mantle of African Anglican leadership in the wake of the retirement of the liberal Desmond Tutu[10] – a highly significant power shift. One Nigerian bishop became the public face of the deep ugliness that pervaded the Conference. As Stephen Bates reports it, Bishop Emmanuel Chukwuma, in full view of the world's media, confronted a gay rights activist, and attempted to exorcize him of his homosexuality. 'You have no inheritance in the kingdom of God', he shouted. 'You are going to hell.' Claiming he was the 'voice of God talking', he said that the church in Europe was dying because it condoned immorality. 'You are killing the church', he charged.[11]

The 1998 Lambeth Conference was the sea-change for the Anglican Church in terms of sexuality, though few liberals actually realized at the time how significant it was. Many, I believe, thought it was a blip that would be readily reversed. But in fact the process has accelerated, to the point where the conservative forces have now achieved a critical level of influence. A series of what have turned out to be inflammatory events has fanned the flames.

In England in 2003, the appointment of a celibate gay man as an assistant bishop unleashed the dogs of war. Jeffrey John, a quiet, gentle priest with an outstanding reputation as a theologian, was nominated as the new Bishop of Reading, an assistant bishopric in the Diocese of Oxford, after a careful and thorough selection process. Though he had once been in a committed, active same-sex relationship, he was now in a celibate relationship with his partner – and had been for years. This was no protection when his appointment was announced. On the grounds that he had not publicly repented of his past relationship, he became the target of an astonishingly bitter and hysterical campaign. If his appointment went ahead, the church would split, his detractors threatened. At the very least, there would be a wholesale withdrawal of funds from the Church of England by dissident English parishes. At the same time, long-term plans to approve the blessing of same-sex relationships were approved in a Canadian diocese, and in TEC in the United States, a gay man in an ongoing same-sex partnership had been elected a diocesan bishop.

---

[10] Ibid., p. 136.
[11] Ibid., p. 137.

The Diocese of Sydney strode swiftly and defiantly into battle. For three decades as we shall discuss below, it had opposed homosexuality vehemently, to the extent of opposing government moves to decriminalize it. In this regard it took a diametrically different stance to other parts of the Australian church. So this was a struggle it was more than ready for. In June 2003, the Sydney leadership issued a public statement, condemning all three developments but most particularly the appointment of Jeffrey John. Archbishop Jensen and his five assistant bishops said the moves had 'created a tragic disruption of fellowship and led to a watershed in relationships within the [Anglican] Communion'. These events were 'the culmination of over thirty years of compromise with western culture and plain disobedience to the teaching of Holy Scripture'. The moment for silence was past, the statement declared, and they called on their fellow bishops in the Anglican Communion to 'join with those who are making clear their abhorrence of adultery and all sexual immorality'. The threat of schism hung over the document, though the details were vague. The Diocese of Sydney would remain in communion 'with those who oppose these developments', and would not 'welcome into our Diocese those who have abandoned the teaching of Scripture in such a flagrant manner'.[12]

Peter Jensen was fortuitously in England at the time. Though his media office was quick to insist that his lecture tour had been planned years in advance, it must have seemed a happy coincidence that he was there. The Sydney Anglican Media statement made sure it alerted British press to his presence in England and offered contact information for him. The British press duly reported the Sydney statement.[13] In Jensen's absence from Australia, however, one of his assistant bishops, Dr Glenn Davies, became the local media spokesperson. He interpreted the Sydney statement as meaning that the Archbishop of Canterbury himself would not be welcome in Sydney if he proceeded with Jeffrey John's consecration. Jensen moved swiftly from England to 'clarify' his comments, saying that though such a ban might be logical, he nevertheless wanted to preserve the unity of the church. Rowan Williams would therefore not be unwelcome.[14] At the same time, Bishop Davies defended the tolerance of polygamy in Nigeria and elsewhere. Polygamy was not adultery, he said, but rather part of their culture.[15] Compromise with African culture was acceptable, it seems, in a way that compromise with Western culture was not.

In the end, the threats of schism from conservative Anglicans outside Britain – including the outspoken Primate of Nigeria, Archbishop Peter Akinola – and threats of withdrawal of funds from English conservatives were so great that the

---

[12] 'Bishops from Sydney Speak About the "tragic disruption of fellowship in Anglican Communion"', 20 June 2003, http://www.sydneyanglicans.net/archive/bishop_tasker/907j/.

[13] See for instance 'Anglican Split on Gay Bishop', *The Daily Telegraph* (UK), 25 June 2003.

[14] 'Rift over Bishop Intensifies', *The Age*, 25 June 2003.

[15] ABC Lateline, 23 June 2003.

Archbishop of Canterbury pressured John to decline the appointment. Moderate Anglicans were appalled, given that John's appointment had been supported by a range of English bishops and other senior clerics. It seemed especially tragic for Rowan Williams personally. Previously he had been openly supportive of gay people, to such a degree that his appointment as Archbishop of Canterbury had attracted complaint from conservative English Evangelicals. Already under pressure, he would lose many of his most loyal supporters over this move, British moderates feared. He had cut his own throat, one lamented. His back down, rather than quietening the forces of discontent, probably encouraged them; they now knew that their threats of schism had real bite, as quickly became clear.

Even though Williams took this unfortunate step in response to the concerted campaign waged against him as much as against Jeffrey John, it did not end the personal attacks against him. More than a year later, the Dean of Sydney caused uproar when press reports emerged of inflammatory comments he had allegedly made at a conference in England. *The Guardian*'s religion reporter Stephen Bates reported that Phillip Jensen had accused Rowan Williams of 'theological and intellectual prostitution' for his privately-held views on homosexuality. The Dean had also allegedly described Prince Charles as a 'public adulterer' and King's College Chapel, Cambridge, as a 'temple to paganism' because it sold CDs of its choral music in the chapel's entrance.[16]

Dean Jensen claimed he had been 'grossly misrepresented', and once back in Sydney, defended himself in a lengthy speech to Sydney Synod which happened to be meeting at the time. Whatever the truth of the detail of the newspaper reportage, it nevertheless emerged from his own defence that Phillip Jensen *had* said that 'when those who hold high office and receive a stipend in the Church of England publicly uphold one set of beliefs while privately believing differently, they should resign'.[17] The reference, as even Jensen's defenders acknowledged, was clearly to Rowan Williams. The Archbishop of Canterbury, like Jeffrey John, was not acceptable on any terms. His official support of the Anglican Communion's majority position on same-sex relationships, as it had supposedly been expressed at the 1998 Lambeth Conference, rather than winning the approval of conservatives, was instead condemned as some form of hypocrisy. It was clear that both Jensen and his English conservative supporters wanted Williams to resign, despite the Dean's furious insistence that he had been misrepresented.

The controversy drew public attention to the fact that Jensen had not only attended a conference held by Reform, the most conservative church organization in Britain, but had actually been an honoured guest there. He told Synod that he 'went to England at the persistent invitation, and under considerable pressure,

---

[16] Stephen Bates, 'Evangelicals Call Williams a Prostitute', *The Guardian*, 13 October 2004.

[17] See report of Jensen's comments in a supportive letter sent to *The Sydney Morning Herald* by a group of conservative Evangelical English clergy, 18 October 2004, reprinted in Phillip Jensen's Synod speech, 19 October 2004.

from our friends at Reform who paid for the trip'. He went on to say how 'thrilled' his hosts had been with the conference's outcomes, with the conference members warmly endorsing a range of matters 'they had invited me over to persuade their members to adopt'. These 'matters' were principally Reform's radical agenda to promote 'deep change' in the Church of England, involving strategies such as the withholding of money from dioceses and/or bishops with whom they disagreed over the 'fundamental' issue of homosexuality; the refusal of the ministry of such 'unorthodox' bishops; and the active support of the conservative African and Asian Primates.[18]

If the conservative coalition had been upset by the Jeffrey John affair, the decision by TEC to consecrate a gay man as bishop left them enraged. This time there was no ambivalence about the status of Gene Robinson's sexuality. Unlike the celibate Jeffrey John, Robinson is publicly in a gay partnership, and proud of it. Just before TEC's General Convention in July 2003, at which Gene Robinson's election as Bishop of New Hampshire was to be ratified, conservative Anglican leaders gathered in the United States. The self-described 'unprecedented gathering of worldwide Anglican mainstream leaders' issued a statement condemning the move, and declaring that if it went ahead, it would 'precipitate a dramatic realignment of the church'. Peter Jensen was one of the signatories, along with the Primates of African, Asian and South American Anglican Churches, and some prominent clergy members of Reform.[19] The list of signatories on this one document indicates the scope of the worldwide conservative Anglican coalition, and that Sydney is in full partnership with it.

Though an emergency meeting of the Primates of the Anglican Communion subsequently called on the Americans to desist for the time being, Gene Robinson's consecration went ahead in November 2003. He had been elected bishop through the exhaustively democratic processes of TEC, and that church – having debated gay clergy for many decades – was in no mood to rescind its decision. After the consecration, the threats of schism became extremely serious, particularly from the conservative coalition, by then generally known as the 'Global South'. Its members had formed a very strong and cohesive pressure group which did not hesitate to make its views known publicly.

Nor was the United States the only target. The Canadian Anglican Church was attacked over plans by one diocese, New Westminster, to formally condone the public blessing of gay unions. A leading dissident there is a former Sydney priest, the Revd David Short, rector of St John's, Shaughnessy, a large conservative evangelical parish in New Westminster. The parish has since effectively broken away from the diocese, and David is no longer officially a priest of the Canadian Anglican Church. The son of a retired Sydney assistant bishop, David has been in Canada since 1991. Sydney Diocese has consistently offered him overt support

---

[18] *Church Times*, 15 October 2004.

[19] 'A Statement from the Gathering of Worldwide Anglican Mainstream Leaders on the Crisis in the Episcopal Church', 24 July 2003.

for his dissent, with the diocesan Standing Committee issuing a strong supportive statement in July 2002. As noted elsewhere, some in Sydney see him as a possible successor to Archbishop Jensen.

As a consequence of the uproar and the talk of schism, the Anglican Primates established the international Commission which produced the Windsor Report, which later led to plans to establish an Anglican Covenant. Both the report and the Covenant proposals have met with mixed responses from all sides with their plan for mechanisms for containing fall-out from divisive events in the Anglican Communion. The major solution is a greater degree of centralism for the worldwide body of churches, which would effectively mean that the independent churches would have to forgo some of their autonomy. Given the nature of the Anglican Communion, the Covenant process is a slow one and no definitive decision is likely for years. Australia's General Synod was lukewarm in its response in 2010; it declined to 'welcome' the Covenant proposal, instead voting merely to 'receive' it. It has asked the Australian dioceses to discuss the proposal before further consideration in 2013.

In an attempt to salvage the Communion, the Primates held a special meeting in Northern Ireland in early 2005 and called on the American and Canadian churches to withdraw voluntarily from international Anglican meetings while further consideration of the situation proceeded. This they reluctantly but graciously agreed to do, and put on hold any further moves to ordain gay bishops or condone the blessing of gay marriages. In 2010, however, their voluntary moratorium came to an end with the consecration in May of Mary Glasspool, a partnered lesbian, as a suffragan bishop in Los Angeles. Once again, media reports suggested the possibility of schism, but again, nothing eventuated.[20]

In one of the few media statements he has issued since his diocese's financial troubles hit, Archbishop Jensen said that the election of Bishop Glasspool was a 'decisive moment' which made it 'absolutely clear to all that the [Episcopal Church] has formally committed itself to a pattern of life which is contrary to Scripture. The election of Bishop Robinson in 2003 was not an aberration to be corrected in due course.' What he called a 'middle group' of people both inside and outside the American Church had waited patiently for a change of heart. 'But to wait longer would not be patience – it would be obstinacy …', he said. He concluded that the middle group now needed to make two things clear: 'First, that they are unambiguously opposed to a development which sanctifies sin and which is an abrogation of the word of the living God. Second, that they will take sufficient action to distance themselves from those who have chosen to walk in the path of disobedience.'[21]

By 2010, an alternative Communion was already in place, ready to welcome dissenters such as Jensen's 'middle group'. It grew out of the global south alliance

---

[20] It should be noted that there are significant minority voices in TEC and the Canadian Church that oppose the direction their churches have taken in regard to homosexuality.

[21] Peter Jensen, 'The American Episcopal Election', 18 March 2010.

that had its origins in the early 1990s, before the Anglican Communion turmoil began. Archbishop Jensen was invited to attend the alliance's third conference, held in Egypt in 2005; the earlier conferences had been held in 1991 and 1997. The 2005 conference was where the alliance formalized its role of opposition. Jensen was obviously delighted to be there. In a statement he released in December that year, he said he was one of just a few invited guests; it was a 'special privilege' to be there. 'Global South', he explained, 'is not so much geographic as a cultural and theological expression. It includes the churches founded as a result of the great missionary movements of the 19th century. Thus there were delegates from Africa, Asia, South America and Central America.' And one from Australia, not from a church founded as part of the nineteenth-century missionary movements! He was also clear that this meeting was about opposition to Western churches such as TEC. The Communiqué from the meeting made it 'perfectly clear that the delegates are deeply concerned about the unbiblical practices of many of the churches of the West. They wish to continue to offer support to Western Christians who are making a stand for biblical truth.'[22]

So the ground was set for the creation of GAFCON – initially a Global Anglican Future conference held in Jerusalem ahead of the 2008 Lambeth Conference. Tensions began to build significantly in the year before the GAFCON conference, as the Sydney bishops delayed responding to the Archbishop of Canterbury's invitation to attend the Lambeth Conference. Archbishop Jensen had already signalled that being part of the Anglican Communion was 'much more than a matter of formal conformity with a particular see or institution, or attendance at a specific gathering within the communion, no matter how venerable'.[23] This was a clear sign that he disputed the traditional definition of 'Anglican' as being in communion with the Archbishop of Canterbury, and with the notion that attendance at the Lambeth Conference was a further sign of Anglican legitimacy for bishops. There was in fact what looked like an orchestrated build-up to the final refusal of the Sydney bishops to attend Lambeth.

In June 2007, the Sydney Synod Standing Committee encouraged the diocese's bishops to consult 'orthodox' Anglican Communion bishops about the possibility of holding an 'alternative Lambeth'. An alternative meeting would provide for 'Christian fellowship and the planning of joint action within the Anglican Communion to contend for the faith of the Apostles once delivered to the saints', according to a report posted on the diocese's website.[24] The Standing Committee also urged the Archbishop and the five Sydney regional bishops to make clear Sydney's protest at the Lambeth guest list if they did decide to attend

---

[22] Peter Jensen, 'Archbishop Writes – Will We Support Them in Their Hour of Need?', 6 December 2005.

[23] Reported in Linda Morris, 'Sydney Bishops Snub Anglican Chief in Gay Row', *The Sydney Morning Herald*, 11 August 2007.

[24] Natasha Percy, 'Sydney Ponders Parallel Lambeth', 27 June 2007, http://www.sydneyanglicans.net/news/stories/archbishop_canterbury/.

the Lambeth Conference. The invitees to whom they should object are those who 'agreed to or participated in' the consecration of Bishop Gene Robinson. The Archbishop of Canterbury was attempting to 'maintain union with the unrepentant while continuing to refuse fellowship to faithful and orthodox Anglicans such as the Church of England in South Africa', the statement said. (The Church of England in South Africa is a conservative Evangelical church that has been closely aligned with Sydney Diocese since it was formed in 1938; it continues to receive ongoing support from the diocese. It grew out of churches which did not join the mainstream Church of the Province of Southern Africa, now the Anglican Church of Southern Africa. It is not a member church of the Anglican Communion.) At the end of July, Jensen and his regional bishops made public their letter to the Archbishop of Canterbury, which explained why they were delaying a response to the Lambeth invitation. It was 'in view of the real hesitations that we experience in joining with those who have consecrated Bishop Gene Robinson …', they said.

Finally, in February 2008, Jensen announced that he and his bishops would not be attending Lambeth. According to press reports, they had 'agonised' over their decision for months, apparently because not all the regional bishops were prepared to boycott Lambeth. The decision was effectively taken out of their hands when Archbishop Peter Akinola of Nigeria told a press conference in Lagos that he would not be going to Lambeth – and nor would Sydney. A letter was hastily despatched to Lambeth declining the invitation, and an announcement made. Reportedly two of the regional bishops remained unhappy with the decision.[25] So too was the Australian Primate, Archbishop Aspinall, who learnt of the Sydney decision from media reports. He issued a formal statement of regret.[26] Even Sydney's premier daily newspaper editorialized against the Sydney decision.[27]

Not surprisingly, the Sydney Synod Standing Committee endorsed the decision 'wholeheartedly'. Jensen made a full statement to the committee, later issued publicly. First, while he remained committed to the Anglican Communion, he did not believe that its good health would be advanced by a conference 'which seems to give credibility and influence to those who have introduced false teaching and continue to commend it'.

Second, the Sydney bishops could not have deep fellowship with the ones responsible for the innovations concerning homosexuality. 'To do so would betray conscience and our fellowship with those who have resisted at great cost to themselves', he said.

Third, the Anglican Communion had been irreversibly changed by these developments and this Lambeth Conference could not turn the clock back. He said: 'The best way of exerting influence is by not attending'; 'absence is a decisive,

---

[25] David Marr, 'The Great Schism: Is This the End of the Anglican Church as We Know It?', *The Age*, Good Weekend magazine, 7 June 2008.

[26] Statement from the Office of the Primate, 4 February 2008.

[27] 'Absence is No Argument', *The Sydney Morning Herald*, 5 February 2008.

though painful way of casting a vote, a way which is sometimes necessary when the issues are of great significance.' Fourth,

> we need to have pastoral care for those who have been hurt ... a number of the foremost leaders from Africa and South America, standing on conscience, have declared that they cannot attend Lambeth ... Given the fellowship which we enjoy with these leaders and their people it is inconceivable that we should not join them in standing aside. We must support those who have been so courageous.

Fifth,

> we have a duty of pastoral care to the Anglican Christians in North America and elsewhere who have made their protest against the local innovations ... Faced with the terrible choice between unity and truth, they have chosen to live by the truth. Should we not be witnesses that their choice is right?[28]

By then, plans were well underway for the alternative Lambeth, GAFCON, to be held in Jerusalem in June, just before Lambeth. The Bishop in Jerusalem, Bishop Suheil Dawani, who was visiting Australia in early 2008, called on Archbishop Jensen and the other organizers of GAFCON to cancel the conference. He told ABC Radio that Jerusalem was an inappropriate location for the conference. 'We are dealing with many different issues and we have other priorities there', he said. In a later press release, he said he had not been consulted about the conference, learning of it only through a press release.

But GAFCON went ahead as planned in Jerusalem, and Jensen and his bishops were among the more than 1,000 people who attended. Around the rest of the Anglican world, the air was thick with talk of the Communion splitting. In the end though, as with so many other moments of threat, the result was more of a splintering than a split. The statement released at the end of the conference on 29 June supported what it described as the 'realignment' that had occurred. Various 'provincial bodies' in the Global South were out of communion with bishops and churches that had promoted a 'false gospel'; 'faithful Anglican Christians' had left their territorial parishes, dioceses and provinces in 'certain Western churches' (that is, in Canada and the United States) to join other dioceses and provinces under alternative episcopal oversight. So there was really nothing new in this realignment.

What *was* new was the establishment of two ongoing bodies, a GAFCON Primates' Council and a Fellowship of Confessing Anglicans. The Primates' Council was urged to take on itself a role previously unique to the Archbishop of Canterbury – they were asked to 'authenticate and recognise confessing Anglican jurisdictions, clergy and congregations'. The GAFCON Primates would also need

---

[28] *Church Times*, 22 February 2008.

to 'put in place structures to lead and support the church', particularly a province in North America. The Fellowship of Confessing Anglicans (FCA) would be the ongoing structure for the new alignment, an organization that parishes, individuals, dioceses, provinces and even para-church organizations could join, so long as they subscribed both to the Jerusalem Declaration and the goals of FCA.[29] And the general secretary of GAFCON/FCA, and secretary of the GAFCON Primates' Council, is none other than Peter Jensen, with the secretariat based in the Sydney Diocesan offices.

Press reports depicted Jensen as the star of GAFCON, and pinpointed the moment when the new star was born. In a press conference where Nigeria's Archbishop Akinola and Uganda's Archbishop Orombi, both known for outbursts of homophobia, were being pressured about violence against gay people in their countries, Jensen moved in to save the situation. When neither Akinola nor Orombi would acknowledge there was a problem, Jensen offered a conciliatory answer. Violence against any person was always wrong, he said, adding that he had condemned, and would continue to condemn, 'any violence against any people and in particular gay and lesbian people'. As one commentator noted, Akinola presented the 'ugly face of homophobia' whereas Jensen offered 'a smiling face of homophobia, a more palatable messenger'. Jensen moved seamlessly into the limelight and so was discovered by the British press.[30]

But the new face of GAFCON was not advocating a breakaway church. This was a movement like earlier movements in the Anglican Church such as the eighteenth-century Evangelical and nineteenth-century Anglo-Catholic revivals, he said. Like the earlier movements, this too would be 'containable' within the Anglican Communion. Criticizing the Archbishop of Canterbury for his lack of leadership, he commented that his moral authority had been diminished, but not destroyed.[31] As Theo Hobson wrote in *The Guardian* newspaper, this new movement had no desire to be a breakaway church. 'Their desire is to take over the Anglican Communion, and you don't achieve that by walking away', he wrote.[32] In the same way, Sydney Diocese, for all its threats over decades, will never break away from the rest of the Anglican Church of Australia. Their agenda is ultimately to take it over by recasting it in their mould, and to do that, they have no choice but to stay inside the tent.

In the Australian church the pressure is on to impose conformity with the new alignment, via the Jerusalem Declaration. As might be expected, Sydney Synod

---

[29] The Jerusalem Declaration can be found at http://fca.net/resources/the_jerusalem_declaration/ and the Goals of the Fellowship of Confessing Anglicans can be found at http://fca.net/resources/goals_of_the_fellowship_of_confessing_anglicans/.

[30] Connie Levett, 'The Battle for Hearts and Souls', *The Sydney Morning Herald*, 5 July 2008.

[31] Barney Zwartz, 'A Church Divided', *The Age*, 1 July 2008.

[32] Theo Hobson, 'The Evangelicals are Moving in for the Kill', *The Guardian*, 1 July 2008.

swiftly moved to endorse it at its 2008 Synod, and called on all Anglicans in Australia to endorse it.[33] They brought it to the General Synod meeting in 2010, seeking a similar endorsement, but instead it was merely noted and commended for study by the dioceses and parishes of the Australian church to 'assist our understanding of some of the current issues facing the Anglican Communion'. The declaration itself is, in many respects, an unexceptional document. It upholds many of the tenets of Anglicanism to which few would object. As the Archbishop of Canterbury has commented, the tenets of orthodoxy spelled out in the document 'will be acceptable to and shared by the vast majority of Anglicans in every province, even if there may be differences of emphasis and perspective on some issues'. He offered a terse comment: 'Despite the claims of some, the conviction of the uniqueness of Jesus Christ as Lord and God and the absolute imperative of evangelism are not in dispute in the common life of the Communion.'[34] The only section of the declaration that would be in serious dispute is clause 13: 'We reject the authority of those churches and leaders who have denied the orthodox faith in word or deed.' Clearly the framers of the declaration meant here the North American churches, but that depends on the interpretation of 'orthodox faith'. If it means orthodoxy in relation to the historic creeds of the church – the Nicene Creed and the Apostles Creed primarily – then the vast majority of Anglicans, whatever their view on homosexuality, would be able to support the declaration wholeheartedly.

It is not the Declaration that is the problem for the future of the Anglican Communion. Rather, it is the goals of FCA that are quite confronting. There are two goals – the first goal is 'missional', the second is a 'consequence', as the online document describes it. The first goal, to preach the biblical gospel, includes defending 'the gospel and the people of God against their spiritual adversaries, notably the revisionist theology which has become so prevalent in the West'. The second is 'to provide aid to those faithful Anglicans who have been forced to disaffiliate from their original spiritual homes by false teaching and practice'.[35] The FCA then is a political movement designed to perpetuate and even foster division across the Anglican Communion. Lining up with the Declaration, as innocuous as it seems, nevertheless has the effect of supporting the tendentious goals of the FCA and the whole GAFCON movement.

Following hard on the heels of GAFCON, Jensen was in England with other GAFCON leaders to speak to a large rally of Evangelical clergy in London. The most interesting report of that gathering came from Bishop Tom Wright, then the Bishop of Durham. A fervent supporter of those North Americans who feel alienated by the liberal agenda of their churches, he was nevertheless scathing in his criticism of Jensen's role at the London rally. The Archbishop of Sydney's agenda, he implied, was that he and a 'very small group of hard-line, right-wing

---

[33] Resolution 28/08, Sydney Synod.
[34] Statement of the Archbishop of Canterbury in response to the GAFCON declaration.
[35] http://fca.net/resources/goals_of_the_fellowship_of_confessing_anglicans/.

English Evangelicals' were called to 'take over the C of E by aggressive planting of new churches under the nose even of existing Evangelical churches and bishops, and insisting that they are the only real "evangelicals", that they alone are true to scripture'.[36] The agenda was in hand before Gene Robinson was even proposed as a bishop, he said, citing evidence that the agenda was on the table before that. If Wright is correct, this is megalomania writ very large.

All of this, sparked supposedly by concerns over homosexuality? Those behind this radical agenda are fond of claiming that it is not homosexuality as such but the failure to uphold scriptural teaching on the issue that is the problem. Faithfulness to the plain teaching of 'God's Word written' is the catch-cry. This position deliberately ignores the reality that good, faithful Bible scholars around the world, including in Australia, interpret scripture rather differently on this matter, as we shall see.

Homosexuality, or more precisely, the gay lobby, has, however, been a long-running concern for Sydney Diocese. With feminism, it is one of the two ideological evils that contemporary Sydney Anglicans see as the enemy of religion and the cause of the disintegration of modern society.[37] In that view, these two movements are responsible for the widespread abandonment of the strictly-regulated male/female relationship claimed to be mandated by God. Their pursuit of a 'pure' Church – and a 'pure' society – requires a return to the old moral order.

Women's ordination is where the Diocese of Sydney has focused its dissent from feminism, and through it developed and promoted its theory of wider female subordination, as will be discussed in Chapter 6. Gay clergy, and the church blessing of same-sex partnerships, are where they focus their dissent from the gay lobby. Women's ordination, though over the past few decades it has placed an enormous strain on internal Anglican relations both internationally and locally and has led to threats of schism, is nothing in comparison with the minefield of homosexuality.

Homosexuality came onto the agenda of all the churches because of debates about its legal status from the 1950s and the subsequent growth of a public gay lobby. It is interesting and somewhat surprising to note that church leaders in general were prominent supporters of the decriminalization of private, consensual sex between adult males, both in Britain and in Australia. While they did not

---

[36] Tom Wright, 'Further Thoughts on GAFCON and Related Matters', http://www.fulcrum-anglican.org.uk.

[37] Peter Jensen said: 'The twin ideologies of the gay and feminist movements, not to mention greed for money, became far more important in shaping society than the teaching of the Bible', in his speech – entitled 'Build on the Past, Seize This Moment, Create the Future' – to the Anglican Church League annual Synod dinner, 9 October 2000. Greg Callaghan, 'Jensen's Crusade', *The Weekend Australian Magazine*, 14–15 May 2005, comments: 'Like many ultra-conservatives, Jensen blames feminists and homosexuals for the decline of the family since the 1960s, the decade when, in his view, society started to go helter-skelter.'

abandon the traditional claim that same-sex activity was, as one English bishop put it, 'morally evil and sinful in the highest degree' because it was 'a violation of natural law', the Church of England nevertheless argued that it should not be regarded as criminal behaviour.[38] Ten years of intense public debate and repeated Parliamentary attempts finally resulted in the repeal of the law concerning homosexuality in Britain in 1967.[39] Australian states repealed similar laws between 1972 and 1997.

In Australia the debate over the decriminalization of homosexual activity revealed the same deep divisions between Sydney and the rest of the Anglican Church as have been revealed by the women's ordination debate. The Diocese of Melbourne followed the line taken by the Church of England. In 1971 – a decade before the Victorian state law was repealed – Melbourne Diocese's Social Questions Committee recommended the decriminalization of homosexual acts between consenting adults in private. Melbourne Synod endorsed the recommendation in 1972. It was one of the first Australian church bodies to take such a stance. However, the Diocese of Sydney's Ethics and Social Questions Committee, reporting the next year, took the opposite position. It called for a continuation of criminal sanctions against homosexuality.[40] Sydney Synod even passed resolutions opposing government moves towards decriminalization, or towards the protection of homosexual people from discrimination. The role of Broughton Knox was influential in Sydney's response, as it had been to the ordination of women debate and many others.[41] God, he argued, had created sex for men and women to use in the lifelong marriage bond. Because it was outside that relationship, homosexuality was for self-satisfaction, and therefore contradicted God's purposes for sex. For this reason, both the Old and New Testaments made it very clear that 'God abominates homosexual acts', he argued. He went further: those who deliberately took part in same-sex acts could not be Christians and should not have any place in the Christian fellowship. Knox's arguments were aired early in 1973, the same year the Sydney Ethics and Social Questions Committee

---

[38] Bishop F.R. Barry, Bishop of Southwell, cited in Peter Coleman, *Christian Attitudes to Homosexuality* (London: SPCK, 1980) pp. 166–7.

[39] Homosexual activity, termed 'sodomy', was a vice under church law in England until the Reformation, when it became subject to secular law, punishable by hanging, first under Henry VIII and later under Queen Elizabeth I. This law was repealed in 1861. A last-minute addition to the Criminal Law Amendment Act of 1885, however, opened the floodgates to prosecution of homosexual activities between consenting adult males in private. It was this Act, under which Oscar Wilde was tried, that was repealed in 1967.

[40] *Report on Homosexuality*, Diocese of Melbourne Social Questions Committee 1971; *Report on Homosexuality*, Diocese of Sydney Ethics and Social Questions Committee, Sydney, 1973.

[41] David Hilliard, 'Gender Roles, Homosexuality, and the Anglican Church in Sydney', *Gender and Christian Religion*, Studies in Church History, 34 (Suffolk: Ecclesiastical History Society, 1998), pp. 516–17.

produced its report. He was a member of that committee; its chair was a member of his staff at Moore College.

The report saw the demand for homosexual acceptance as posing a very real danger to society. It said that 'overt homosexuality' was a basic contradiction of the heterosexual pattern of relationships because it 'defies the polarities of sex'. The ramifications of the gay lobby's demands were enormous, demanding 'nothing less than a radically new society'. The threat was 'real and not imagined'. Peter Jensen's recent claim that homosexuality has assisted the disintegration of Australian society is directly descended from that dire warning; presumably, he would believe the committee's stance on the issue has been validated.

Not that that was Knox's last word on the subject. In 1977, he whipped up continued opposition to decriminalization in Sydney Synod with a motion that claimed that the state laws against homosexual practice were not unjust because they reflected 'the Creator's prohibition of homosexual acts which is so strongly expressed in his Holy Word'. Historian David Hilliard has commented that it would have been hard then for the diocese to modify its position 'without losing face'.[42] How much more difficult would it be for Sydney to soften its approach on homosexuality now – even if it wanted to – after more than three decades of determined opposition, and in the light of the stance taken by Broughton Knox, the central figure in the development of its unique theological mindset. In my estimation, all attempts to engage Sydney in dialogue on the issue – attempts such as those instigated by the General Synod Doctrine Commission under the leadership of Peter Carnley in recent years – have been doomed to failure.

In 1985 – a year after the NSW law was changed – a sub-committee of Sydney Diocese's Standing Committee, in a report on homosexuality and ministry, claimed that homosexual people who engaged in homosexual acts could not occupy any office or perform any ministry in a parish. This prohibition covered everything from churchwarden and synod representative to organist, choir member or Sunday school teacher.[43] This entrenched Knox's view that active homosexuals had no place in a Christian congregation. These prohibitions were enacted in some parishes, reinforcing the pattern of homosexual people gravitating to parishes more likely to be sympathetic to their situation and not minded to ask questions that invaded personal privacy. There were also recorded instances of parishioners being denied Holy Communion because of their 'unrepentant' homosexuality.[44] These reports and actions reveal a far stronger antipathy to homosexual practice in Sydney Diocese than exists in other Australian dioceses.

The 1985 report was prompted by more than the repeal of the government legislation. It was also a response to AngGays, a small but effective gay lobby group in the diocese formed a few years earlier. AngGays gained some publicity

---

[42] Ibid., p. 517.
[43] Ibid., p. 518.
[44] David Hilliard, 'Sydney Anglicans and Homosexuality', *Journal of Homosexuality*, 33(2) (1997), pp. 117–18.

because one of its founders, an outspoken member of Sydney Synod, also led a Sydney chapter of the Order of Perpetual Indulgence, an 'order' of gay male nuns originating in San Francisco. This was in the spirit of the Sydney Gay and Lesbian Mardi Gras, a lavish annual city gay pride parade that initially was extremely controversial, and was regularly denounced by Sydney's conservative mainstream churches. These days it is generally treated as just another event in the annual city calendar. AngGays was not the first lobby group for Anglican homosexuals. In the early 1970s 'Cross+Section', an inter-denominational group of gay Christians, had been formed. The convenor, who was also secretary of a Sydney Anglican parish, was dismissed from his job after a televised interview in 1972, leading to large-scale demonstrations outside his church during Sunday worship.[45]

The 1998 Lambeth Resolution 1.10 effectively silenced the gay debate in the Anglican Church of Australia. The occasional skirmishes that have occurred since have been provoked by attempts to require obedience to that resolution. The 2004 General Synod, after a brief, low-key debate, passed minimalist motions saying that the Australian church did not condone the blessing of same-sex unions or the ordination of homosexual people in relationships. In the face of the international furore and Sydney's role in it, moderate Australian Anglicans have gone quiet. Although a series of surveys and anecdotal evidence suggested that only a minority of Australian Anglicans hold hardline attitudes on homosexuality, moderate Anglicans have not wanted to provoke an over-reaction from Sydney that might endanger gay Anglicans in other dioceses. Nor have many felt brave enough to face the wrath of the conservative juggernaut. In fact, the relentless conservative demands on this issue and others have effectively silenced moderate bishops, clergy and lay people in Australia. Most of them have enough to do just coping with too few resources, and the seemingly intractable problems that beset their dioceses and parishes. They seem to have lost the energy, confidence and courage to respond adequately to the conservative threat.

The General Synod Doctrine Commission did, however, try to engage the debate in a carefully nuanced academic fashion, in the hope of encouraging dialogue. *Faithfulness in Fellowship: Reflections on Homosexuality and the Church*, published in 2001, offered ten essays by theologians, Scripture scholars and church historians on various aspects of the issue. A 2003 study book based on the essays was designed for parish use. Neither the book nor its study guide was much used, however, as Anglicans continued to shy away from raising the subject. Another Doctrine Commission publication, *Lost in Translation? Anglicans, Controversy and the Bible* (2004), offered more essays reflecting on aspects of biblical interpretation concerning homosexuality. Again, it sparked little interest.

In response to the Lambeth 1998 call to listen to the experiences of gay people, three of the 23 Australian dioceses undertook diocese-wide listening programmes either in Synods, clergy conferences, or in parishes. These proved to be very difficult, with gay people increasingly feeling too vulnerable to speak of their

---

[45] Ibid., pp. 107–9.

experiences publicly, given the angry, insensitive responses they provoked from some quarters. In one diocese, the listening process turned into what has been described as a time of shouting rather than of listening. Other dioceses, possibly alarmed by these reactions, avoided a listening process altogether.

The General Synod Standing Committee, however, decided to include a formal listening process in the 2007 General Synod programme. As a member of the Standing Committee, I was asked to formulate an audio presentation, following guidelines prepared by the committee. Four categories of participants were agreed by the Standing Committee: a gay person who had left the church because of the church's attitude; a gay person still in the church in a longstanding monogamous relationship; a gay person in the church who had chosen celibacy in obedience to the church's requirements; and a person who once identified as a gay person but who, through a Christian experience, had become heterosexual. The identities of the four people who participated were kept entirely confidential. Their stories were read for a professionally-prepared audio disc by four anonymous volunteers.

The presentation came at the end of a Synod session, with the auditorium dimly lit and Synod members asked to listen in prayerful silence. There was no debate on the presentation. Many Synod members found the stories moving and appreciated the opportunity to hear first-hand the experiences of gay people. With widespread media interest, excerpts of the stories appeared in various publications around the country. The stories were very different, but each reflected the staggering price that individuals have paid for the church's inability to deal compassionately and generously with the issue of homosexuality. Together, they sum up the price the church has also paid in terms of its loss of integrity and the loss of significant ministry gifts. The hope was that each diocese and many parishes would make use of this carefully-prepared material made freely available to them, but that has not been the case. The church either does not want to listen, or is frightened of listening.

In the midst of this, without any real discussion, conservatives have been able to require that gay clergy refrain from any form of sexual relationship. They have used the uproar over clergy sexual abuse scandals to insert into the national church's recently-developed clergy code of conduct the requirement that clergy and all church workers and officers must be chaste in singleness. The code does not refer to same-sex relationships specifically, but it does not need to. The code applies equally to homosexual people as to heterosexuals, who at least have the option to marry if they do not want to live without sex. This development has not come just from Sydney Diocese; the whole church has been galvanized into action after the devastating effects sexual abuse has had on the reputation and morale of Christian churches worldwide. The Anglican Church of Australia has not, however, been affected to the same degree as the Catholic Church, and while some dioceses have been seriously hurt, other parts of the church have been relatively unscathed.[46]

---

[46] Muriel Porter, *Sex, Power and the Clergy* (Melbourne: Hardie Grant Books, 2003).

Opposition to feminism and homosexuality are clearly linked in the Sydney mindset. Both of them, for Sydney, are flagrant denials of their teaching that God has created patriarchal, heterosexual marriage as the only template for male/female relationships and as the only arena for acceptable sexual activity. Sydney Anglicans claim that their opposition to both ideologies – and the practice of them – is drawn exclusively from their obedience to Scripture. And yet, while their opposition to equality for women is certainly strong enough, it is nevertheless not as passionate as their revulsion for homosexuality. This can partly be explained as cultural. Overt opposition to female equality has long been a dead letter in Australian society generally, though misogyny is still alive and well in subterranean ways. It would be suicidal for any church to oppose the full participation of women in the wider community, regardless of their rules as far as the church is concerned. But homosexual practice has been out of the closet only for a few decades. As recently as 1997 it was still illegal in one Australian state (Tasmania). Old prejudices and homophobia are still close to the surface. Despite anti-discrimination laws, they erupt from time to time in thoughtless or ill-considered remarks on radio talkback, for instance. Overtly gay people are in a minority, and because many prefer discretion, the minority seems even smaller than it really is, despite what some might claim is their over-representation in contemporary films and television programmes.

But there is even more lurking behind the Sydney mindset. Certainly there is a strong element of power politics in their position; opposition to same-sex marriages and gay clergy is, for the very cultural reasons I have just outlined, the ideal 'line in the sand' for conservatives to draw in their bid for ascendancy in the church. But there is more. Some have suggested that the extremely masculinist nature of Sydney society is one factor. As I explained in Chapter 3, Sydney the city had its beginnings in a convict colony overwhelmingly dominated by men. For decades the male/female imbalance was very high. Such a concentration of men in the early days of the colony would almost certainly have led to covert homosexual relationships, as happens in all locations – such as in prisons – where women are unavailable. This may well have instilled repugnance for homosexuality in the Sydney religious psyche, particularly given the Anglican Church's counter-cultural, self-protective responses to its environment.

Stuart Piggin has argued that the masculine dominance of early Sydney created an 'aggressively anti-woman culture', particularly in the churches.[47] While he was arguing this in the context of a discussion about the ordination of women, homophobia is usually found in the same places as anti-woman sentiment. A fear of the feminine is the common thread. It has also been claimed that psychological revulsion for male homosexuality is related to an abhorrence among men for 'playing the woman', that is, men who adopt the passive role in sexual activity. Among the ancient Greeks who openly practised homosexual sex, only boys or

---

[47] Stuart Piggin, *Evangelical Christianity in Australia: Spirit, Word and World* (Melbourne: Oxford University Press, 1996), p. 155.

slaves were expected to take the passive female position. This is one reason why lesbianism is so little regarded in all debates about homosexuality, even in the churches; there is no issue there of male 'degradation'.

While all these elements could well be factors, I suspect the real reason for Sydney's angst on this issue is somewhat simpler. As David Hilliard has suggested, Sydney Diocese, early on in the 'gay debate', threw down the gauntlet of absolute opposition in a way that made it hard for them to retreat later. More, the gauntlet was wielded by that iconic figure, Broughton Knox. As we have seen in earlier chapters, it was he who shaped the diocese's distinctive doctrine of the church – a doctrine unique in Anglicanism. Knox taught Sydney to reject women's ordination, when other significant and highly-respected Australian Evangelical leaders such as Leon Morris of Melbourne supported it. Knox instilled in them the theory of female subordination, in both the church and the home. And Knox was one of their first public advocates for a level of opposition to homosexuality that went far further than that of conservative Christians in other places. He not only demanded a continuation of criminal sanctions against homosexuals, but also argued against practising gay people having any place in the Christian congregation. Sydney Anglicans would, I am sure, reject this analysis swiftly: it was not Knox per se who was responsible for their position, but the Bible to which he pointed, they would protest. It is their utter reliance on 'God's Word written', on the 'plain teaching' of Scripture, that has informed – no, required – their stance, they would claim. And so it would seem. Look at the debates about women in the ministry, as discussed in Chapters 5 and 6. Look at their insistence that the Bible repudiates all homosexual activity.[48]

Other eminent theologians and Bible scholars, some of them Evangelicals, have, however, come to very different interpretations to Sydney's on the issue of the ordination of women. As mentioned above, Melbourne Evangelical scholar Leon Morris, a man deeply-respected among all Australian Evangelicals, supported the ordination of women at least from the time of its first serious debate. He was a member of the Doctrine Commission that produced the seminal 1977 report, *The Ministry of Women*. While Broughton Knox – also a member of the Commission – refused to accept the Commission's conclusions in favour of the ordination of women, Morris did. A year earlier, a paper Morris had written supporting women's ordination, together with two other supportive documents, was printed in a booklet entitled *A Woman's Place*.[49] Interestingly, the other Sydney member of the Commission – a layman, Dr A.M. Bryson – agreed with the majority conclusion.

---

[48] For concise explanations of the Sydney Diocesan theological understanding in relation to homosexuality, see Peter Jensen, 'Ordination and the Practice of Homosexuality' and Glenn Davies, 'Homosexuality in the New Testament', in The Doctrine Panel of the Anglican Church of Australia, *Faithfulness in Fellowship, Reflections on Homosexuality and the Church* (Melbourne: John Garratt Publishing, 2001).

[49] Leon Morris, John Gaden and Barbara Thiering, *A Woman's Place: Anglican Doctrine Commission Papers on the Role of Women in the Church* (Sydney: Anglican

Outside Sydney, opposition to women in the ministry, in those early days, came principally from Anglo-Catholics. Evangelicals outside Sydney were generally in favour. Leon Morris was principal of Melbourne's Evangelical theological college, Ridley College, and a highly influential scholar. A Moore College-trained priest-scholar, Kevin Giles, based first in Armidale NSW and then in Adelaide, was writing prolifically in favour of women's ordination in the late 1970s and early 1980s.[50] (Giles had done postgraduate study in Durham University, UK, and at Tubingen University, West Germany, gaining a more generous theological perspective than his initial Moore Theological College training might suggest.) A Melbourne Evangelical archbishop, David Penman (Archbishop 1984–89) was one of the most determined proponents of women's ordination in the country. Prominent Melbourne clergy Alan Nichols and the late John Wilson, a former Melbourne bishop, were consistently strong in their support.[51] Teaching with Leon Morris at Ridley College, John Wilson and theologian and scholar Charles Sherlock ensured their biblically-based support for the broader women's cause permeated the theological formation of Melbourne Evangelical clergy. This meant that Evangelical clergy and lay people in Melbourne – a diocese where there has historically been a strong Evangelical presence – could be relied on to vote in favour of women's ordination. That is not the case any longer. Sydney's influence has extended into other dioceses to such an extent that these days opposition to women in ordained ministry is more likely to come from some Evangelicals than Anglo-Catholics. That was certainly the case when Melbourne Synod debated women bishops in 2007; the only public opposition came from Evangelical speakers in the 'Sydney mould'.

Some have suggested that it was this strong support for women's ministry among Evangelicals outside Sydney that helped prevent any real threat of schism on the part of Sydney. While they remained firmly opposed to women clergy, they nevertheless respected Evangelicals such as Morris too deeply to sever their relationships with them. If they did not publicly acknowledge it, it seems many of them privately accepted that there might be two respectable interpretations of the biblical position. While they believed their position to be the right one, they were nevertheless willing to entertain the prospect that another view was seriously held. Sadly, that situation changed with the ugly confrontations and resort to civil law that characterized the final stages of the women priests debate in the 1990s. Sydney's intransigence has hardened at the same time as its influence has strengthened across the Australian Church. It seems harder now for all but a few Evangelicals outside Sydney to oppose them publicly on this or any other

---

Information Office, 1976).

[50] Kevin Giles, *Women and Their Ministry: A Case for Equal Ministries in the Church Today* (Melbourne: Dove, 1977) and *Created Woman: A Fresh Study of the Biblical Teaching* (Canberra: Acorn Press, 1985).

[51] See papers published in Alan Nichols (ed.), *The Bible and Women's Ministry: An Australian Dialogue* (Canberra: Acorn Press, 1990).

issue. On homosexuality, however, it seems impossible for Sydney Anglicans to accept that there might be another view. This is not substantially different to the view taken by most Evangelicals, it must be said. But for moderate Evangelicals it has not become a yardstick by which they judge the biblical credentials of other Christians.

What lies at the heart of this ugly dispute? Ostensibly it is all about the Bible. Those who oppose any liberalizing of official church views on homosexuality claim that the issue is about the authority of Scripture. This is not the place for a full biblical exegesis on this topic, but we need to note that there are just a few biblical references to homosexuality, none of which can actually be claimed to be central to Christian teaching. Homosexuality is not mentioned in the Ten Commandments, for instance, and Jesus himself had nothing at all to say about the topic. Of the seven texts traditionally associated with homosexuality, only three are now regarded as indisputably about the subject.[52] These references come down to two in the Old Testament book of Leviticus, in a section termed by scholars 'the Holiness Code', and one in St Paul's letter to the Romans. St Paul's comment is the one that scholars on both sides of this debate would argue is the key reference, and yet the meaning of that text is not agreed. In the first chapter of Romans, St Paul cites homosexual behaviour in a list of unacceptable sins. However, the only kind of homosexual behaviour known to St Paul was most likely predatory, cultic, or at the very least promiscuous, all of which are also condemned by modern Christian defenders of same-sex partnerships.

Biblical scholars of significant international stature claim that St Paul's writing is not necessarily a bar to faithful, ongoing committed relationships between two adult people of the same sex. In fact, these scholars say that since the very notion of such relationships was foreign to the world the biblical writers knew, the Bible actually has nothing at all to say about monogamous same-sex unions. To the biblical writers, as to theologians, law makers, doctors and everyone else up until relatively recent times, homosexual activity was presumed to be a variant on immoral human sexual behaviour in general. It was like adultery or bestiality, a form of lust. It was not connected with love or intimacy or emotional need, let alone with sexual orientation, a concept not even understood until the late nineteenth century.[53]

---

[52] For instance, the destruction of the city of Sodom, told in the Old Testament book of Genesis (chapter 19), comes about because of the attempt by the townspeople to rape male visitors to the city. The town's punishment was traditionally linked with the sin of homosexuality. The term 'sodomy' is derived from this story. However, biblical scholars now point out that the wickedness for which the people of Sodom were punished was the violent mistreatment of strangers, a sin against the Middle Eastern code of hospitality.

[53] For a useful survey of the variety of views concerning the homosexuality debate in the Church, see The Doctrine Panel of the Anglican Church of Australia, *Faithfulness in Fellowship: Reflections on Homosexuality and the Church* (Melbourne: John Garratt Publishing, 2001).

But then, heterosexual sex was not formally linked with love or intimacy either for most Christian theologians until relatively recent times. It has been almost entirely forgotten that the Christian Church taught for many centuries that the best form of love even between husbands and wives was platonic, asexual. Any sexual activity even within marriage should be limited to the express purpose of procreating children, they taught. The reality is that the Christian Church has changed its mind, and changed it often, over the course of history, and has set aside some quite specific Scriptural teachings in the process.[54] But these changes have not led to schism.

If biblical authority is the yardstick, why is it then that conservative forces have not destabilized the Anglican Communion over the ordination of women? And what about divorce?[55] In most parts of the Anglican Communion, there is now recognition that marriages can and do die, and that new marriages can bring healing and grace. Remarriage in church is now almost universally acceptable in some form in the Anglican Church. But that was not always the case. The non-conformist churches have long been generous in their provision of remarriage in church for divorcees, a generosity to which many Anglicans can testify, because the Anglican Church was until just 25 years ago in this country, extremely harsh on divorce.[56] Divorced Anglicans had to resort to other churches if they remarried, which many found deeply hurtful.

Divorce is no longer a divisive issue for Anglicans, but for decades it was a cause of major friction in the Anglican world. It was an ongoing debate in Australia for the best part of 100 years, as it was internationally, a debate based almost entirely on the teaching of Scripture. The 1888 Lambeth Conference of Bishops pointed out that 'Our Lord's words expressly forbid divorce', and they were right. There is no ambiguity in Jesus' strict teaching against divorce. In three of the Gospels he is reported as saying that anyone who divorces his wife and marries another, commits adultery, and whoever marries a woman divorced from her husband commits adultery.[57] Strictly speaking, the only ambiguity is whether Jesus allowed remarriage even for the 'innocent party' in a divorce occasioned by adultery.[58]

Eventually, the growing consensus among church members and the wider community that divorce was acceptable, if regrettable, forced the Anglican Church

---

[54] Muriel Porter, *Sex, Marriage and the Church: Patterns of Change* (North Blackburn: Dove, 1996).

[55] I have written about the issue of divorce in more detail in 'Scripture and the Breaking of Communion: An Historical Overview', in Scott Cowdell and Muriel Porter (eds), *Lost in Translation? Anglicans, Controversy and the Bible* (Melbourne: Desbooks, 2004).

[56] The Anglican Church of Australia's The Marriage of Divorced Persons Canon was finally approved in 1985.

[57] Luke 16:18; Matthew 5:31–2 and 19:3–9; Mark 10:2–12.

[58] Matthew 5:32.

to rethink its position. It was coming under immense pressure from within its own ranks, not to mention outside, as divorce law reform progressed around the Western world. Theologians and scriptural scholars then argued successfully for a more lenient approach to divorce and remarriage than Jesus' specific teaching allowed. But the Anglican Church was not threatened with schism over divorce.

Sydney Diocese, as has been noted, has taken a more conservative position in relation to divorce than other Australian dioceses. It is possible for someone deemed to be the 'innocent party' to a divorce, to be married in a Sydney church, but certainly not for those considered to be at fault in the breakdown of the original relationship. Clergy, however, cannot be divorced, let alone remarried, no matter if they were 'innocent'. The breakdown of a clergy marriage usually leads to a swift requirement that they move out of ministry, which is not the case in other dioceses. The Australian Church has had two divorced and remarried diocesan bishops, yet there is no indication that Sydney bishops regarded themselves as out of communion with them. So the significant difference between Sydney's attitude to divorce and that of other dioceses has not been a cause of any public friction. Divorce it seems is, despite the diocesan strictures, regarded as a 'second order' issue in Sydney, one where there is more room to manoeuvre than is the case with homosexuality, even though Jesus' own words on the subject were so explicit. But as a Sydney Diocesan leader once said in my presence, he would not allow the gay American bishop Gene Robinson even to hand out the hymn books in a Sydney parish!

So biblical authority alone seems unlikely to be the reason why homosexuality has become the 'line in the sand' in world Anglicanism. I suspect it is respectable window-dressing for the exercise of blatant power-politics. As Stephen Bates has argued, homosexuality is the 'line in the sand' for conservative Evangelicals because 'it is the issue that they have chosen': 'It has not been thrust upon them – they spotted it as the rallying point more than a decade ago. They see it as a way to unite their constituency in opposition to the shifting sands of belief and secular culture.' For them, he writes, there is no room for 'dialogue, doubt or debate'. Theirs is nothing less than 'a takeover bid, to create a pure church of only one sort of believer'.[59] I would add that the rallying point might just as easily have been women's ordination or even divorce. There was not, however, the same degree of Evangelical unity on those subjects, and in any case, there are rather too many women and too many divorcees, both in the church and in the wider community, for either issue to have gained the necessary traction.

The gay issue does however connect with the women's debate because opposition to it has the effect of shoring up the conservative view of the subordinate place of women in the church and family. Acceptance of gay men would threaten everything in the conservative frame of reference. If gay clergy and same-sex partnerships were accepted, even reluctantly, even in other parts of the Anglican world, then the arguments for female subordination would be shattered. Patriarchal

---

[59] Bates, *A Church at War*, p. 222.

headship would be overturned. The resort to Scripture to prove male headship would be a dead letter. It is, then, an absolutely crucial battle for conservatives such as Sydney Diocese to win.

Chapter 5
Tensions:
Sydney and the Australian Church

The Diocese of Sydney's relationships with the rest of the Australian Anglican Church have always been strained. When most of the other Australian dioceses were Anglo-Catholic in character, Sydney's severe low-church Evangelicalism kept them inevitably at odds, and bred something of a ghetto mentality. As we have seen in Chapter 3, this marked difference in churchmanship, and the suspicions it bred on both sides, was the chief reason why it proved such a long and difficult exercise to achieve a national church constitution. But in recent decades, the strains between 'Sydney and the rest' have become even more marked, leading at times to speculation of a possible schism.

As we have seen, the 1990s saw the development of border incursions, as Sydney-style churches were planted in other Australian dioceses. The mid-1990s also saw the end of any form of prayer book uniformity across Australia as Sydney rejected the 1995 *A Prayer Book for Australia*. But two issues in particular have exacerbated those strains to almost intolerable levels – the ordination of women, and lay and diaconal presidency. These issues have, in varying ways, encouraged the diocese's increasing ideological attachment to an ecclesiology that insists that the local church is paramount. The national church, in this scenario, is little more than an administrative arrangement, the expectations and statutory obligations of which can legitimately be challenged and even avoided. Underlying this ecclesiology, and the diocese's attitudes particularly to both the ordination of women and lay and diaconal presidency, is the radical teaching of Broughton Knox.

Knox, a theologian with radically conservative theological views, was the central figure of Sydney Diocese in the second half of the twentieth century. On the Moore College teaching staff from 1947, he continued lecturing at the college for several years after his retirement, in all a period of more than 40 years. His influence over generations of ordinands was profound, and continues still, as those he impacted at Moore are now the leaders of the diocese. A recent biography describes him as the 'father of contemporary Sydney Anglicanism'.[1] If anything, 'father' is rather a benign term for someone with his extraordinarily pervasive influence. He was not just father to his successors at Moore and the Sydney leaders he taught, but guru and prophet as well. And he was far more than college principal and theological lecturer: he passed on to his students the political skills

---

[1] Marcia Cameron, *An Enigmatic Life: David Broughton Knox, Father of Contemporary Sydney Anglicanism* (Brunswick East: Acorn Press, 2006).

he exercised so effectively himself, and largely selected who would be ordained in Sydney Diocese, a prerogative usually belonging to the bishop of a diocese.[2]

For Knox and his disciples, the local congregation is the church, 'that real and physical expression of the heavenly fellowship'.[3] The diocese and the national church are merely 'networks' or 'associations' of churches that exist to serve the local congregations. In the words of Mark Thompson, a Moore College lecturer, 'the denomination is a service organization but the local congregations are the church of God on earth'.[4] If the denomination does not serve the needs of the gathered congregation, then it can be ignored, it seems. This is a radical Protestant concept of 'church', rather than the traditional Anglican understanding. Rejecting a larger concept of institutional church can conveniently sanction political behaviour of a less than godly kind in diocesan and national church assemblies.

Knox was not alone in promulgating this teaching. It was also taken up with enthusiasm by his Moore College colleague, Donald Robinson, later Archbishop of Sydney. Generations of Moore graduates have been imbued with this particular ecclesiology, which has progressively strengthened the diocese's distancing itself from the national church. It justifies keeping it at arms' length at best and at worst, treating it with contempt. On the other hand, Sydney Diocese itself, despite this rhetoric, continues to command significant loyalty from its local congregations.

Sydney Diocese increasingly insists that the national church operate purely in accordance with its very limited 1961 constitution. For instance, it argues that the Primate should function only within the stipulated provisions of the constitution, which would require him to do little more than convening and chairing General Synod and Standing Committee meetings, and carrying out other limited specified statutory roles. The notion of Primate as a significant national church leader, as it has progressively become since 1961, is anathema to them. On the basis of this stance, Sydney Diocese has refused to contribute its share towards the costs of a research assistant to the Primate.

Sydney has also for years refused to pay the voluntary 'special assessment' contribution levied by the national General Synod. Other dioceses, many of them strapped for cash, pay their contribution, even though it is often a struggle for them. But Sydney takes refuge in the strict legal position that the fund is voluntary. The special assessment fund is used principally to pay the national church's contribution to the administration of the international Anglican Communion, through its legal entity, the Anglican Consultative Council, as well as its contribution to the National Council of Churches and the World Council of Churches. Together, these contributions total about three quarters of the money raised by the special

---

[2] For an excellent brief resume of Knox's influence, see Bruce Wilson, 'The Father of Contemporary Sydney Anglicanism', *Market-place*, 11 October 2006.

[3] See Mark D. Thompson, 'The Church of God and the Anglican Church of Australia', in Bruce Kaye (ed.), *'Wonderful and Confessedly Strange': Australian Essays in Anglican Ecclesiology* (Adelaide: ATF Press, 2006), p. 237.

[4] Ibid., p. 243.

assessment. Because of the size of its General Synod representation, Sydney would be expected to pay about a quarter of that amount.

Sydney bases its refusal to pay on the grounds that it cannot in conscience support all the purposes for which the fund is used. It takes issue with certain aspects of ecumenism in particular, as represented by the National Council of Churches and the World Council of Churches, and with some of the work of the Anglican Consultative Council. Its opposition, however, has not impacted on its involvement in Anglican Communion-funded bodies, particularly membership of the Anglican Consultative Council, and attendance by its bishops (pre-2008) at the Lambeth Conference. To ameliorate criticism, Sydney Diocese has generally made separate, specific financial contributions to the Lambeth Conference. But the reality is that the national church is regularly out of pocket to the tune of about one quarter of its special fund because of this ideological stance. This refusal is debated regularly at every General Synod meeting, but no headway is ever made in changing its mind.

More seriously, the diocese also seems to be looking for ways to sidestep its statutory financial and other obligations as well. Media reports in late 2010 revealed unheralded proposals by the diocese's Standing Committee to ask the New South Wales (NSW) Parliament to amend the state's Anglican Church Property Trust Act to require that the diocesan Synod specifically agree to each financial payment levied by the national church. If the Parliament were to agree, this could severely constrain the operations of the national church. In effect, it would allow the diocese to bypass the General Synod's constitutional authority to impose financial levies on dioceses.

Hearing of the proposal, the Primate wrote to the Attorney-General, to the shadow attorney general, and to the director general of the NSW Department of Justice, alerting them to wider church concern. He also asked the Archbishop of Sydney and the Sydney Standing Committee to delay the proposal so there could be consultation. Following some significant media interest, the proposal was postponed, with Sydney Synod 2010 agreeing by resolution that any such moves be brought to Synod for approval before promotion to the NSW Parliament. In any case, the NSW Attorney-General apparently assured the Primate that the Government would want general consensus within a church community on any changes to church legislation. The matter is clearly now dead in the water.

The parliamentary route to avoid statutory assessment might be closed but other avenues are being investigated. Sydney Synod 2010 passed a resolution criticizing several financial decisions of General Synod, and asking Sydney Standing Committee to 'enter into urgent consultation with the General Synod Standing Committee to negotiate a more equitable financial outcome for the dioceses of the Australian Church'. Further, it asked the Sydney Standing Committee 'to consider whether it should report on these matters to the 2011 session of Synod before arranging for payments to the General Synod in 2011'. If Sydney Standing Committee does decide to report back to Sydney Synod in 2011 before paying its financial dues to the General Synod, it might well be said to be acting provocatively in terms of the national constitution. In a voluntary body relying entirely on goodwill among its members for its operation, there would be little General Synod or its Standing Committee could do about it.

The Ordination of Women

At the very time that Sydney Diocese's Evangelicalism was changing into a more rigidly Calvinistic mode under the influence of Broughton Knox, the rest of the Anglican Church – in Australia as well as around the world – was grappling with the question of the ordination of women, an issue that would almost tear it apart. We will look in detail at Sydney's theological stance on the ordination of women in the following chapter, but here we need to note that a fundamental division over the issue was apparent from the outset of the debate in the Australian church. When the General Synod Doctrine Commission presented its first report on the subject to the 1977 General Synod meeting, 11 of its 12 members supported its finding, that there were no theological reasons why women should not be ordained to all three orders of ministry – deacon, priest and bishop. The one dissentient, author of a minority report opposing the Commission's findings, was Broughton Knox. Effectively, the view of this one man was to lock up the view of his diocese, not just then but for the future. So the one dissentient was not merely one, but rather signalled the stance his diocese's leaders would inevitably take.

From 1977, Sydney's opposition to women in ordained ministry has been implacable.[5] Its archbishops and Standing Committee have, in general, maintained the line with energy and determination, although its Synod was not always so hardline. Sydney Synod passed the General Synod legislation for women deacons a couple of times in the late 1980s in the face of the direct opposition of Archbishop Donald Robinson. He was not opposed to women as deacons per se. Rather, his concern was that, once women were deacons, claims might be made that they were entitled to progress to priesthood as well by virtue of their diaconal ordination. Archbishop Robinson had made it clear on numerous occasions that his view was that to ordain women as priests was to be disobedient to Christ himself. The male presbyterate was 'essential for the integrity of the church' and non-negotiable, he said in 1987.[6] He eventually gave his assent to the legislation once a careful proviso was added, stipulating that women deacons could not become priests in the diocese without Sydney Synod's explicit approval.

The leadership for the women deacons' ordinance came from the Sydney Synod itself, and principally two of its lay members, Keith Mason (then the

---

[5] For a comprehensive overview of Sydney Diocese's engagement with the subject, see 'Review of the Synod's Consideration of the Law of the Church of England Clarification Canon 1992 and the Ordination of Women as Presbyters', a report from the Standing Committee to Synod 2008, http://www.sds.asn.au/Site/103913.asp?a=a&ph=sy.

[6] Ibid., p. 191.

Sydney Solicitor-General, now recently retired as President of the NSW Court of Appeal) and Colleen O'Reilly (then a lay reader in the diocese, now a prominent vicar and Cathedral canon in the Diocese of Melbourne). Subsequently, though the Synod refused to pass the 1992 General Synod legislation for women priests, there was nevertheless a significant minority vote when the legislation came before the Synod once more in 1996. On that occasion, while it lost clearly in the House of Clergy – predominantly the men trained at Moore College under Broughton Knox and Donald Robinson – it lost by just ten votes in the House of Laity.[7]

In 1999, when another attempt was made to have the legislation debated, 12 of the 24 women deacons in the diocese appealed in writing to the Synod to agree to women priests. Despite their appeal, and a passionate plea from one of their number on the floor of Synod, the Synod narrowly decided it was a 'waste of time' to debate the bill and so declined to do so. No doubt Archbishop Harry Goodhew's signal the previous year that he would approve the legislation if it were passed – and would actually ordain women priests – was enough to make the diocese's politicians ensure the bill was not even debated.[8] But certainly among the laity, who had not been so exposed to the influence of Moore College, the possibility of women priests was not entirely anathema at the end of the twentieth century. In hindsight, it can be seen from this example alone, that Sydney Synod and the diocesan leadership even at this late stage had not entirely capitulated to the absolute power of what would soon become known as the 'Jensenites'. (Attempts to revisit the issue during Peter Jensen's episcopate have come to nothing.)

Between 1977 and 1992, the Diocese of Sydney effectively waged war against the national church over the ordination of women priests. It was not the only opponent of women clergy; its 'satellite' dioceses of North West Australia and Armidale were opposed, as were traditionalist Anglo-Catholic dioceses such as Ballarat, The Murray and, to a lesser extent, Wangaratta. But these other dioceses were small, and because of their size, had few representatives to General Synod. The leadership in opposition to women clergy, particularly in political terms, came from Sydney Diocese, which also had the largest number of representatives to the national body. This alliance, together with a few isolated opponents among other dioceses' representatives, ensured that legislation for women priests was not passed by the General Synods of 1985, 1987 and 1989. Sydney had also tried hard to ensure the 1992 General Synod was likewise futile for the women's cause. The pressure building up in the rest of the Australian church at that time, however, coupled with the ordination of women by Perth Diocese in March 1992, meant that by then the tables had been turned. Whereas pleas to protect the unity of the national church had once been an effective argument for some to resist the legislation, now national unity required it, as we shall see.[9]

---

[7] *The Sydney Morning Herald*, 15 November 1996.

[8] *The Sydney Morning Herald*, 9 and 20 October 1999.

[9] See Muriel Porter, *Women in the Church: The Great Ordination Debate in Australia* (Ringwood: Penguin, 1989) and Muriel Porter, 'The End of the "Great Debate": The 1992

By 1999, when Sydney Synod refused even to debate the issue of women priests, there were considerable numbers of women clergy in active service in the rest of the Australian church. Among those who had been priests from the time of the first ordinations in late 1992 were clergy in dioceses such as Melbourne who had been deacons since 1986, and some of these women had been in full-time lay ministry positions for some years before that. Had they been men, these women would have been ordained for more than 15 years by 1999. With that level of experience, they should have been on the lists of those to be considered for consecration as bishops when vacancies arose. So by 1999, the national church had moved well beyond the issue of women priests, to a consideration of women as bishops.

At the turn of the twenty-first century, the Anglican Church of Australia was being confronted once more by its failure to sort out the question of women's ordination in its entirety from the outset. The 1977 Doctrine Commission report had not differentiated between the three orders of ministry when it found there were no theological reasons for not ordaining women. Ideally, the question should have encompassed all three orders from then on. It could have been, if the findings of the church's highest court, the Appellate Tribunal, had been heeded in 1985. That year, the Tribunal had said that the ordination of women to any of the three orders was not inconsistent with the church's constitution. At the time lawyers were divided about what the Tribunal opinion[10] meant in practical terms. In 1988, however, the General Synod Standing Committee concluded that the Tribunal decision meant that no specific legislation for the ordination of women was necessary, meaning there was nothing to stop a diocesan bishop from proceeding to ordain women immediately.

However, in 1985 two archbishops passionately committed to the cause of women's ordination decided not to proceed on the basis of the Tribunal opinion alone. Archbishops Peter Carnley of Perth and David Penman of Melbourne brought last-minute legislation for women priests to the 1985 General Synod because, as Penman argued, women priests should not be introduced by default. Rather, it should happen 'prayerfully, deliberately, and synodically', he said. Their move, though well-intentioned, was politically naïve. The legislation was controversial enough even without being rushed to synod without any opportunity for discussion beforehand. Even supporters felt they were being steamrollered

---

General Synod Decision on Women Priests', paper presented to the Studying Australian Christianity Conference, Sydney 14–16 July 1993, published in Mark Hutchinson and Edmund Campion (eds), *Long Patient Conflict: Essays on Women and Gender in Australian Christianity* (Sydney: The Centre for the Study of Australian Christianity, 1994).

[10] Appellate Tribunal decisions on such matters are technically 'opinions'. Sydney Diocese claims the decisions are advisory only. (See, for example, the wording of Resolution 16 of Sydney Synod 2010 and the argument from Sydney lawyer Neil Cameron, 'Appellate Tribunal Does It Again', *Australian Church Record*, October 2010.) As noted earlier, this is not the view of one of Australia's most senior judges, Justice Keith Mason AC.

by the archbishops. Because the legislation came without proper notice, a 75 per cent majority vote by General Synod members was required even to allow it to be debated, ensuring a highly-charged process. Wily opponents, principally from Sydney Diocese, eventually voted to allow the legislation to be considered, having sown sufficient doubt during the preliminary debate to ensure that it was defeated. Had the legislation not even been drafted, let alone debated, the way would have been clear for any bishop to ordain women on the strength of the Tribunal decision.

The defeat of the legislation, on the other hand, given the archbishops' own rationale for bringing it, effectively removed that possibility. A golden opportunity to proceed immediately was given away and with it, the pathway for women to progress seamlessly from deacon to priest to bishop, as male clergy do. After all, the Anglican Church of Australia has no specific legislation for male clergy. Instead, the 1985 General Synod passed legislation for women deacons only, almost as a consolation prize. That move opened the door for women clergy in full orders in due course, but only the door into the hallway, we might say. The inner doors to priesthood and episcopate remained tightly shut, with the door to women bishops not finally opened until 2007. If women had been ordained in 1985 on the strength of the Tribunal decision alone, opponents would no doubt have made an almighty fuss about it, and tried all kinds of stalling tactics, possibly taking the matter to the secular courts, as they did in later years. But in the end, the ordinations would have been declared valid, and women would have proceeded to the next two orders of ministry without subjecting the church – and to themselves – to the ongoing battles that plagued it for more than 20 years.

General Synod legislation for women priests failed again in both 1987 and 1989. The 1987 attempt came to a 'special' meeting of the General Synod, called to deal specifically with the 'woman problem', given it had become so pressing. In 1987 those in favour of women priests mustered just under 66 per cent of the vote, but the required majorities of two-thirds in each House were not met; the Houses of Laity and Bishops had achieved the two-thirds figures, but not the House of Clergy. In 1989 the vote in favour had dropped, with an overall vote of 61.5 per cent. It was still a healthy majority, but not enough.

The level of frustration was growing rapidly across the church, with some bishops in favour of women clergy openly describing themselves as 'the oppressed majority'. Fearing that subsequent attempts would continue to fail, they looked for alternatives. After the failure of the 1987 canon, Archbishop David Penman of Melbourne suggested that one way forward lay through legislation enacted by diocesan synods rather than General Synod. Consequently a committee was established to bring legislation to Melbourne Synod in 1988. The legislation, passed convincingly by a high margin, nevertheless contained a clause that it would not be acted upon until the Appellate Tribunal decided it was valid. But the Tribunal's judgement was that it was not valid, a decision which came as a bitter disappointment given that the legislation's chief backer, Archbishop Penman, had died following a massive heart attack just a month before the Tribunal's decision was announced in November 1989.

The Tribunal ruled that the Melbourne Act was invalid not because it was diocesan legislation per se, but because Melbourne Diocese's constitutional foundation in a parliamentary act of 1854 did not permit legislation of this kind. The Tribunal's judgement did not, however, rule out the possibility that other dioceses, with different constitutions, might use local legislation to achieve an end still denied the church by General Synod.[11] The battleground, since 1985, had been the issue of local diocese versus General Synod, and the Tribunal's judgement served only to intensify it.

The Tribunal's 1989 decision rendered Melbourne, historically the leader of the women's ordination movement, helpless, leaving other diocesan bishops to assert leadership. The first substantial move came from Owen Dowling, the Bishop of Canberra and Goulburn, in an address to his Synod on 31 August 1990. In that address, Bishop Dowling announced that he would ordain women priests on 24 February 1991, under the terms of diocesan legislation passed by his Synod in 1989. The legislation was constitutionally valid, according to his legal advisers, he said. He told Synod that 'at an informal meeting held recently between the bishops of some dioceses and their legal advisers, the same point of view emerged ... [that] a Canon of General Synod is not necessary'. Those other bishops present at the informal meeting almost certainly included Bruce Wilson of Bathurst, Alf Holland of Newcastle and George Hearn of Rockhampton.

After a lengthy excursus presenting theological arguments in favour of women priests, Bishop Dowling then said that he had no intention of testing the validity of his Synod's legislation before the Appellate Tribunal (as Melbourne had done, to its cost). If others wished it tested, it was up to them. Effectively, he said that he intended to proceed unless stopped. Others did wish it tested. Keith Rayner, then Archbishop of Adelaide and Acting Primate, quickly formulated a set of 11 questions for the Tribunal, covering a wide range of possible diocesan moves. It soon became clear that the Tribunal's response would not be available in time for the planned February ordination; it would take at least a year, the Tribunal President, Mr Justice Cox, announced. Just two weeks after his momentous announcement, Dowling had suspended his plans, though he denied that he had been in any way intimidated.[12]

The church settled in yet again for the long wait for a Tribunal judgement. The only bright spot came from the West, where Archbishop Peter Carnley, always unpredictable, announced some changes to the constitution of the Diocese of Perth. With the agreement of Perth Synod, the constitution would explicitly provide for an 'equal opportunity' church, where women could not be excluded. Such a change required 12 months' notice, so could not be implemented until

---

[11] David Bleby QC, 'What Does It Really Mean?', *See* (Melbourne Diocesan monthly newspaper) December 1989.

[12] Owen Dowling, Charge to Synod of Canberra and Goulburn, 30 August 1990; *Church Scene*, 14 September 1990; media release of the Diocese of Canberra and Goulburn, 19 September 1990.

1991. The constitutional change had in fact been made by the time the Appellate Tribunal's judgement was finally published. Perth is a long way from the rest of Australia, so while the constitutional changes might have seemed important close to home, most of the country ignored them. The tyranny of distance allowed Perth's astute archbishop to play his cards close to his chest, until he finally took everyone by surprise in March, 1992, and ordained Australia's first women priests.

Before that event, the Tribunal, after taking 14 months to deliberate, announced its findings. But they offered no real answer to the problems plaguing the Australian church. The four senior judges and three bishops who comprised the Tribunal, brought down bewilderingly different answers to the 11 questions. Initially, it seemed that their effective answer on the most pressing question – can a diocese lawfully act on its own legislation? – was a clear 'no'.[13] But the Tribunal members were in fact divided on that question in such a way as to give no answer at all. (Two lay members and two bishops need to agree on a point of ritual or discipline to constitute an answer; in this case, three lay members and one bishop said 'no', while one lay member and two bishops said 'yes'.) The Tribunal had not said 'yes' to diocesan legislation, but neither had it said 'no'. In the West, Peter Carnley was quick to see the implications, and announced that he would 'be seeking advice from his legal advisers concerning the next steps to be taken'.[14]

Archbishop Rayner saw further implications. The pressure on the 1992 General Synod to resolve the issue was now immense, and he recognized his responsibility as Primate: 'I shall certainly see it as a very important part of my role as Primate to try to lead the church towards a resolution that will enable our unity to be maintained and the church to move forward', he said.[15] This signalled his own considerable shift towards the need for a prompt and final national resolution; as the situation grew more urgent, his own leadership of the situation also grew. This, together with Rayner's considerable stature in the national church, was one of the factors that must not be discounted in any assessment of why the General Synod finally passed the legislation.

The situation quickly became more urgent. A couple of days before Christmas 1991, Owen Dowling once again announced an ordination date. He would ordain 11 women to the priesthood on 2 February 1992. This time he had the backing of five other diocesan bishops with whom he had met, together with their legal advisers, a few days earlier. Archbishop Ian George of Adelaide, and Bishop Phillip Newell (Tasmania) joined Bishops Wilson, Holland and Hearn, who all declared they would also seek to ordain women soon. One of the leading opponents, Dr Ian

---

[13] 'Tribunal Says "No" to Immediate Ordinations', media release from Anglican Media, Melbourne, 6 December 1991; Statement by the Primate of the Anglican Church of Australia, the Most Reverend Dr Keith Rayner, on the Release of the Opinion of the Appellate Tribunal, 6 December 1991.

[14] 'Anglican Appellate Tribunal Unable to Give Ruling on Vital Ordination of Women Question', media release, Diocese of Perth, 6 December 1991.

[15] Quoted in *The Age*, 7 December 1991.

Spry, a Melbourne QC, chairman of the Association for the Apostolic Ministry, a body formed in 1989 to oppose women priests, warned that there might be legal action through the civil courts to prevent Dowling's 'proposed illegality'. Rayner, meanwhile, called for calm.

Some believe that similar threats of legal action had held back individual bishops from proceeding for some time; the costs, financial and otherwise, were just too high. So Bishop Dowling and his supporting bishops were in no doubt as to what might lie ahead. In the aftermath of the inconclusive Tribunal decision, they doubtless believed that they had come to a point of no return. Without some further action, the General Synod of 1992 would almost certainly be as powerless as its predecessors. It was abundantly clear that theological and academic debate alone would not sway those last crucial votes.

The legal threat was finally activated, with significant orchestration from Sydney. In mid-January 1992, the matter was brought to the Supreme Court of NSW by three individuals whom the secular press persisted in calling 'two ministers and a parishioner'. The clergymen were David Robarts, a Melbourne rector with a long history of vehement opposition to women priests, later made a bishop in a breakaway traditional church, and Dalba Primmer, then rector of Bega in NSW, one of the few opposed clergymen in the Diocese of Canberra and Goulburn. The 'parishioner' was Dr Laurence Scandrett, a member of Sydney Diocese's powerful Standing Committee, no less. 'We expected this would happen, but we were living in fond hope that it wouldn't', Dowling was reported as saying.[16]

The week leading up to 2 February was tense in the extreme. At first the Supreme Court refused an injunction to stop the planned ordination, and the women's movement was gleeful. But the trio quickly lodged an appeal, which was just as swiftly heard. Just two days before the ordination was due to take place, it was stopped by an interlocutory injunction issued by the NSW Court of Appeal. Instead of ordaining the women, Owen Dowling took them, robed ready for priesting, through the service in Goulburn Cathedral up to the point of ordination – and then proceeded to ordain the male candidates alone. It was harrowing, and very public.

The media exploded. The non-ordination received saturation coverage, as had the court hearings. There were TV specials, comment columns, editorials, features and endless 'letters to the editor'. The mood was overwhelmingly one of outrage from journalists, from ordinary citizens and more importantly, from ordinary Anglicans. They were appalled to see a bishop and a group of earnest churchwomen dragged through the civil courts, and they said so. Church leaders can have been in no doubt that the church had to get its house in order, and quickly. A pastoral letter written to Sydney parishes by Archbishop Donald Robinson, an arch opponent of women priests, is evidence of how the issue was affecting ordinary Anglicans. He asked them 'not to be disturbed in their Christian duty and

---

[16] *The Age*, 17 January 1992.

witness', which suggests that many Anglicans, even in conservative Sydney, were in fact deeply disturbed.[17]

Some reporters delved behind the surface. Was this court case really the work of just three aggrieved individuals? *The Age*'s Margo Kingston revealed the role of the Association for the Apostolic Ministry in the court challenge, in both organizing it and appealing for donations to fund it.[18] Later, it became clear that the Diocese of Sydney had helped bankroll the plaintiffs in the case. Following public questioning, the Archbishop of Sydney advised his Synod that he had thought 'the interests of the diocese in the Dowling issue were such that it should consider some engagement in the legal process initiated by people testing the powers of the bishop in the Supreme Court'. After his advice to the Standing Committee, both the plaintiffs and Bishop Dowling had been offered up to $100,000 each. The plaintiffs had accepted; Bishop Dowling had refused.[19] The Goulburn events were without doubt the pivotal point in the long-running women's ordination debate. Ironically the opponents of women priests so overplayed their hand at several points in those last critical months, that they effectively forced the pace of change.[20]

Archbishop Keith Rayner once more struggled to restore order to the church, recognizing the significant change of mood. He took the rare step of issuing a pastoral letter to the clergy and laity of Australia, which was published in full in several major daily newspapers. In the letter, Rayner warned that if General Synod could not 'find a way through the impasse', then he could not 'guarantee that the church can be contained within the existing constitutional framework'.[21] His prose was measured as always, but Rayner nevertheless was warning that the Australian church would break up if the General Synod could not find a way for women to be priests. It was an exact reversal of the many earlier predictions that ordaining women priests would be the cause of the disintegration of the Anglican Church; it was this reversal of opinion which led to the Australian General Synod decision in late 1992.[22]

In his pastoral letter, Rayner also called for a moratorium both on further attempts to ordain and on legal proceedings. Neither happened. The Goulburn plaintiffs did not withdraw their continuing court case, and in Perth, Archbishop Carnley continued quietly to plot his own moves. In January he had announced that he would ordain ten women in Perth's St George's Cathedral on 7 March.

---

[17] 'Letter from the Archbishop to the Congregations of the Diocese', February 1992.

[18] *The Age*, 5 February 1992.

[19] Presidential Address to Sydney Synod, 12 October 1992.

[20] *Church Scene*, 14 February 1992. See also editorial, *Church Scene*, 27 November 1992.

[21] *The Age*, 6 February 1992.

[22] Archbishop Robinson gave evidence in the NSW Supreme Court that women priests would be a 'recipe for short-term chaos and the long-term disintegration of the church', quoted in *The Australian*, 24 January 1992.

In the east, where the drama of the court case was about to begin, no one took much notice. But the Goulburn plaintiffs, with the addition of a Perth priest, nevertheless brought the matter before the Supreme Court of Western Australia in the week leading up to the ordination. This time the court refused to play ball, and the planned ordination went ahead, stunning and delighting the still-smarting supporters of women's ordination on the east coast. Australia had its first women priests, ordained under the authority of a diocesan constitution. There could be no turning back now.

Now it was the turn of opponents to erupt. Preventing the ordination ceremony in Goulburn had been a major victory for them, but Carnley had turned it into a Pyrrhic victory. Those opposed claimed that the Perth ordination had been illegal, and quickly moved against both the Archbishop and the women on those grounds. Within weeks, they had the matter back before the courts, this time as part of the case still proceeding in NSW. Effectively, they wanted the ordinations annulled. They did not succeed; the matter was ruled out of order.[23]

More seriously, trouble erupted at the heart of the church. Six Australian diocesan bishops publicly deplored Carnley's action. Donald Robinson of Sydney, Barry Hunter of the Riverina, Peter Chiswell of Armidale, John Hazlewood of Ballarat, Robert Beal of Wangaratta and Graham Walden of The Murray claimed Carnley had 'precipitated this threat to the unity and stability of our church by an action taken outside our present constitutional agreement'. Tensions between Robinson and Carnley, at the few public occasions they were together, were palpable, as Robinson claimed they were no longer in full communion. Rumour had it that Carnley was not invited to celebrate Holy Communion during the annual bishops' conference in May to prevent conflict.[24] Carnley remained suspect in Sydney's eyes throughout the rest of his episcopate, including his time as Primate in succession to Keith Rayner.

Meanwhile, the Canon Law Commission and a special 'monitoring committee', set up by General Synod Standing Committee, were preparing for the General Synod meeting in early July 1992. The two groups, working together, eventually came up with two proposals. The first had originally been floated by Archbishop Ian George of Adelaide. He suggested a change to the constitution of the national church, devolving power over ritual, ceremonial and discipline to the dioceses. Many in Sydney saw its possibilities. While they certainly would not want to use it to ordain women, as other dioceses would, they might be able to use it to legalize lay presidency at the Eucharist, for instance. Some suspected a political deal lay behind the proposal: 'you give us women priests, we'll give you lay presidency',

---

[23] *Church Scene*, 8 May 1992. Archbishop Rayner had in fact publicly already declared that Carnley had not acted illegally in ordaining the women, given that the Tribunal had not found either way on the question of diocesan legislation; *Church Scene*, 20 March 1992. Ian Spry took issue with him in a letter to *Church Scene*, 3 April 1992, in which he said the women 'were not priests and could not act as such'.

[24] *Church Scene*, 3 April 1992.

though there is no evidence for that. Possibly some in Sydney simply saw potential for their own needs in this strategy.

The proposed constitutional amendment continued to cause real controversy right up until the General Synod, and effectively allowed a smoother passage for its official alternative, a canon repealing any inherited law of the Church of England that might prevent the ordination of women in Australia. The 1991 Appellate Tribunal decision had claimed a vague, inherited law from the Church of England might still stand in the way, despite the Australian church's autonomous status. Repealing any possible inherited law was originally the suggestion of David Bleby QC from Adelaide, until recently chair of the Church Law Commission, and now a Supreme Court Judge. It was nothing short of a stroke of genius, for it united all those who supported women's ordination. There were a few supporters who had maintained that, as there was no specific legislation for male clergy, any form of legislation for women was in itself discriminatory. This proposal, as a means of 'clarification', removed that concern and so allowed them to support the legislation. As it was also about clarifying the legal situation, it was not overtly legislation for women clergy; it might have proved acceptable to some who did not personally want women priests but could support clarification. That canon was finally passed by the requisite majorities – by the slimmest of margins – in November 1992, opening the door to women priests in Australia at last.

The question of women bishops was firmly on the church's agenda by the end of the twentieth century, as the numbers of women priests grew around the country. Diocesan synods began calling on General Synod to make it possible, leading to an 'in principle' debate at the 1998 General Synod. The same arguments in relation to women priests were aired again on both sides. The only significantly different arguments concerned practical matters, such as confirmation and ordination: would people confirmed and ordained by a woman bishop, find that they were not recognized as truly confirmed or truly ordained in other parts of the Anglican Communion? And would the presence of women diminish the collegiality of the bench of bishops? How would those opposed to women in holy orders cope with a woman bishop? If they objected to a woman priest in their parish, they could always move to another parish, but moving to another diocese would not be a realistic option.

These concerns quickly gave rise to demands for alternative forms of episcopacy for those opposed to women bishops. In the Church of England, those opposed to women priests can choose to bar women clergy from their parish entirely, and can elect to come under the care of sympathetic male 'flying bishops', but the Australian church had resisted similar moves with women priests. The situation is significantly different in Australia in any case. In the Church of England, church legislation applies across the board, whereas in Australia dioceses enjoy high levels of autonomy, as we have noted. Those dioceses which do not support women priests, are not obliged to experience their ministry. Similarly women bishops will only be appointed in dioceses where there is strong support. In a diocese such as Sydney, women priests or bishops from elsewhere cannot exercise their full ministry in the diocese; they can function merely at the level of a deacon. So any alternative forms of episcopal care mooted in Australia would apply only to tiny minorities within dioceses strongly supportive of women bishops.

The first attempt at legislation at the General Synod of 2001 came after a General Synod working group had done a substantial amount of work discussing the possibilities.[25] One suggestion from a Sydney participant was to change the constitution to allow parishes in one diocese to elect to join a different diocese. So parishes opposed to women bishops could elect to join a diocese likewise opposed. The effect would be that parishes physically next door to each other could belong to different dioceses. Though some preliminary ideas of the legislative changes needed were provided, there was no substantial thought given to practical issues, such as who would pay for all the travel involved in a country so vast as Australia for the bishop in a far-off diocesan centre to visit the parish or offer pastoral care to its clergy? At a political level, would this provide a means for Sydney Diocese to do exactly what it liked within its own virtual borders and to attract in significant numbers of parishes from around the country, thus bolstering its own position and weakening its neighbours? Needless to say, this proposal would have required a vast amount of constitutional change and could have taken years, if not decades, to achieve. Not surprisingly, it did not gain any real traction.

Instead, the working group brought legislation, again in the form of a 'clarification' canon to remove any inherited law of the Church of England preventing women bishops. It also provided a form of alternative episcopal oversight for those opposed to women bishops, once a woman bishop had been elected or appointed. It meant that the General Synod of 2001 quickly became bogged down over the issue. Those in support of women bishops were generally not prepared to concede to the alternative oversight provisions, as they feared the model on offer would undermine the authority of women bishops. On the other hand, those opposed were adamant that alternative options to their liking should be provided. The divisions became so protracted that the legislation had to be withdrawn, and another working party was subsequently formed to prepare for the next General Synod.

Consequently General Synod 2004 was presented with legislation that contained options much more acceptable to women's supporters, all of whom managed to unite around the mooted provisions. Nevertheless the legislation failed, though by a very small margin, because the Sydney-led opposition resolutely refused to give way on their principal objection, that women were forbidden by Scripture to hold authority in the church. The writing was on the wall. No matter what efforts were made to hand out olive branches in the form of alternative provisions, there would be no compromise. As long as Sydney dominated General Synod with its large representation, there could be no progress. So in the following year, some in the

---

[25] I chaired the working group at the request of the General Synod Standing Committee, and presented the doomed legislation at the 2001 General Synod.

church decided it was now time to test whether legislation really was necessary. We had been left with no other option.

Doubts about whether legislation for women bishops was actually necessary had persisted since women had become priests. If any inherited laws from the Church of England preventing women priests had been removed, surely women priests' orders were the same as men's, and they could therefore be considered for election or appointment as bishops. Some dioceses open to the possibility of women bishops, wondered whether they could legally consider women priests when they came to elect new diocesan bishops. In the Diocese of Adelaide, as it prepared to elect a new archbishop in 2004, some women clergy in Australia were initially considered. However, given the persisting doubt, the diocese commissioned legal advice. The advice has not been made public, but as they decided not to proceed with the names of women candidates, presumably it was at least cautious. In Melbourne Diocese, following the retirement of Archbishop Peter Watson in 2005, the Board of Nominators was faced with the same dilemma. The Board reported to Melbourne Synod that, 'with regret', it had decided not to consider nominating female candidates, 'given that the constitutional position concerning women in the episcopate in this country is not clear'.[26]

What was clear was that there was a significant level of doubt about whether further legislation was required for women bishops, once women could be priests. The church's constitution contains a 'canonical fitness' definition that spells out the fundamental requirements for a bishop. That definition requires bishops to be 'persons in priests' orders', which certainly suggested that legislation was not necessary. And if it was not, then trying endlessly to get legislation through the labyrinthine processes of the General Synod was not just a waste of time and energy. It condemned the church to a continuing and damaging war of attrition, which reinforced a sense of real grievance among what has been accurately described as the 'oppressed majority' in most of the Australian dioceses.

So it was clearly worthwhile establishing whether legislation was in fact necessary. In April 2005, I organized an approach to the Appellate Tribunal under a constitutional provision that allows a minimum of 25 General Synod members to ask for constitutional clarification.[27] The question we posed to the Tribunal was framed in appropriate legal terminology, but in essence it was quite simple: were the canonical fitness requirements[28] gender neutral as the use of the term 'person'

---

[26] 'Report on the Proceedings of the Board of Nominators', presented in St Paul's Cathedral, Melbourne, 13 February 2006.

[27] For a full account of the reference to the Appellate Tribunal see Muriel Porter, 'Women in Purple: Women Bishops in Australia', *Voices: Quarterly Essays on Religion in Australia*, 1(2) (2008).

[28] Section 74(1) of the Constitution of the Anglican Church of Australia states:
'Canonical fitness' means, as regards a person, that:
(a) the person has attained at least 30 years of age;
(b) the person has been baptized; and

suggested? Or did 'person' in this context really mean 'male persons only'? This seemed to the lay mind to be highly unlikely, because the canonical fitness definition had been formulated by General Synod as recently as 1989, coming into force in 1995. 'Person' surely always meant both men *and* women in the latter decades of the twentieth century. If 'person' was gender neutral, was there anything else in the constitution which would prevent a woman priest, who met the canonical fitness criteria, from becoming a bishop?

It came as no surprise that the Diocese of Sydney Standing Committee entered the lists to argue against the case that the word 'person' in this case included women, and they fought their case hard in every way. Their lawyers claimed that Archbishop Roger Herft of Perth, a member of the Tribunal, should disqualify himself from hearing the matter, accusing him of bias against Sydney. He had demonstrated bias in public statements supporting women bishops and in comments he had made on Sydney's stance on women's ministry, they said. Archbishop Herft did not accede to the demands. What was not suggested in any of the formal documentation around this skirmish was that this attempt to remove Archbishop Herft might have been motivated by political considerations. For a definitive finding, two of the three bishops on the Tribunal, and two of the four lawyers, have to agree. In this reference, Archbishop Phillip Aspinall of Brisbane and Bishop Peter Brain of Armidale took different positions. Archbishop Aspinall found in favour of the pro-women case (supported by Archbishop Herft), while Bishop Brain decided against it. If Archbishop Herft had disqualified himself, the Tribunal would not have been able to come to a definitive answer. In the event, Archbishop Herft's continuing on the Tribunal was crucial to the outcome: the Tribunal found in favour of the pro-women case by four to three. It has been criticized as a very narrow win, but most Appellate Tribunal decisions in fact have been by a similar margin.

The submissions made by the parties to the reference ranged over a wide area, as did the responses of the individual Tribunal members. But central to the issue was the interpretation of the canonical fitness criteria as defined in the constitution. Debate concentrated not just on the plain meaning of the actual definition, but also on what was intended when change to the definition was set in train by a General Synod canon in 1989. That change was an interesting story in itself, and has been the subject of ongoing debate since the Tribunal brought down its opinion. When the national Anglican church came into being on 1 January 1962, its constitution said that canonical fitness was defined as 'the qualifications required in the Church of England in England for the office of a bishop, at the date when this Constitution takes effect'. The problem was that no one was very sure what those qualifications were, because the constitution came into force before the introduction of a new code of canon law in England later that decade. For the first time, the new English code then included a canon specifically dealing with the canonical fitness of

---

(c) the person is in priests' orders.

bishops, but because that post-dated the Australian Church's Constitution, it had no effect in Australia.

The Canons of 1604 – the definitive canon law in England until the 1960s and therefore in Australia until 1962 – did not provide any such definition. Until very recent times, the appointment of bishops in the Church of England has been the sole prerogative of the Crown, that is, bishops were appointed by the Sovereign. So until the canon law was revised in England in the 1960s, there was no codification of the minimum requirements for bishops in the Church of England, leaving the issue open to considerable confusion. For instance, was there a prohibition on illegitimacy or physical deformity as had been the case in pre-Reformation canon law?

Robert Phillimore, the nineteenth-century English canon lawyer generally relied on for the legal view that women could not be ordained in the Church of England, had also commented that illegitimacy was an impediment to ordination, along with 'any corporal infirmity which would impede the exercise of [the priest's] spiritual functions, and tend to repel and alienate the laity'.[29] Illegitimacy has been an issue in Australia in the past; at least one bishop, born illegitimate, sought legal advice before accepting the invitation to episcopal office. There were apparently other questions that arose from time to time about what constituted an impediment in terms of canonical fitness, leading the General Synod Canon Law Commission to draft an alternative definition, the one now in place. The question of gender seems not to have been their focus. Some commission members have argued that the commission intended no significant change to the old definition, intending only to provide clarity. Nevertheless, though these same people have insisted that maleness was an absolute requirement in the old definition and was therefore fully intended in the new, they framed the new definition in gender-neutral language, using the term 'person' without a gender qualification.

At the Tribunal and subsequently, there has been debate over this issue, with opponents of women bishops claiming that the commission (and the General Synod) really meant male persons when they used the word 'person'. It is now impossible to know whether that is true or not, even if it were relevant. Whatever drafters and even legislators might intend, is not usually the over-riding interpretative principle. But whatever they meant, any politically astute commission member would have realized that to cast the change in exclusively male terms would have spelt certain defeat on the floor of the 1989 General Synod. That same General Synod meeting had before it, as we have noted, legislation for women priests – the third time such legislation had come before General Synod in four years. It was a time of high controversy and enormous public interest over the issue, given there were at that time 90 women deacons across 16 dioceses eligible for priestly ordination. That same General Synod even passed a resolution which, among other things, noted the possibility that some bishops might proceed to ordain women to

---

[29] Robert Phillimore, *The Ecclesiastical Law of the Church of England* (2 volumes, London, 1873), pp. 114–15.

the priesthood without waiting for legislation, a sure indication of the heightened feelings. Although the legislation for women priests did not pass at that synod, it gained more than 60 per cent support, a significant majority. That same majority would have swiftly rejected a canonical fitness change that enshrined a male-only episcopate. In its neutral form, the new definition passed the 1989 General Synod with little if any debate.

But changes to the constitution, rightly, require a particularly high level of support. Once agreed by the General Synod, they need to be passed by three-quarters of the Australian dioceses, including the five metropolitan sees (Adelaide, Brisbane, Melbourne, Perth and Sydney). And that is where the changed definition nearly came unstuck. It easily passed 75 per cent of the dioceses, including four of the metropolitan dioceses. The stumbling block was Sydney, where although the synod readily passed the change in 1990, it was held up by the then archbishop, Donald Robinson. He vetoed Sydney Synod's assenting ordinance on the grounds that he 'believed that the definition of the term "canonical fitness" proposed ... was deficient'.[30] His grounds, according to a later statement, were that he believed the changed definition would 'alter the basic qualification for canonical fitness namely, that a person should be male'.[31] After Archbishop Robinson's retirement, his successor, Archbishop Harry Goodhew, agreed to the change after Sydney Synod had once more passed the assenting ordinance in March 1995. The new definition was then able to come into effect. The Sydney assenting ordinance contained a clause which said that 'nothing in this ordinance is to be interpreted as indicating an intention by the synod [that is, Sydney Synod] to legislate on the issue of the ordination of women as priests or the consecration of women as bishops'.[32] It seems clear that the Sydney leadership at the time believed that the changed definition did not carry within it any inherited gender bar, if indeed there actually was one in the original definition. It is interesting to note that the Church of England's current canonical fitness law, adopted after 1962, also uses the term 'person', as well as the male pronoun. But a clause specifically barring women bishops was added in 1988, when the debate about women's ordination was in full swing in that church.

In its submissions to the Tribunal, Sydney's legal representatives claimed that maleness had been a requirement of the original vague canonical fitness definition, and that nothing had changed in that respect in the new definition. Since the Tribunal decision, a number of Sydney people have claimed that Sydney Synod had no inkling that the changed definition might permit women bishops when it agreed to the change in 1995, the implication being that otherwise it would not

---

[30] 'Archbishop's Power to Withhold Assent to Ordinances', an interim report from the Standing Committee to Sydney Synod 2002.

[31] 'General Synod – Constitution Alteration (Canonical Fitness) Canon and Bill 1989 Assenting Ordinance 1994 – Explanatory Statement' issued on behalf of the Standing Committee of Sydney Synod, 3 February 1995.

[32] Ibid.

have agreed. This was the substance of a number of speeches in General Synod 2007. Presumably the speakers had forgotten about their own former archbishop's warnings and the rider their synod added to the assenting ordinance. Other complaints about the decision have been that it was a 'change by judicial sleight of hand',[33] that it was made by a narrow majority all of whom are 'known public supporters of female ordination'[34] or that a 'change of this significance should have been the consequence of mutual agreement in General Synod rather than legal fiat'.[35] There were also veiled threats that a subsequent Tribunal might reverse the decision, a view strongly discredited on the floor of General Synod 2007 as 'extremely unlikely' by the then Tribunal President, Justice Peter Young. Others have said that as it was technically only an 'opinion', it carried no real weight.[36]

In October 2007, Sydney Synod Standing Committee passed a resolution denouncing both the Tribunal decision and the Tribunal itself in terms that could be described as inflammatory. The resolution claimed that material presented by Sydney Standing Committee to the Tribunal had 'mostly' been ignored. Consequently Sydney Standing Committee would not seek constitutional clarification from the Tribunal on any matter, and it was 'unlikely' that it would in future 'participate in the consideration of questions on the Constitution put to the Tribunal'. The resolution was sent to the General Synod Standing Committee, as well as to the members of the Tribunal.[37] True to its word, Sydney Standing Committee did not defend Sydney Synod's stance on lay people and deacons presiding at the Eucharist in a subsequent Tribunal reference, as we shall see.

It was a significant risk asking the Tribunal for clarification on the canonical fitness definition. If the Tribunal's decision had gone the other way and decided that the definition explicitly meant 'men only', then not even General Synod legislation for women bishops would have overcome the barrier. Another change to the constitution, amending the definition explicitly to permit women as bishops, would have been needed. This time, Sydney Synod would not have approved the alteration, even with the rider appended to the 1995 ordinance. Women bishops

---

[33] This is the heading on an article by Sydney lawyer Neil Cameron criticizing the decision in the December 2007 edition of *Southern Cross*. The heading was in turn criticized in the following edition by one of the Tribunal members, Bishop Peter Brain of Armidale, even though he voted against the Tribunal decision: 'To impute deception is altogether unworthy of Christians', he wrote.

[34] This point was among others made by another Sydney lawyer, Robert Tong, in a letter to the February 2008 edition of *Southern Cross*. Mr Tong neglects to mention that earlier Tribunal decisions making women's ordination more difficult were made by majorities consisting of public opponents, such as Archbishop Robinson.

[35] Archbishop Peter Jensen, writing in the December 2007 edition of *Southern Cross*.

[36] For example, Robert Tong has claimed the decision is merely an 'advisory opinion' which is 'neither binding or [sic] final ... only a civil court can make binding decisions': *Southern Cross*, February 2008.

[37] As reported in the 2008 Report of the [Sydney Synod] Standing Committee.

would have been off the agenda for the Australian church for the foreseeable future.

Those of us who initiated the reference were reasonably confident in our case, however, and trusted that the word 'person', in an alteration formulated so recently, carried the modern dictionary meaning of referring to both men and women. If it did not, then women were not 'persons' in the eyes of the church, and that would have been an extremely embarrassing and damaging conclusion for the Tribunal to reach. Nevertheless, it reached its conclusion by just one vote! We were also aware that though the reference was risky, we had no other alternative course of action, given Sydney's ever-increasing dominance of the General Synod.

By an odd quirk, while the Tribunal decision meant women priests could legally have been elected as diocesan bishops immediately, the same was not true for assistant bishops. Most dioceses govern the appointment of assistant bishops through the 1966 General Synod assistant bishops' canon which, because it dates from before the change to the canonical fitness definition, still contains within it the original definition with its presumed bar on women. But diocesan synods could easily rectify that through local legislation; Melbourne Synod did so in November 2007. All that then stood in the way of the appointment of the first woman bishop was the issue of protocols for those opposed, which were discussed by the Australian bishops at their April 2008 meeting. A simple protocol was agreed, and by May 2008, Australia had its first two women bishops. Kay Goldsworthy, one of the first women priests ordained in Perth in March 1992, was consecrated an assistant bishop in the same city on 22 May. On the other side of the country, one of Melbourne's first women priests, Barbara Darling, was consecrated an assistant bishop on 31 May.

Despite the furore over the decades, the two women have taken their place among the bishops of the Australian church with few difficulties. They attend the national bishops' meetings, are both members of General Synod and also of its Standing Committee, and are received in all these situations with courtesy. Sydney representatives at the 2010 General Synod even included Bishop Darling – a moderate Evangelical – on their voting ticket, ensuring her election to the General Synod Standing Committee. In this case pragmatism trumped ideology! Thankfully the anger that erupted from Sydney Diocese after the Tribunal decision has not translated into personal animosity to the women concerned.

The ordination of women priests and then their consecration as bishops might not have caused the outright schism that was widely predicted and feared, but it has undoubtedly energized Sydney Diocese's ideological determination to keep itself at a distance from the rest of the national church and to be uncooperative whenever possible. The Tribunal's rejection of Sydney's arguments in the reference concerning women bishops provided a golden opportunity for the diocese to try to position itself effectively outside the Tribunal's authority. Its claim that the Tribunal's decisions are merely 'advisory' underscores that position, as does its subsequent decision not to participate in future Tribunal deliberations.

The Sydney view on Tribunal decisions needs to be challenged. One of Australia's leading legal luminaries, the former President of the NSW Court of Appeal, Keith Mason, who is a member of the Tribunal, has insisted that Tribunal opinions are binding on the church. 'It is quite contrary to the fair reading of the [church's] Constitution' to say that opinions of the Tribunal are 'no more than provisional, personal utterances that are open to be disregarded by any member of the Church who is not happy to abide with them', he has written.[38] The problem the national church has is how it can enforce the Tribunal decisions, a matter that has now become a pressing issue with Sydney Synod's decision to ignore the Tribunal's decision on diaconal presidency.

Lay and Diaconal Presidency

The controversy over the ordination of women saw Sydney constantly frustrating the desire of most of the rest of the Australian church for women clergy. In a reverse pattern, the national church has refused to entertain Sydney's long-standing desire for lay and diaconal presidency at the Eucharist. A 2010 Tribunal reference on the matter offered the diocese not only the opportunity to carry out the threat to ignore the Tribunal, but to defy it openly as well. Unlike the ordination of women debate, on this matter Sydney does not have the support of many of the other conservative world Anglican leaders, suggesting that these 'new Puritans' are deeply radical indeed. Lay presidency,[39] or as Sydney prefers to term it, lay administration, is a somewhat arcane matter difficult to explain to anyone outside the church's inner sanctum. Unlike the role of women, homosexuality or even divorce, it does not touch key human issues. It is about the rules governing church order and worship, and so is both an internal matter and an intensely academic one. The debate is about who is permitted to preside at the service of Holy Communion (also called the Eucharist, Mass or Lord's Supper), which is the central act of Christian worship. In the mainstream Christian churches, only bishops, priests or other fully-ordained ministers can preside. This is true for the Orthodox churches, the Roman Catholic Church, and for the Anglican Church, as well as for some non-conformist churches such as the Presbyterians. (In some other non-conformist churches, such as the Uniting Church in Australia, lay presidency is permissible under certain circumstances.) At first glance, it might seem that lay presidency is a democratic move, offering the broad lay membership of the church, and its deacons, a full and equal role within its sacramental ministry. But that is certainly

---

[38] Keith Mason, 'Believers in Court: Sydney Anglicans Going to Law', The Cable Lecture 2005, p. 14.

[39] Until recently, when Sydney Diocese switched its emphasis to diaconal presidency, the debate about non-priestly presidency has been termed the 'lay presidency' debate. The term encompassed diaconal presidency as well. For ease, I will generally continue to use 'lay presidency' to refer to the whole debate.

not its purpose in the Sydney context. Rather, it is a hierarchical manoeuvre designed to achieve, once and for all, the Puritan objective of ridding the church of ancient rituals and ceremonies that are deeply important to mainstream Anglicans, and particularly to those of an Anglo-Catholic or high-church persuasion. It is also designed to reinforce the primary 'headship' role of the male priest as 'head' of a parish rather than sacramental minister and in the process, underscore the ideology of the church as the local gathered community presided over by this male 'head'.

At the time of the Reformation, the Anglican Church, despite considerable pressure from its extreme reform wing, retained the three-fold order of ministry: bishops, priests and deacons. This pattern, though it is nowhere clearly required in the Bible, evolved in the early centuries of the Christian church. There are finely-nuanced theological perspectives on the three-fold order and how it functions, but for our purposes, we need only to note that in the traditional pattern, it is bishops and priests alone who preside at the altar in Anglican services of Holy Communion. (It should also be remembered that not so long ago, only priests were expected to lead any kind of church service, and were generally expected to do almost everything within the service.)

Sydney Diocese began working towards a change in this pattern at some stage in the early 1970s, though lay presidency did not become a major issue until the 1990s. By the 1970s, Broughton Knox's teaching on revelation as anti-sacramental and the ordained ministry as primarily a preaching role was bearing fruit. Non-priestly presidency then became the subject of examination by Sydney's doctrine commission, with significant support from theological scholars from Moore College. On several occasions there were attempts in Sydney Synod to pass their own diocesan legislation to permit the practice of lay people and deacons presiding at Holy Communion. This prompted the then Primate, Keith Rayner, to ask the Appellate Tribunal whether lay and diaconal presidency was constitutional, and if it was, could it be authorized by a diocesan synod? They persisted with these attempts despite the Tribunal's answer, handed down in 1997, that lay/diaconal presidency could be introduced only with the support of General Synod legislation. Diocesan legislation, the Tribunal said, would not be sufficient. The decision that even a General Synod canon could authorize such a break with Anglican tradition was a surprising and disturbing one for many, including Keith Rayner.

The lay presidency legislation brought to Sydney Synod before that had received high levels of support from both clerical and lay synod members. However, Jensen's predecessor as archbishop, Harry Goodhew, resisted the move as had his predecessor, Donald Robinson. Because diocesan bishops have to agree to any synod legislation to make it operative, this opposition prevented the legislation from becoming diocesan law. Goodhew, who was committed to the norms of Anglican polity, was personally opposed to the practice. But he had another reason for his veto: he recognized that lay presidency would seriously harm Sydney's standing in the wider Anglican Communion, where the innovation is widely abhorred as 'unAnglican'. That, in turn, would limit Sydney's involvement in the fast-developing international conservative coalition. Delivering his presidential address to Synod in 1998, Goodhew commented that the diocese did not need to carry 'that extra bit of lead in our saddlebags when we try to be an influence beyond our own borders'. It was in fact the same reason why Sydney Synod abandoned a further move for lay presidency in 2004.

It is interesting to note that while the rest of the Australian Church was diverted by the spectre of lay presidency and fearful of its potential to divide the national body, Sydney was already immersing itself in the international tactics that have brought the Anglican Communion to the brink of schism. In his same synod address, Archbishop Goodhew called on Sydney to abandon its 'isolationist mindset and resolve to be an active participant in the life of the Communion'. He indicated that he was involved in the development of a 'network of bishops' committed to mission and evangelism. 'What we have in common is loyalty to the Bible and to the fundamentals of supernatural religion as expressed in our Creeds', he said. Goodhew, as we have seen, had been a speaker in the well-resourced and highly-organized conservative programme that had such an enormous influence on the outcomes of the 1998 Lambeth Conference earlier that year. Up until the end of his term of office, he continued to be involved in the international discussions.

The extent of his involvement took many by surprise. He is an irenic, softly-spoken man who, as archbishop, always avoided the politics of confrontation and who worked hard to keep Sydney from adopting too separatist a position on potentially divisive issues. As well as vetoing lay presidency, he had come close to supporting women priests, and had advocated a more generous tolerance on Sydney's part of the different churchmanship practices of other dioceses. But clearly, the low-key archbishop laid the groundwork for his successor's much more high-profile activity in the conservative world alliance. Ironically, his rejection of lay presidency obviously helped immeasurably.

It seems likely that Peter Jensen hoped to be able to deliver both lay presidency and involvement in the 'Global South'. He was fully expected to affirm further moves in the direction of lay presidency in the 2004 Sydney Synod. But at the last moment – literally – the move was withdrawn. In his printed address to Synod, Jensen said he was 'looking forward to the thinking of the Synod on the matter', though he warned Synod that it needed to be fully informed of the situation the diocese faced. He indicated that one of the diocese's regional bishops, Peter Tasker, had been 'very active this year in visiting bishops in Africa and Asia on our behalf and discussing this matter as well as other Anglican Communion issues with them'. He continued that he had been 'authoritatively informed that there are many in the Anglican Communion who would see a move to endorse lay administration in any way as equivalent to the consecration of an active homosexual'.

This must have been deeply shocking, carrying with it the implied threat that Sydney might find itself excluded from the Anglican Communion in the same way as TEC and the Canadian Church. But by the time Jensen delivered the address, the planned Synod move had been withdrawn by its mover, though obviously in consultation with the Archbishop, as he referred to the withdrawal move in the pre-released address. It seems likely that Bishop Tasker's report of the responses from other members of the Global South strongly recommended not proceeding, given that the Windsor Report on the international situation was imminent.[40]

But lay presidency could not be sidelined forever. The push for its formal introduction is too strong, and it is widely rumoured that it is informally happening in any case. Jensen, as a product of the Broughton Knox teaching at Moore Theological College, is deeply committed to it. In his first Synod address in 2001, making crystal clear his different perspective from that of Harry Goodhew, he championed lay presidency as flowing 'naturally and properly from the theology of the Bible and our reformed heritage'. He continued: 'The theological importance of the congregation and its significance as an agent for mission also calls for this development',[41] a comment that indicates a clear connection between lay presidency and the ideology of the supremacy of the local congregation as taught by his mentor, Knox.

This link to Knox's teaching seems to signal one important reason why lay presidency has become such a consuming issue in a diocese where, ironically, Holy Communion is actually not celebrated as often as in other parts of the Anglican world. Whereas in other places, the main Sunday service is now almost invariably a service of Holy Communion – additional Sunday services of Holy Communion and weekday celebrations are also common – in Sydney that is not the case. Usually only the few more conventional parishes, all of them resolutely opposed to lay and diaconal presidency, would adhere to that pattern these days. Most parishes, as a quick surf of individual parish websites will reveal, restrict Holy Communion to the early morning Sunday service, though a number do not seem to offer the sacrament even that regularly. The major services, often called 'meetings', are labelled 'family' or 'contemporary' services, and from the website information provided, do not seem to follow any of the approved Anglican formularies either. The Communion service, where it is held, is often described as 'classic' or 'old style' by contrast.

Peter Jensen has argued that lay presidency was necessary because of the demands of the Sydney 'Mission', which required a vast multiplication of congregations to cope with the influx of converts. The work entailed in pastoring the new congregations will go well beyond what one person, the parish rector, could do, he said, so lay people would need to be authorized to preside at Holy Communion in these additional places. 'We are aiming to develop a theologically shaped, pastorally responsible method of achieving a sacramental life for our people', he said.[42] Given the evidence of the parish websites, however, it seems that few Sydney clergy are actually celebrating the Holy Communion very much

---

[40] Peter Jensen, Presidential Address to Synod 2004, delivered on 18 October, both original and subsequent pre-released version.

[41] Peter Jensen, Presidential Address to Synod 2001, delivered on 26 October 2001.

[42] Peter Jensen, 'The Pastoral Need for Lay Administration of Holy Communion', www.sydneyanglicans.net/mindful, posted 12 October 2004.

at present, and that extending sacramental ministry at that same level into new congregations would scarcely be a time-consuming exercise. Unlike rural dioceses where declining numbers of clergy are so thinly spread that weekly Communion services are increasingly difficult to provide, Sydney – with more than 700 active licensed priests, 200 more than in Melbourne, for example – has more than enough ordained clergy to meet its extremely limited sacramental needs.

This point was made in response to Peter Jensen by a Melbourne theologian, Dr Andrew McGowan, in the debate about lay presidency held before and during the 2004 General Synod.[43] Dr McGowan said that the argument based on multiplying pastoral needs was 'interesting but also quite curious', given 'a general sense of Anglican liturgical practice in Sydney':

> It is far from clear why we should imagine that ministers and communities in the Sydney Diocese who have not hitherto been accustomed either to using the Holy Communion as a central aspect of pastoral ministry, or to viewing it as an essential expression of Christian community, would suddenly do so simply because they have been authorized.

Suggesting that the development of more congregations would create a need for lay presidency was really only a debating point, McGowan commented: 'It is tempting at this point to see the drive for "lay administration" as a sort of sacramental Cinderella seeking a theological Prince Charming at the ball, deftly changing partners and rationales as the dance progresses.'[44]

Following the back down at the 2004 Sydney Synod, it seemed as if the issue was off the official agenda. But Sydney then changed tack in two ways. It began to focus on diaconal presidency rather than lay presidency, as we shall see, and it changed its ordination strategy quite markedly. It created a permanent diaconate by restricting priestly ordination to men who were to be rectors of parishes. This both underscored the Sydney view that 'presbyters' are parish leaders first and foremost rather than presiders over sacraments, and it created a pressing need for diaconal presidency.

Traditionally, deacons could be expected to be ordained priests within a year or so of their diaconal ordination. That meant that second-year curates, other assistant clergy, and chaplains would all be, in the normal course of events, priests and thus authorized to celebrate Holy Communion. A permanent diaconate, which functions in other dioceses on a small scale, is very different, carrying with it the expectation that these deacons would not normally become priests. It would be rare in other places for parish curates and most chaplains to remain deacons. In

---

[43] The 2004 General Synod passed a resolution on lay presidency that said in part: '[This General Synod] does not condone the practice of lay and diaconal administration/presidency at the eucharist in this Church.' Resolution 74/04.

[44] Andrew McGowan, 'Is Lay Presidency Necessary?', www.sydneyanglicans.net/mindful, posted 12 October 2004.

Sydney it is quite different. Permanent deacons there include traditional parish curates, youth workers, church workers for the anticipated growth of church plants, and chaplains. With the number of priests severely limited, the number of clergy permitted under church law to celebrate Holy Communion is also severely limited. This has the potential to cause a 'Communion drought', even in a diocese where Holy Communion is as infrequent as it is in Sydney. A way had to be found to authorize deacons to celebrate Holy Communion. But the 1997 Appellate Tribunal decision had said that such a change required General Synod legislation, and it was highly unlikely that General Synod would ever pass such legislation.

A diocesan committee had already been looking into the possibility that some existing General Synod legislation might provide a loophole, even if that had not been the intention of the legislation. It came to the conclusion that 'several General Synod canons may already exist which authorise or provide for the authorisation of lay persons or deacons to administer the Lord's Supper, namely the Ordination Service for Deacons Canon 1985, the Canon Concerning Services 1992, and the Lay Assistants at Holy Communion Canon 1973'.[45] This report, energized by the Appellate Tribunal's 2007 decision concerning women bishops, formed the basis for a motion brought to Sydney Synod in 2008 by Bishop Glenn Davies. Synod was asked to accept the conclusions of the sub-committee's report, by affirming again 'its conviction that lay and diaconal administration of the Lord's Supper is consistent with the teaching of Scripture; and … that the Lord's Supper in this diocese may be administered by persons other than presbyters'.[46] Sydney passed the motion unamended.

It soon became clear that regional bishops were authorizing rectors in their region to allow diaconal presidency if they wished, and that at least some rectors were acting on this authority. A deacon in charge of a parish also publicly referred to the Synod resolution as authorizing him to celebrate Holy Communion. There was also some evidence that lay people may have been allowed to preside, on the basis of the resolution, which was described as being 'an important statement of moral force'.[47] More seriously, Archbishop Jensen was implicated. In a document entitled *Full-time Paid Ministry in the Diocese of Sydney*, published by the Diocese's Department of Ministry Training and Development, and bearing the Archbishop's imprimatur, the Synod resolution was referred to as the basis for its advice that deacons could administer the Lord's Supper. By reproducing the 2008

---

[45] 'Lay and Diaconal Administration of Holy Communion: Legal Impediments', revised edition, presented to Sydney Synod 2008, p. 164.

[46] Resolution 27/08 of Sydney Synod, passed on 20 October 2008.

[47] See the 'Submissions of the 28 Signatories' to the Appellate Tribunal: Reference in the matter of lay and diaconal presidency, 18 November 2009, and 'Supplementary Submission of the 28 Signatories', 16 December 2009. These submissions can be accessed at http://www.anglican.org.au/Web/Website.nsf/content/Appellate_Tribunal.

Synod resolution in full, without comment on lay presidency, it could be said to have also implied that lay presidency was likewise authorized.[48]

During the 2008 Synod, Bishop Davies told Synod members that lay presidency would not be authorized by the Archbishop, advice he has repeated on a number of occasions. It is believed that Archbishop Jensen gave similar advice to the 2009 meeting of the Australian bishops. Given his strong advocacy of lay presidency in the past, one can only conjecture that he was either not convinced that the supposed legal authorization existed, or that he did not want to risk upsetting his allies around the world. Possibly some research might have suggested that allowing deacons to preside at Holy Communion would not be so offensive to the international conservative alliance as lay presidency.

The Sydney resolution caused a flurry of concern in Sydney 'stole' parishes, in other Australian dioceses, and further afield. Sydney clergy and laity concerned to uphold Anglican norms were unsurprisingly distressed; some voiced their concern during the Synod debate, to no avail. The Primate, Phillip Aspinall, wrote to Archbishop Jensen asking him to do what he could to postpone any action on the resolution, and to 'use his office to ensure as far as possible that others within the diocese also refrain from acting', at least until the bishops' meeting in March 2009. No such undertaking was given apparently; in any case, diaconal presidency was publicly authorized between the 2008 Synod and the bishops' meeting. The Archbishop of Canterbury, in a letter to the Primate in December 2008, noted that the Sydney resolution was 'an unprecedented departure within the Anglican Communion'. Clearly he was concerned by the development.

The vast majority of Australian bishops made their concern known at the bishops' meeting, and a reference to test the validity of the Sydney claims at the Appellate Tribunal was mooted. Anecdotal reports suggest that Archbishop Jensen was unrepentant about diaconal presidency, even though he assured the other bishops he would not be authorizing lay presidency. He asked the bishops to let Sydney have diaconal presidency, given his assurance about lay presidency. The bishops however were not persuaded. Perhaps what is not understood in Sydney is that to opponents of lay presidency, diaconal presidency is just as serious. Both are breaches of Anglican norms and of catholic order. The bishops themselves were not proactive in organizing a reference to the Tribunal, however. Perhaps they are reluctant to confront Sydney Diocese in so formal and public manner, so some of them decided to approach a lay person instead. They approached me. I had had the recent experience of organizing a reference and as a lay person, I did not have much to lose. At least, that was probably the assumption. I agreed, though with some misgivings. Even organizing a reference is hard work, as under the church's constitution, at least 25 members of General Synod have to support such a move. It also requires not just careful formulation of the actual question or questions,

---

[48] *Full-time Paid Ministry in the Diocese of Sydney*, 2nd edition (Sydney: The Anglican Church Diocese of Sydney Department of Ministry Training and Development, January 2009), p. 13.

but preparation of a full legal submission. Reply submissions are also required. The outcome of the reference, as in all court cases, can depend to a great extent on the quality of those submissions, not to mention the comprehensiveness of the questions. It is a venture not to be undertaken lightly.

Twenty-eight General Synod members from 13 dioceses were organized to sign up to the reference. Eight of them were diocesan bishops. Michael Shand, a distinguished Melbourne Queen's Counsel most generous in his pro bono work for the church, agreed to assist us. Six questions were formulated. The first four dealt with the specific General Synod canons that Sydney had identified as possibly giving authorization to lay or diaconal presidency: did any of these canons permit a lay person or deacon to preside, we asked. A fifth question asked whether any other canon of General Synod gave such authority, while the sixth asked whether the 2008 resolution of Sydney Synod was constitutional. We were supported by separate submissions, one from the Diocese of Newcastle, and one from a group of three Sydney Anglo-Catholic rectors and a parishioner who was a Sydney barrister. The Diocese of Sydney declined to participate, however, leaving Bishop Glenn Davies to defend diaconal presidency in a personal capacity. He declined to make any submissions on the matter of lay presidency, claiming that as the Archbishop of Sydney was not going to authorize it, the resolution affirming it was no more than the majority opinion of the Synod at the time the resolution was passed.[49]

Without any person or party willing to defend the lay presidency affirmation, it seemed possible that the Tribunal would not consider the matter. Certainly that was a matter of some contention during the directions hearing. It was submitted that without a 'contradictor' the Tribunal would not be able to consider it. No doubt it would have suited Sydney Diocese not to have lay presidency examined. However, the Signatories made a strong case that the matter was too important to be ignored, and substantiated that case in the context of their submissions. They even included relevant extracts from the key Sydney defences of lay presidency in the documents appended to their submissions. At the heart of their submission on this issue, they argued that the question was 'of real importance to the church as a whole, whichever side of the debate one takes'.[50]

Not just the Signatories and the Australian bishops but most Anglican observers outside Sydney believed that Sydney Diocese was pulling a very long bow indeed in trying to find authorization for lay and diaconal presidency in existing General Synod canons. The principal claim for lay presidency, for example, was made from the Lay Assistants at Holy Communion Canon 1973, which says that 'lay persons being communicants may be authorised by the bishop to assist the priest in the ministering and distribution of the Holy Communion'. This canon is an authority for lay Eucharistic assistants, that is, people rostered to help distribute the consecrated elements. (It has been superseded by a later canon in force in most

---

[49] 'Submissions of the 28 Signatories ...', p. 20.
[50] Ibid., p. 24.

other dioceses, but Sydney has not adopted the later one.) To claim it actually authorizes lay people to preside at Holy Communion is extraordinarily far-fetched.

The claim for diaconal presidency was based on the Ordination Service for Deacons Canon 1985. This canon authorized an additional form of service for the ordination of deacons; the service it authorizes does not contain any words that either directly or by implication authorize a deacon to preside. Sydney Diocese's claim was based principally on the contention that the new service allowed a deacon to baptize candidates of any age, including in the presence of the priest, as distinct from the 1662 *Book of Common Prayer* provision for the deacon to baptize infants only, and then only in the absence of the priest:

> While no specific mention is made of either baptism or the holy communion [in the 1985 service], a plain reading of the ordinance indicates that whatever assistance the deacon may render in the administration of one sacrament would also pertain to the other. No hierarchy of sacraments is expressed in describing the deacon's role of assisting the presbyter. In particular, there is no dispute that the deacon is authorised to administer the sacrament of baptism in its entirety as a means of assisting the presbyter. In like manner, the deacon is similarly authorised to administer the Lord's Supper in its entirety as a means of assisting the presbyter.[51]

The obvious reply to this argument was that whatever might have been happening in practice, the 1985 service did not authorize deacons to administer baptism more widely than the limited permission given in the *Book of Common Prayer*, let alone preside at Holy Communion.

Bishop Davies offered detailed argument about the precise meaning of 'administration' in the service; the Bishop gives the deacon authority to 'assist in the administration of [God's] holy sacraments'. Bishop Davies' argument was the word 'administration' implied the entire service of Holy Communion, including the central prayer of consecration. The Signatories' reply was that the service authorized the deacon to 'assist in' the administration, which makes clear that the deacon's role is still that of an assistant, rather than a celebrant.[52] In summary, the Signatories pointed out that the role of the deacon in the 1985 service was not substantially different to what it was in the equivalent services in both the *Book of Common Prayer* and the 1978 *An Australian Prayer Book*. If the 1985 service permitted deacons to preside, then so did the other two services.

The Tribunal found in favour of the Signatories and their supporters on the key questions of lay and diaconal presidency by a clear six to one majority. The odd man out was the Bishop of Armidale, Bishop Peter Brain, whose diocese had in the past allowed diaconal presidency. On the matter of lay presidency, the

---

[51] 'Lay and Diaconal Administration of Holy Communion: Legal Impediments', pp. 164–5.

[52] 'Submissions of the Signatories …', p. 18.

majority were extremely succinct: the word 'assist' in the 1973 canon 'means to take a part in the service subsidiary to the priest and not involving the act of consecration', the majority said, definitively ruling out lay presidency.[53] On the matter of diaconal presidency, the majority report said that 'we do not consider that the role of the deacon in the service of Holy Communion has undergone any serious or relevant change by the 1985 Canon'.[54] In a supplementary report, one of the majority, Archbishop Phillip Aspinall, commented that 'in short, Dr Davies presents no evidence of a trajectory of reform of the sort that would sustain the practice of diaconal celebration of the Holy Communion for which he contends'.[55]

Further, the Tribunal offered a caution about obeying church rules, perhaps to warn the Diocese of Sydney against pressing on with diaconal presidency at least, despite the Tribunal decision. Members of the church were entitled to worship God according to the rules of the church, the Tribunal said, 'in respect of many of which the clergy at their ordination swore before God to uphold'. It continued that while many of the rules of the church could be enforced under the law of trusts, few church members could afford to undertake expensive court proceedings. There was also Scriptural authority 'for the view that proceedings of such nature before a secular court are wrong for believers'. The report continued:

> It is thus up to the bishops and this Tribunal to see that the rules of the church are upheld. This is not just a matter of legalism, but a matter of fairness and protection of the ordinary members of the church. The determination of this reference and the publication of these reasons will make it difficult for any member of the church who acts contrary to them ... to argue that such conduct is inadvertent.[56]

There was no formal initial response to the Tribunal decision from the Diocese of Sydney; it waited until its 2010 Synod, when Bishop Davies brought a motion to reaffirm the 2008 resolution that had just been declared unconstitutional. The 2010 motion described the Tribunal's opinion as an 'advisory' opinion, and the tenor of the debate was that Sydney Synod's opinion was as valid as the Tribunal's. That view was stated in no uncertain terms in the Synod by the Dean of Sydney, Phillip Jensen: he said that the way forward was 'to say thank you for your opinion, here is our opinion and that is how we fellowship together in disagreement. The Lord's Supper is a gospel issue and we need to make clear it is a gospel issue in world Anglicanism.' As we have already discussed, this unprecedented situation has caused a great deal of consternation in the national church and created a crisis

---

[53] 'Appellate Tribunal: Report to Primate, Reference on the Legality of the Administration of Holy Communion by Deacons or Lay Persons', 10 August 2010, p. 23.
[54] Ibid., p. 21.
[55] Ibid., p. 31.
[56] Ibid., pp. 13–14.

of authority in the Anglican Church of Australia. How it will cope with it is still unclear.

Between the publication of the Tribunal decision and the commencement of Sydney Synod just two months' later, some leading players in the diocese prepared a professionally-published report disagreeing with the Tribunal decision.[57] The report canvasses the legal and theological issues once again, with no surprises. It does, however, reinforce the Sydney line that the Tribunal's opinion carries no more weight than any other advisory opinion; continues to insist that the 1985 General Synod service for the ordination of deacons authorizes them to preside at Holy Communion; and argues that the issue is at heart theological, rather than constitutional. The practice of lay and diaconal presidency is a theological necessity, it insists. In particular, Bishop Davies rehearses the arguments he presented to the Tribunal in relation to the 1985 ordination service – arguments that six out of seven of the Tribunal members, including all four lawyers, had decisively rejected. The publication is a notable example of Sydney Diocese's over-riding conviction that they and they alone are always right, particularly when it comes to the interpretation of Scripture and church tradition.

Given there are no new arguments canvassed in this report, the intriguing question must be: why was this report written and published in so short a timeframe, and for whom is it intended? It is available free to members of Sydney Synod, so presumably its promoters felt they needed to convince Synod members that the Synod was right to defy the Tribunal's decision. A motion at Synod, brought by one of its editors, asked for copies to be distributed to all members of the Australian General Synod. So clearly they want to ensure that they bring General Synod members onside with their decision. Providing copies for members of Sydney Synod as well as the General Synod must be close to a thousand free copies – a very generous distribution. No doubt copies will also be sent to key players among the conservative forces around the Anglican Communion. As Dean Jensen told Synod, Sydney needs 'to make clear it is a gospel issue in world Anglicanism'. That is probably the most important audience of all that will need to be convinced that Sydney's actions in defying the national church's highest court are justified.

Some people have suggested that the zeal for lay presidency is a form of 'payback' for the ordination of women. The connection can be deduced if lay presidency is seen as a means of downgrading priesthood, given it has already been 'downgraded' by the inclusion of women. There may, at a subconscious level at least, be a kernel of truth in that suggestion. In some quarters, ordaining women might have increased the passion for its introduction, given that the very notion of lay presidency causes a great deal of distress to Anglicans committed to traditional Anglican polity. However, in this case I agree with Peter Jensen, who argues that the 'payback' theory is not the basis for advocating lay presidency. He points out that lay presidency has been on Sydney's agenda for about as

---

[57] Peter Bolt, Mark Thompson and Robert Tong (eds), *The Lord's Supper in Human Hands: Epilogue* (Sydney: Australian Church Record and Anglican Church League, 2010).

long as women's ordination has been discussed in the wider church, and that is a fair point. However, it is hard to see the decision to defy the Tribunal's 2010 determination as entirely separate from what one Sydney bishop has described as the 'deep anger' the diocese felt over the Tribunal's decision that women bishops were constitutional.

It is also certainly true that a growing pressure to allow women deacons a sacramental role has been one of the factors in the recent push for diaconal presidency. At both the 2008 and the 2010 synods, Archdeacon Narelle Jarrett[58] seconded the motion about lay and diaconal presidency. On both occasions she has spoken of the need for women chaplains in schools and prisons to be able to 'administer' Holy Communion, saying it was 'a tragedy' if they could not do so. That pressure has been there for some time. In 1998, a resolution of Sydney Synod called for a five-year experimentation of lay and diaconal presidency 'as a principled means by which we may reduce the tensions and synodical divisions over the ordination of women to the priesthood'. The following year, as we have seen, 12 of the Diocese's 24 women deacons appealed (unsuccessfully) for priesting, suggesting their growing frustration with a non-sacramental role.

Far more significant in explaining the genesis of the issue, however, is its coincidence with the developing Sydney theology of the church as the local congregation, which we have already discussed. Broughton Knox was teaching trainee Sydney clergy at Moore College this novel (for Anglicans) understanding of the church in the 1960s and 1970s. As Jensen has pointed out, lay presidency was first brought to the attention of Sydney Synod in 1970.[59] In Anglican (and more generally, Catholic) polity, priests are not ordained just for one congregation or parish or even diocese: they are ordained as priests in 'the church of God'. This indicates that their ordination is valid across the church, or at least in practice, across the tradition within which they are ordained. So, a priest ordained in the Anglican Diocese of Melbourne can function readily as a priest in all other parts of the Anglican world, subject to the granting of a local licence by the diocesan bishop concerned. While any appointment from outside a diocese will be carefully vetted, for occasional visits a licence is usually granted as a courtesy. There are exceptions. Women priests find their orders not so readily portable, given there are some dioceses and a few national churches, such as Nigeria, which still do not have women clergy. And Sydney Diocese is extremely reluctant to license clergy from outside except for very occasional one-off events.

Lay presidents, however, though they would need to be authorized by the diocesan bishop in the scenario Sydney presents, would presumably not function outside their own congregation. With lay people permitted to preach and lead other forms of worship in their congregation, adding a lay president would allow individual congregations to function from time to time quite independently

---

[58] Archdeacon Jarrett is not a priest; she is a deacon in charge of women's ministry in Sydney Diocese.

[59] Peter Jensen, 'The Pastoral Need for Lay Administration of Holy Communion'.

of ordained clergy. This would be a powerful symbol of the notion that the congregation is the church entire to itself, rather than an expression of the whole church of God. It is also a powerful indicator that the priest's role is as head of the local church, the leader rather than a sacramental functionary.

The roles that the laity are currently permitted to perform in wider Anglicanism, in particular in terms of preaching, has also been used as an excuse for lay presidency. If lay people are able to preach the Word of God, not allowing them to preside at Holy Communion by reserving that role alone to the ordained, seems to exalt the sacrament above the preaching. For a theology so powerfully weighted towards the pre-eminence of preaching as Sydney's, this is unthinkable.[60] The Appellate Tribunal, however, in its 2010 decision, rejected a supposed nexus between presiding and preaching, by arguing that Anglicanism had not historically maintained that nexus. From 1549 (the date of the first *Book of Common Prayer*) until the seventeenth century, preaching other than from the prescribed homilies was not part of church services unless the clergyman held a specific preaching licence. 'The supposition that there is a necessary implication that a person who is authorised to preach must be authorised to celebrate the Eucharist thus needs examination', the Tribunal said.[61]

Introducing lay presidency, then, is scarcely necessary to Sydney's prevailing liturgical practice. Likewise, it is unnecessary in an urban context well endowed with ordained clergy. Ironically, there seems to be little demand for it from lay people! It is the *ordained* theologians and leaders of Sydney Diocese who have demanded it. For these reasons, it is only to be expected that outsiders might imagine its impetus came from a desire for payback, or for downgrading priesthood per se, or even for demonstrating the diocese's extreme difference from the old enemy, the Church of Rome.

I believe, however, that its purpose is much more radical. It is to lay the symbolic axe finally and decisively to the root of traditional church order. Allowing lay people and deacons to preside at Holy Communion would be the culmination of Sydney's relentless drive for Puritan purity. It would effectively rid the diocese of the last vestiges of Catholic order and traditional sacramental understanding that, to the Sydney mindset, should have been removed as part and parcel of the mid-sixteenth-century Reformation of the Church of England. That incomplete Reformation would finally be complete. The new 'reformed' church would be a church that was fundamentally congregational. It would emphasize the Sydney view that the teaching of God's Word is *the* central act of the gathering – or meeting – of Christians, rather than the integrated ministry of Word and Sacrament. It would allow Sydney Diocese at last to reflect fully the vision of Broughton Knox. That is why it has been pursued so vigorously despite the almost

---

[60] See Peter Jensen, 'Theological Reflection on Lay Administration', www.sydneyanglicans.net/mindful, posted 12 October 2004, for a fuller version of his arguments in this area.

[61] 'Appellate Tribunal: Report to Primate …', pp. 17–18.

complete lack of empathy in the rest of the Anglican Church, not just in Australia but worldwide. While it might seem a rather cerebral crusade in contrast with the human passions invoked by debates over women or sexuality, I suspect it is a cause dearer to the Sydney heart than anything else. It makes sense of Peter Jensen's revealing 'vox pox' comment during the 2004 General Synod. Sydney's Archbishop, along with many other delegates to the synod, was asked, on camera, by the inhouse media team, why he was an Anglican. I am not sure, he replied: 'I could just as easily be a Presbyterian.' (Presbyterians, certainly in the conservative Australian Presbyterian Church, are usually regarded by conservatives as having a pure model of Reformed church polity, even though they do not practise lay presidency.)

In the end, what questions about women, sexuality, and lay presidency have in common for Sydney Diocese is an obsession with purity. They would term it Gospel purity, but as I have indicated, their interpretation of the Gospel is not the sole interpretation. While they would not call women clergy impure, it is hard not to detect an underlying hint of the ancient fear of female sexuality behind their highly-nuanced rational arguments against women's ordination, to which we turn in the next chapter. Certainly, a woman preaching the Gospel in a mixed congregation would be deemed to 'taint' the Gospel in some way, because they maintain women lack the Scriptural authority available to men.

Any form of sexual activity outside marriage, and same-sex activity in particular, is overtly regarded as impure, and specially in the clergy. An unrepentant or active homosexual bishop would not be allowed even to hand out hymn books! It has been suggested to me that this reflects the kind of rigour that marked the ancient Donatists. The Donatists were a fourth-century schismatic group formed in opposition to a bishop of Carthage because they believed he had been consecrated by bishops who had themselves betrayed the Gospel under the persecution instigated against Christians, and specially clergy, by the Roman Emperor Diocletian. This rejection of the ministry offered by an ordained person because of some perceived moral or other defect in them in fact flies in the face of Article Twenty-six, one of the Thirty-nine Articles of Religion. Article Twenty-six is labelled, 'Of the Unworthiness of the Ministers, which hinders not the effect of the Sacrament'. Though the Article requires that 'evil Ministers' should be deposed if they have been found guilty of any offence, it also recognizes that clergy minister the Word and Sacraments in Christ's name and by his 'commission and authority', not by their own authority. Clergy therefore are not required or even expected to be perfect. The rigour of Sydney Diocese's expectations, however, comes close to requiring moral purity.[62]

---

[62] Michael Jensen – Archbishop Jensen's son – has commented that a Donatist-style quest for purity can have the effect of damaging the unity of the church. The Reformers, he notes, resembled the Donatists to some degree: 'The Donatists and the Purity of the Church', Sydneyanglicans.net/, 22 November 2010.

Lay presidency represents another kind of purity, Protestant purity. It establishes a church polity fully conforming to the ideals that Sydney sees as established during the English Reformation before it was 'watered down' by the 'compromises' of the Elizabethan Settlement and later, the Restoration under King Charles II. It effectively creates the new Puritanism in church order. Sydney Diocese's drive for purity on so many fronts, while not to be equated with the misguided *individual* 'sinless perfection' preached by various Christian sects, nevertheless comes close to demanding an overall institutional perfectionism. It leaves no room for different perspectives, let alone a more generous response to the full spectrum of human diversity. And no place at all for the inclusive, tolerant broad-church Anglicanism that so many of us cherish.

In summary, it is this obsession with a certain kind of purity, manifested in particular in opposition to women clergy and the pursuit of lay and diaconal presidency, and the associated commitment to the church as local congregation, that has created an unbridgeable gulf between the Diocese of Sydney and the rest of the Australian church. That gulf is deeper, wider and more serious in the twenty-first century than it has been in the half century since the national constitution came into being. So why does Sydney stay within the national church when it resists so many of its requirements and expectations, challenges the authority of its constitution and of a statutory body such as the Appellate Tribunal, and is frustrated in its crusade to authorize lay and diaconal presidency? In an impassioned speech at the 2010 General Synod, Archbishop Jensen assured the General Synod that his diocese was 'completely committed' to the national church. 'To break up the Anglican Church of Australia would be a monumental blow to the cause of the Gospel in this country', he said. However, dioceses should have as much local freedom as possible, with as little interference from, and as few costs imposed by, the national centre, he said. From this I conjecture that the diocese really wants to have its cake and eat it too. It wants freedom from obligations, and freedom to pursue its own agenda, but it remains within the national church structure presumably because it needs the status and name the national body confers.

Chapter 6
Women: Equal but Different

More than two decades ago, on a visit to Australia, the late Monica Furlong – matriarch of the movement for the ordination of women in the Church of England – said that arguments offered against women in ministry were not really important in themselves. What was important was what the arguments hid. Underneath the rhetoric, men and women were very frightened of each other and of what the debate about the ordination of women would reveal, she maintained. The debate about women was just the 'tip of the iceberg'; the real issue confronting the church was sexuality in general, she said.[1] My experience of the ordination of women debate in this country over 25 years is that Monica was absolutely right. The passion and determination with which some opponents of women in leadership prosecute their cause, seems to me to suggest that a deep unacknowledged fear of women (and sexuality) underlies their stance.

This is a view that would be vociferously refuted by those Sydney Anglicans who have spearheaded opposition to women in holy orders over two generations. They maintain their opposition comes solely from their adherence to the Bible, and insist that they have no option but to oppose, on that ground alone. But some years ago a shrewd observer of the first generation of male opponents, whom she knew at close quarters, offered a perceptive assessment. The late Deaconess Mary Andrews, who had been principal of Deaconess House in Sydney (since renamed in her honour), was a fine Christian woman of independent spirit. Formerly a missionary in China, where the first Anglican woman priest was ordained for the Diocese of Hong Kong in 1944, she was a strong and outspoken supporter of the ordination of women. Even in retirement, she regularly sat in the public gallery at synod meetings when the issue was debated, a source of great inspiration to the women protagonists on the synod floor. She told me, with a wry smile: 'I know only too well why some of them [opponents] are against women priests. I knew their mothers, know their wives!'[2] She backed up her comment with anecdotes of the control she had seen these wives and mothers exerting over their husbands and sons, though supposedly they were 'subordinate' women. Perhaps they subscribed to the philosophy of a Sydney clergy wife who once told me that the secret of a

---

[1] Author interview with Monica Furlong in Melbourne, May 1984. Published in *Church Scene*, 25 May 1984.

[2] Author interview with Deaconess Mary Andrews, Sydney, 14 April 1988; published in Muriel Porter, *Women in the Church: The Great Ordination Debate in Australia* (Ringwood: Penguin, 1989), p. 53.

happy marriage was for the wife to make all the decisions, but to let her husband think that he had.

A former Australian Primate, Peter Carnley, speaking in the 1987 General Synod debate on women priests, described opposition to women clergy as as much 'psycho-spiritual' as theological. He said he had a 'funny feeling' it was psycho-spiritual because such deep emotions were obviously stirred by the debate. He suggested that fear of dominance by women may well be involved. The absence of father-figures during World War II may have left many men then in power in the church with a hostility to women, a result of their mothers' strong presence in early childhood. Had too many mothers supervised their sons' baths for too long? he asked.[3] His comments were not well received! But though the point was perhaps not appropriate as a debating tactic, it may well have had some substance. Regardless of whether any or all of the men involved had fathers away at war at a crucial time in their childhood, there is documented evidence that fundamentalist church leaders – who share opposition to women in leadership with conservative Evangelicals – had largely absent fathers. Biographies of American fundamentalist leaders 'offer strong testimony to powerful maternal influence and example', according to an authoritative study. 'In many accounts, fathers were either absent or emotionally distant authority figures', writes Margaret Lamberts Bendroth. 'The testimony of sons to their mother's desire that they enter the ministry was nearly a staple of fundamentalist biography.'[4] Where men either resist or idolize their mothers, or place women on a pedestal generally, it is not unusual to find them also resisting moves to accord real women genuine equality.

As suggested in Chapter 3, the suspicion evoked by the strong female leaders of the Tinker Tailor group in Sydney may also possibly have had an ongoing subterranean influence on the male opponents of both the group and women's ordination. Women's histories indicate that wherever there has been dominant female influence, particularly of a radical kind, conservative reaction is highly likely. This is certainly true of the contemporary situation, where a number of authors have identified a backlash against feminist advances in general society.[5]

Opposition to women as priests and bishops has become what some have termed the 'great cause' to Sydney Anglicans,[6] so much that they have been accused of reinterpreting a central Christian doctrine, that of the Trinity, to support their stance. They are not alone in this. Conservative Evangelical theologians around the world, but principally in the United States, have developed this reinterpretation over the

---

[3] Ibid., p. 131.

[4] Margaret Lamberts Bendroth, *Fundamentalism and Gender: 1875 to the Present* (New Haven, CT and London: Yale University Press, 1993), p. 100.

[5] For example, Susan Faludi, *Backlash: The Undeclared War against Women* (London: Chatto & Windus, 1991).

[6] Kevin Giles, 'The Trinity and Subordinationism', paper given at a symposium held at Trinity College, Melbourne, 20 August 2004, p. 4, henceforth identified as 'Trinity paper'.

past 30 years. (In this as in so many areas, conservative Australian Evangelicals are deeply influenced by contemporary radical North American Protestantism.) It is a reinterpretation that is strongly opposed by mainstream Christian theologians.

This is a highly sophisticated area of theological enquiry, and one that I have neither the space, nor the theological expertise, to deal with in depth. In summary, the standard or orthodox interpretation of the Trinity (Father, Son and Holy Spirit) presents God as three co-equal persons, eternally differentiated but not subordinated in their relationship, bound together 'in a communion of love' which presents 'an ideal for human interpersonal and political relationships'.[7] The new conservative Evangelical view, however, is that 'the Trinity is not made up of co-equal persons' and can therefore 'be quoted to support hierarchical ordering in social relationships'. The Son – Jesus Christ – is fully divine but eternally subordinated to the Father in role or function. As Kevin Giles, a Moore College trained priest who is now a retired Melbourne vicar has argued, this 'novel and dangerous doctrine of the Trinity' has been developed to legitimate, even require, the permanent subordination of women. God the Father has an unchanging and unchangeable 'headship' (leadership) over the Son; so God has given 'headship' to men over women in the church and in the home, the argument goes. Every Evangelical theologian who has agreed with this reinterpretation of the doctrine of the Trinity also supports the subordination of women, Giles has claimed.

What does this mean for the role of women? Women are declared to be equal to men, but different in role. Indeed, so central is this claim that the women's organization set up in Sydney in 1992 to oppose the final stages of the national push for women priests calls itself 'Equal but Different'. This 'difference' is actually a difference as a *result* of female biology, not *because* of female biology. We are not talking here in terms of the evocative French term, 'vive la difference'! This is not about the innate differences between men and women that make life so interesting, challenging and delightful. The difference, in Sydney terms, is that women have a different God-given role to men. In simple terms, women obey and men lead, in the church and in the home. As Giles has pointed out in detail in a major study of this debate, this is actually quite a new position for conservative Christians, who until relatively recent times argued from Scripture that leadership belonged to men in all spheres of public life, as well as the church and the home.[8] But this view is hardly tenable in the twenty-first century, where women are leading politicians, judges, doctors, academics and business leaders. In 2010 in Australia, the towering heights of national governance are in the hands of women exclusively: a female sovereign represented by a female governor-general, with a woman prime minister. To insist on women's subordination across society would expose conservative church leaders to ridicule, though if they were really serious about God-given subordination, they would have no alternative but to suffer the

---

[7] Ibid., p. 1. I am indebted to Kevin Giles's paper for my summary of this debate here.

[8] Kevin Giles, *The Trinity and Subordinationism: The Doctrine of God and the Contemporary Gender Debate* (Downer, IL: InterVarsity Press, 2002), chapter 6.

resulting opprobrium. This limitation of female subordination to the two areas over which the churches continue to have some influence – the family and their own institutions – reveals their true agenda.

However, as Giles points out, to claim that women are still in some way equal to men under the terms of this argument is actually deceptive. 'If women are permanently subordinated in role and their subordinate role can never change then they are the subordinated sex', he writes. This means they are in some ways less than men, which means they are inferior to men. Therefore they cannot be equal to men. He accuses conservative theologians who take this view of circular reasoning: they devised a novel theology to uphold the permanent subordination of women, then developed a novel doctrine of the Trinity on the same terms, and then used the novel doctrine of the Trinity to justify the permanent subordination of women. 'The doctrine of the Trinity has been reconstituted in terms of fallen human relationships to support what was already believed, [that] women are subordinated to men! Instead of correcting human thinking the doctrine of the Trinity has been made a servant of human thinking and ideas, an instrument of oppression.'[9]

Giles's critique of his erstwhile friends in Sydney has created tensions in his relationships with these other, more conservative, Evangelicals. Peter Carnley has also experienced tough confrontations over his assessment of Sydney's espousal of the novel doctrine. He accused Sydney Diocese's Doctrine Commission (which produced a 1999 report entitled 'The Doctrine of the Trinity and Its Bearing on the Relationship of Men and Women') of seeming to be 'prepared openly to embrace' the heresy of Arianism.[10] Arianism is an ancient church heresy, named after a fourth-century protagonist, which holds a strict subordination of the Son to the Father, to the point of denying the full deity of Christ. To call someone an Arian is a term of significant abuse in theological circles. A Melbourne conservative Evangelical priest and theologian, Canon Dr Peter Adam, has particularly taken issue with Carnley for attacking T.C. Hammond, Principal of Moore Theological College from 1935 to 1953, as a subordinationist. 'To attack T.C. Hammond is to attack someone who is of iconic significance in the Diocese of Sydney', he said, complaining that Carnley had titled his paper to a Melbourne symposium on subordinationism, 'Was T.C. Hammond an Arian?' Even to ask the question was to 'spread ill will and fuel resentment', Adam said.[11] But in the Sydney Doctrine Commission's 1999 report, a quote from T.C. Hammond – that 'the subordination of the Son and the Spirit to the Father' was a necessary part of 'full Christian

---

[9] Giles, Trinity paper, pp. 1–3.

[10] Peter Carnley, *Reflections in Glass: Trends and Tensions in the Contemporary Anglican Church* (Sydney: HarperCollins, 2004), p. 235.

[11] Peter Adam, 'Honouring Jesus Christ', paper given at a symposium held at Trinity College, Melbourne, 20 August 2004.

doctrine' – certainly suggests that Carnley's question is a reasonable one.[12] If it is emotive, then that in itself speaks volumes. Whether or not Arianism is a fair description of T.C. Hammond's position, or indeed of the Sydney Doctrine Commission's report, it is worth noting that Peter Jensen subsequently called on the Doctrine Commission to review the controversial report. He has since said that the commission 'gave careful consideration to these charges, and rejected them decisively'.[13]

The recent discussion about women's ordination in direct relation to the doctrine of the Trinity has lent new energy to an internal church debate that had grown rather stale. After all, there is nothing new in the insistence that women cannot be priests or bishops. A host of reasons have been predicated for barring them down the centuries. The Roman Catholic Church, together with traditionalists in the Anglo-Catholic stream of the Anglican Church worldwide, opposes women in holy orders mainly on the grounds of claims that Jesus did not include women among his 12 apostles, he did not ordain any women, and that only men can represent (the male) Jesus in presiding at the central Christian rite of the Eucharist. Therefore, these arguments claim, the Christian churches have been right in insisting that men only can be ordained. Mainstream Protestant churches traditionally barred women from the ordained ministry because of a handful of biblical texts enjoining women to be submissive to male authority, and a generalized assumption that women were inferior to men in terms of leadership, not just in the church. These same (Protestant) arguments used against women in ministry were traditionally used against women in public life generally, including the right even to vote.

Supporters of women's ordination have refuted these arguments on a number of grounds, but mainly on the basis that the biblical teaching on female submission/inferiority was principally cultural, in the same way that the New Testament expectation of slavery was culturally-conditioned. They point to another Scriptural verse that claims full equality for women (and indeed slaves), St Paul's famous claim that 'there is no longer Jew or Greek, there is no longer slave or free, there is no longer male and female; for all of you are one in Christ Jesus' (Galatians 3:28 NRSV). This is clear evidence that human particularity – of race, class or gender – has no significance 'in Christ', that is, for Christian people. It is a fundamental biblical truth that transcends any cultural conditioning, though it has been scandalously overlooked in Christian history. Christian people argued in favour of slavery in the eighteenth and nineteenth centuries; the Afrikaans Church maintained apartheid on religious grounds in South Africa. Conservative Christians continue to argue for female subordination.

---

[12] The full 1999 report 'The Doctrine of the Trinity and Its Bearing on the Relationship of Men and Women', is reproduced in Giles, *The Trinity and Subordinationism*. The Hammond quotation is on p. 126.

[13] Peter Jensen, 'Caleb in the Antipodes: The Pivotal Role of T.C. Hammond', a lecture presented to the Irish Church Missions, Dublin, in June 2005.

Supporters of female equality also argue that there is strong biblical evidence that there *were* women among Jesus' apostles, and in particular, Mary Magdalene, who was the first witness of the Resurrection. In fact, serious scholarship has offered compelling evidence of female leadership in the early Christian Church, with some women identified as priests and even bishops.[14] As to the notion that only men can 'represent' Christ, it is argued that the critical fact of Jesus as the Son of God incarnate as a human being was his humanity, not his maleness. If Jesus can be represented only by the particularity of his gender, then presumably these representative men need also to be bearded, circumcised Jews. And if his maleness was the key to the Incarnation, then God could not have identified with women, and they could not therefore have been redeemed by God's sacrifice on the Cross. As a women's ordination slogan says, 'If you will not ordain us, then don't baptise us'.[15]

As I have suggested above, there is far more to the Christian gender debate than theological argument. In my experience, the rhetoric is the publicly acceptable face of a deep misogyny that the Christian Church has been party to fostering. Inheriting a dualist understanding of the body and sexuality from the Graeco-Roman world, it also imbibed the ancient suspicion of women inherent in most human cultures. Part of that suspicion is related to a misunderstanding of female bodiliness, particularly as regards menstruation. When the ordination of women debate was first raised at a significant level in the Anglican world, at the 1920 Lambeth Conference of bishops, it was pointed out to the assembled hierarchy that a major reason why women were kept away from the altar and pulpit was the superstition that they were ritually unclean when they menstruated.[16] Both Orthodox Judaism – out of which Christianity sprang – and some branches of Eastern Orthodox Christianity, as well as other faith traditions, still observe ritual restrictions on menstruating women.

For all these reasons, the Christian Church quickly abandoned the early equality it seems to have originally granted women in line with Jesus' own example of his treatment of women, and developed the dichotomy of woman as either Madonna or whore. The exaltation of the Virgin Mary, particularly in popular medieval devotion and even some theology, created a model of feminine perfection that no other woman could emulate: who else could be both virgin and mother? Even the most virtuous Christian mother, by virtue of her (marital) sexual experience, could never match that ideal. And her sexual experience, no matter

---

[14] For the most recent scholarly discussion, see Charlotte Methuen, 'Vidua – Presbytera – Episcopa: Women with Oversight in the Early Church', *Theology*, May/June 2005, pp. 163–77.

[15] There are a number of full discussions of this debate from the pro-women perspective. In particular, I recommend Ruth B. Edwards, *The Case for Women's Ministry* (London: SPCK, 1989).

[16] Paper presented by Dr Letitia Fairfield, quoted in Brian Heeney, *The Women's Movement in the Church of England 1850–1930* (Oxford: Clarendon, 1988), p. 72.

how lawful and restrained, nevertheless touched her with a tinge of the whore. Only virginal women who effectively denied their womanliness and acquitted themselves as honorary men, were able to avoid the stigma. The development of clerical celibacy from the fourth century also exacerbated the notion of women as dangerous temptresses, as they had to be avoided at all costs if a priest were to maintain his ordination vows. Compulsory celibacy also ensured that clergy lived lives effectively divorced from significant female influence, further compounding any latent misogyny.

Contrary to a view often expressed by present-day opponents of women's ordination, the contemporary women's movement in the Christian Church is not a product of the secular feminist movement of the 1960s. Far from it. There is compelling evidence that the opposite is in fact the case: the struggle for female equality in all areas of life grew out of a concern to establish women's equal place before God. The modern-day story of women's emancipation began with American women who spoke publicly against slavery in the first half of the nineteenth century. They quickly found themselves criticized as 'unnatural' by male clergy in particular. 'The appropriate duties and influence of women are clearly stated in the New Testament', wrote the outraged clergy authors of a 'pastoral letter' aimed at such women. 'The power of woman is her dependence, flowing from the consciousness of that weakness which God has given her for her protection ....' When a woman assumes the role of a public reformer, she yields the power God has given her and 'her character becomes unnatural', they argued.[17] This is contorted, artificial reasoning by any standard, but as we will discuss below, it is not dissimilar to that being promoted today by many conservative Evangelicals.

Nothing daunted, women concerned about slavery continued their public campaign, but found themselves forced to defend their God-given rights as women in the process. This came to a head in 1848, when a woman's rights convention was held in Seneca Falls, New York. The convention's stated aims were to discuss 'the social, civil and religious rights of woman'. Five of the 12 resolutions passed by the convention dealt with religious issues directly, and included a claim for the inclusion of women in the ministry. The call for female suffrage was actually a late addition to the list of resolutions, and met with some resistance, mainly on the grounds that it would derail the other concerns.[18] Women's equality before God and in the church was an important original and integral component of the first manifesto of the first organized women's movement in history. The women

---

[17] The New England Council of Congregational Ministers 'pastoral letter' in response to the public oratory of Sarah and Angelina Grimke, quoted in Elizabeth Clark and Herbert Richardson (eds), *Women and Religion: A Feminist Sourcebook of Christian Thought* (New York: Harper & Row, 1977), p. 206.

[18] Donna A. Behnke, *Religious Issues in Nineteenth Century Feminism* (New York: Whitston Publishing, 1982), p. 66; Judith Hole and Ellen Levine, *Rebirth of Feminism* (New York: Quadrangle Books, 1971), pp. 429–33.

who authored these claims were mostly devout Christian women. The modern women's movement is their descendant, not vice versa.

The struggle for women's ordination began in earnest in the second half of the nineteenth century in some American mainline denominations, with the first woman ordained generally claimed to be Antoinette Louisa Brown. She was ordained a minister in the First Congregational Church in Wayne County, New York, in 1853. Such was the opposition she faced that she lasted just one year in the ministry. In the second half of the nineteenth century, in Protestant Europe and in the Church of England, women were being admitted to newly-formed orders of deaconesses, quasi-religious orders whose members dressed in a drab uniform and whose duties were pastoral visiting and the like. Deaconesses were introduced into Australia from the 1880s beginning, ironically, with Sydney, where it was made clear their role was to be a 'supportive' one.[19] The Salvation Army, formed in London in 1878, gave women an equal role in leadership from the beginning.

In the twentieth century, as the daughters and granddaughters of the first Christian feminists were at last gaining the vote, mainstream churches were forced to look seriously at women's ministry. In the main, however, they resisted, generally along the lines of female inferiority. For instance, the bishops of the Anglican Communion, meeting at the 1920 Lambeth Conference, were convinced that while women would one day share a spiritual equality with men in the spiritual world that was to come, in the 'present world of action ... man has a priority'. Marriage and motherhood remained women's central, God-given vocation, they said.[20]

The bishops' views were not far removed from those of fundamentalists, who argued vociferously against women in leadership. From its beginnings, the fundamentalist movement was deeply anti-feminist, with early leaders viewing women not as partners but as a threat, a 'pernicious influence to be silenced and subordinated': 'without serious restraints, they believed women would only impede the quest for doctrinal purity'.[21] American fundamentalists took issue with the women's movement's claims to God-given female equality, claiming biblical inerrancy as their justification. It is interesting to note that, at the time the women's movement was beginning, the same theologians who opposed female equality on biblical grounds, also supported slavery for the same reason.[22] For the fundamentalists, female subordination was regarded as 'inevitable as death'; women in authority were an 'unmistakable sign' of 'failure and apostasy'.[23]

One historian of fundamentalism and gender has mounted a case for seeing Christian fundamentalism as responding primarily to the gains of the first-

---

[19] Muriel Porter, *Women in the Church*, p. 44.

[20] *Conference of Bishops of the Anglican Communion* (London, 1920), pp. 39–41, 95–105.

[21] Bendroth, *Fundamentalism and Gender*, p. 32.

[22] Ibid., pp. 34–5.

[23] Ibid., pp. 45–6.

wave women's movement, resulting in the 'dismantling of the Victorian gender ideology'.[24] Betty A. DeBerg writes: 'In popular fundamentalist literature, theological orthodoxy – salvation itself – was inexorably connected to the morality and social conventions of the Victorian middle-class.' By 1920, fundamentalists were blaming higher criticism of the Bible 'for the revolution in manners and morals. Much of this material consisted of commentary on changes in the attitudes and behavior [sic] of women.'[25] DeBerg's basic thesis is that it was the changes brought about by first-wave feminism that provided the psychological reason for the entire movement.

However true that interesting hypothesis might be it is clear that part of the fundamentalist anti-feminist response was conditioned by the development of a 'more self-consciously masculine posture' as the movement grew more defensive.[26] And in the 1920s, as liberated women assumed unheard of freedoms as 'flappers', fundamentalist reservations seemed to be confirmed. Increasingly, fundamentalist literature reflected a concern about female intellectual weakness and psychological vulnerability,[27] though fundamentalists, like churchmen of all persuasions, were always perfectly happy to have women working alongside them in subordinate ministries. Sydney Diocese has developed a wide range of such ministries for women, with some claiming that more than 50 per cent of all their ministries are occupied by women. But these are all subsidiary ministries. While women attend lectures at Moore Theological College, their theological training is designed to train women to minister to *other women* and to children. It is generally not expected that women will minister to men, and certainly not teach them in any church capacity. Sydney Diocese has adopted the General Synod legislation for women deacons, but not many women are ordained. At the February 2010 ordination of deacons in Sydney, six women were ordained alongside 50 male deacons, with one other woman commissioned as a 'stipendiary lay worker'. Out of the 925 licensed clergy in Sydney in 2010,[28] just 45 are women (including two women priests ordained outside the diocese, who are licensed in Sydney as deacons only). Women cannot lead the church in any significant way in Sydney.

Anecdotal evidence suggests younger male clergy in particular have taken an increasingly hard line against women having any leadership role in public worship in Sydney, even to the extent of forbidding them from publicly reading lessons from the Bible. Preaching to mixed congregations (that is, of men and women together) is unacceptable in many parishes. Some suggest the new restrictions stem from the influence of the Ministry Training Strategy, an initiative developed

---

[24] Betty A. DeBerg, *Ungodly Women: Gender and the First Wave of American Fundamentalism* (Minneapolis, MN: Fortress Press, 1990).
[25] Ibid. pp. 126, 132.
[26] Bendroth, *Fundamentalism and Gender*, p. 40.
[27] Ibid., p. 63.
[28] This figure includes retired clergy.

in the student-focused conservative mega church of St Matthias', Centennial Park, and discussed in Chapter 1.

Peter Jensen's predecessor as Archbishop, Harry Goodhew, recognized the situation for women had become more restrictive even during the time of his relatively generous and open archiepiscopate. Although it was none of his doing, women who might formerly have sought ordination as deacons were increasingly feeling inhibited, either because they were fearful of the reaction of male rectors for whom they must work, or because they believed themselves they should minister only to women and children. Increasingly, even during his term of office, women were being commissioned as 'parish sisters' instead of being ordained deacons. 'Parish sister' is an ambiguous and clearly subsidiary role, not to mention curiously outdated in its terminology. In an interview on the eve of his retirement, Goodhew said he 'would want to continue to ordain women as deacons, and to licence them to preach and leave it up to the individual rector to decide whether he wanted her to preach'. Clearly he was worried that restrictions might be enforced by a more conservative successor.[29] It seems further restrictions are not required, given the increasing ideological support for women's subordination in the parishes and clergy of the diocese, and in the women offering themselves for training.

The Sydney attitude to women draws on the conservative fundamentalist literature post World War II, which 'emphasised God's "order of creation" as a way of negotiating sex roles', influencing the growing conservatism in Evangelicalism. This terminology of female subordination and male authority as being ordained as part of God's order, became dominant in conservative Evangelical literature from the 1960s, and remains so, as we will discuss below.[30] It is interesting to note that during his Australian 1959 crusade, Billy Graham, whose influence on contemporary Sydney Anglicanism has been so profound, preached male headship in the home. Further, he promoted the conservative family ideal with the woman staying at home with the children, keeping herself attractive for her husband, maintaining a clean house, restraining household expenditure, and refraining from nagging or complaining.[31]

In mainstream Protestant churches, however, the issue of women's equality would not be so readily suppressed. In the United States they had admitted women to authoritative ministry by the middle of last century. In Australia, the Methodist Church ordained its first women clergy in 1969; the Presbyterian Church followed in 1974 (though since then, the continuing Presbyterian Church – formed of those who did not enter the Uniting Church when it was formed in 1977 – has ceased ordaining women).

In the Anglican Church, the issue was only just being taken seriously at the end of the 1960s, despite the fact that the first Anglican woman priest had been

---

[29] Author interview with Archbishop Harry Goodhew, March 2001.

[30] Bendroth, *Fundamentalism and Gender*, p. 112.

[31] Judith Smart, 'The Evangelist as Star: The Billy Graham Crusade in Australia, 1959', *Journal of Popular Culture*, 33(1) (Summer 1999), p. 165.

ordained in the Diocese of Hong Kong under the exceptional circumstances of Japanese occupation in 1944. Li Tim Oi's clandestine ordination by Bishop R.O. Hall met a critical pastoral emergency, as the Revd Li was left alone to minister in Macao to a church packed with war refugees. Her ordination was roundly condemned once word leaked out, and for many years she was forced to lay aside her orders.

It was the Diocese of Hong Kong that took up the cause of women in the priesthood again in the early 1970s, ordaining two more women priests in 1971. Later in the 1970s, women were ordained in the United States, Canada and New Zealand, and the Australian Anglican Church decided by General Synod resolution that theological objections did not constitute a barrier to the ordination of women as either priests or bishops.[32] The Australian resolution, made by the 1977 General Synod, followed the reception by the synod of one of the most important theological documents on women's ordination to be produced in the Anglican Church of Australia. *The Ministry of Women: A Report of the General Synod Commission on Doctrine*, had recommended the decision to the General Synod. The report was the work of a stellar cast among Anglican theologians. Chaired by the then Primate, Melbourne's Archbishop Sir Frank Woods, it included three who would later serve as Primate (John Grindrod, Keith Rayner and Peter Carnley) as well as theologians such as Bishop Max Thomas and Dr John Gaden. More significantly, the commission included a leading Melbourne Evangelical theologian, Leon Morris, who also promoted its conclusions. As mentioned earlier, their conclusions were denounced by just one of the commission's 12 members, the Sydney theologian Broughton Knox.[33] Knox wrote a one-person minority report in which he presented the full range of arguments against women's ordination still current in Sydney to this day.

Knox's report is worth examining in some detail. Following the conservative Evangelical view, he argued that 'the question of the ordination of women hinges on the relationship of men and women'.[34] He continued: 'This relationship was

---

[32] The resolution was passed by the 1977 General Synod with comfortable majorities. However, because of the high voting requirements for legislation, it took 15 years between the passing of the 1977 resolution and the 1992 legislation for women priests.

[33] Knox's father, Canon D.J. Knox, had argued against admitting women as members of Synod in Adelaide in 1921, claiming it 'was not in keeping with the spirit and letter of Holy Scripture or even common sense', admitting women would 'reduce the manliness and virility of Synod', he argued: Peter Sherlock, '"Leave it to the Women": The Exclusion of Women from Anglican Church Government in Australia', *Australian Historical Studies*, 39(3) (2008), pp. 288–304, at p. 301. In the 1970s, Knox's son would use similar arguments in Sydney Synod against women as churchwardens. This Knox family connection suggests that biography is at least as influential as theology in debates about gender in the Church.

[34] *The Ministry of Women: A Report of the General Synod Commission on Doctrine*, Volume 1 of Reports to the General Synod of the Church of England in Australia, 1977, p. 29. This discussion of Knox's views is taken from this document, pp. 29–33.

formed in the divine mind and expressed in creation and is testified to throughout Scripture. The relationship does not change, though the form of its expression may change with changes in culture.' In creating humanity, God gave a 'headship to man which he did not give to woman'. This headship of man to woman was 'in every sphere of life', though it is in marriage 'that this relation of headship and subordination is most clearly expressed and experienced'. Beyond the Bible, 'nature itself teaches us, that man is the head of woman'. Women must not lead in the Christian congregation because a woman who is subordinate to her husband must not 'be over him in the things of God in the congregation'. And in case unmarried women think this particular argument has no relevance to them, Knox is quick to point out that that is not the case, though interestingly he offers no reasons (or mechanisms) for this claim.

The subordination of women was related directly to the Trinity in Knox's view, because Christ is 'himself subordinate to the Father', he maintained. This indicates the direct line of inheritance of this particular argument from Broughton Knox. This inheritance alone would make it extremely difficult for contemporary Sydney theologians now to abandon either their view of some measure of subordination within the Trinity, or the implications of that subordination for women.

More important than esoteric debates about the Trinity are the implications for women of the claims that God requires them to be subordinate to men. In a society now alerted to the reality of domestic violence and abuse of all kinds in even seemingly respectable marriages, this poses significant problems. But even in the 1970s, before domestic violence was seriously on the public agenda, its Sydney proponents were clearly aware of the difficulty of 'selling' such a doctrine. Knox, like his successors, claimed that male headship was modelled on the 'headship' of Christ. This meant that male 'headship' of woman was not to be about dominance. Rather, Knox insisted, male headship 'consists in the obligation to take the lead in serving', and had 'as its only object the true welfare of woman'. Men, being sinful human beings, however, had often misused their leadership role, provoking rejection by women of the subordinate role. This rejection by women 'characterises modern society', Knox continued, but is an ancient tendency, which is why the New Testament requires women to 'recognise the order of headship and subordination by being obedient to their husbands'.

Oh the contortions required to defend the indefensible! What on earth did Knox mean when he claimed that male leadership's only object was the 'true welfare of woman'? It can only mean that women are, at some level, child-like, *needing* to be cared for, protected and led. It implies inferiority and a certain helplessness on the part of women, assumptions that were once integral to patriarchal Western society. These are the very misunderstandings about women – and about the Bible – that the first (Christian) leaders of the modern women's movement came together to tackle in the mid-nineteenth century. If they were serious, then it would not be women's ordination they would be resisting, but women's involvement in the entire public arena. If women are so created by God that they require male leadership, then it is ludicrous (and possibly disobedient!) to limit that leadership claim to the church and the home. How can these theologians seriously accept a female sovereign, let alone women politicians, judges, professors, university vice-chancellors and the like? Or, closer to home, women as churchwardens or as members of synods? Earlier generations of Christians who insisted on female inferiority were at least consistent, limiting women to home and hearth and their 'proper' duty as carers of husbands and children.

If it is bad enough to have male theologians arguing for female subordination, it is even worse to listen to women making the same contorted arguments. 'Equal but Different', the Sydney anti-women's ordination lobby group, is a women's organization. Its committee includes Christine Jensen, whose husband is the Archbishop, and Helen Jensen, married to Phillip, the Dean of Sydney. The website proclaims

> ... the absolute equality of men and women in His [God's] purposes with respect to status, honour and dignity; that both men and women are equally fallen before our Creator and Judge, and that both are equally loved and able to be rescued from God's deserved wrath through the death and resurrection of the Lord Jesus Christ; that God's purposes for humanity include complementary relationships between the genders; that men are called to loving, self-denying, humble leadership, and women to intelligent, willing submission within marriage; that within the church, this complementarity is expressed through suitably gifted and appointed men assuming responsibility for authoritative teaching and pastoral oversight; and that we unconditionally reject the use of God's purposes for marriage as an excuse for violence against women, whether physical, emotional or spiritual ...[35]

Both the organization's name and this belief statement pose more questions and problems than they solve. If women must submit to men, how are they in any manner, equal? (The slogan 'equal but different' sounds close to one of the descriptions of the place of women in Islam: not inferior, just different.)[36] The statement suggests they are equal because both are sinful and both are able to be 'saved' by Jesus Christ, a curiously limited and unsatisfactory form of equality by any measure. Over two thousand years of Christian history, when women were clearly denoted as inferior human beings in all mainstream Christian theology, few seriously suggested that women were more sinful than men, even if it was often claimed that their intrinsic weakness made them more vulnerable to temptation. Nor was it generally asserted that salvation through Christ was not available to them, though there were occasional claims that women did not have souls. Baptism has always been equally available to women and men, which implies the need for and availability of Christian salvation for both. Is this the only equality the Sydney

---

[35] http://www.equalbutdifferent.org/.
[36] Quoted in Geraldine Brooks, *Nine Parts of Desire: The Hidden World of Islamic Women* (Sydney: Doubleday, 1996), p. 10.

women acknowledge? What about equality under the (secular) law? Equality in terms of democratic rights and freedoms? Equality in employment and education? The absence of such affirmations is alarming from twenty-first century women.

And what about the 'difference' they claim? This seems to be a matter of 'distinctive roles', though that is not spelt out other than the opaque, nonsensical terminology of 'loving, self-denying, humble leadership' for men and 'intelligent willing submission within marriage' for women. It is not apparent just what loving male leadership means in this context, let alone intelligent and willing submission. It is a rhetoric that belongs to an earlier age, when citizens in a full democracy such as Australia were nevertheless called 'subjects' in a strange hangover from a hierarchical, even feudal society. Thankfully, that terminology has long gone from the secular world, and with it the outdated concepts of owing fealty to the sovereign. The hereditary nature of the monarchy is the only surviving link with the notion that biology inevitably governs destiny. In every other area of modern democratic life in societies such as ours, biology is *not* necessarily destiny. In theory at least, both men and women from every race, class and creed can aspire to every role and occupation available. Our relationships to each other in society are mediated through roles that are not dictated by biology or personal status. Judges who send criminals to prison might one day become prisoners themselves, if they flout the law of the land. A politician who governs will only do so as long as he or she holds office. Even when in office, they also belong to the governed. Respect and obedience (in terms of the law) are required, but are required from and by *all* citizens, not men only or women only, let alone black people only, for example.

If the woman's role is to submit to her husband's leadership, where and how is the level of submission mediated? Is it left to each couple to work out for themselves, which has obvious dangers? Does it simply mean that when the chips are down in any marital disagreement, the man's view prevails? And is that the same in a disagreement over how many children to have, where to live and how to spend money as well as what to have for dinner tonight? What about sexual relations in marriage? St Paul offered some guidelines that suggest that men and women alike need to respect each other's sexual needs,[37] but in cases of disagreement, must the husband's need prevail over the wife's need? Could the end result sometimes amount to rape in marriage? Where does male leadership and female submission begin and end? And how on earth is female submission both willing and intelligent? It is a contradiction in terms. All the 'feel good' rhetoric about 'right relationships' and proper male leadership being expressed in 'self-

---

[37] 'The husband should give to his wife her conjugal rights, and likewise the wife to her husband. For the wife does not have authority over her own body, but the husband does; likewise the husband does not have authority over his own body, but the wife does. Do not deprive one another except perhaps by agreement ...', 1 Corinthians 7:3–5, NRSV. This sounds very much like a biblical expectation that men and women are completely equal in marriage. There is no hint here, in this most intimate and central of male/female relations, of female submission to male headship.

denial' cannot overcome the fundamental problems for women that are posed by a marriage that is not overtly and entirely a marriage of equals. That there are inherent dangers for women in an unequal marriage is apparent from the rider the authors of the 'equal but different' statement have obviously felt compelled to add: 'we unconditionally reject the use of God's purposes for marriage as an excuse for violence against women, whether physical, emotional or spiritual ....' Domestic violence can all too readily be an outcome of unequal marriages.

The website statement seems to restrict female submission to married women, but is not explicit about the situation for single women. That must be because it could not possibly relate to single women, given they are no longer subject to laws such as those that kept unmarried women under the control of their fathers or other male relatives until the late nineteenth century. Take the case of a single woman, perhaps a well-paid career woman, living alone and handling all her own financial and legal affairs, long since independent of her birth family. How is she to exercise intelligent, willing submission to any man? And which man? More to the point, how does any of it relate to Christian ministry, which is supposed to be a ministry of submission to the will of Christ and of service to Christ's people? Surely submissive women are the ideal clergy!

The difficulty involved in the practical outworking of this ideology is clearly demonstrated in an interesting recent online discussion on the Sydney Diocesan website.[38] Nicky Lock wrote an article entitled 'Submission in practice' in which she outlined the concerns of a young Sydney woman, engaged to be married. 'So what does submission look like in practice?' the young woman asked the (male) minister at a church service where he had been preaching on the subject. 'Sharing was invited from mature Christian couples about their own marriages', the author wrote. Their answers were telling. One couple explained that 'they worked very closely in partnership and saw almost no occasions when there had been any necessity for the husband to take the lead about any decisions, other than an imposed work-related example'. Another man said his wife had completed postgraduate education in theology so he would 'submit to her wisdom in that area at times since her knowledge exceeded his'. In modern society, so different from the Graeco-Roman world of the New Testament, 'gender roles in marriage have been released from the traditional patterns', Ms Lock continued. So, she asked her readers, how do modern couples live out submission? Responses poured in, revealing that most respondents were as confused as the author. One obviously older woman said that her husband took the lead in every area of their marriage, including financial. She has her pay put into his bank account; if she needs money, she asks him for it. She was, however, the exception; most of the other men and women who answered revealed that, though they all enthusiastically espoused the ideology of wifely submission, in reality their marriages were actually as equal in practical matters as those of any other modern couples.

---

[38] http://www.sydneyanglicans.net/life/relationships/submission_in_practice/.

To justify the 'submission' requirement, Sydney Anglicans offer up two texts from the Bible about women not being permitted to teach, about keeping silent in church, and learning from their husbands.[39] In the past, these very texts were used to prevent women teaching in schools and universities, from participating even in hymn singing in church, and from having any education outside the home. In the modern world, such interpretations are nonsense and in any case, biblical scholars outside Sydney usually see these texts as culturally conditioned. They argue two possible scenarios. One is that the texts reflect concern with women's extremely limited role in society in the first Christian centuries, when for women to speak publicly in mixed gatherings, or to assume any degree of equality with their husbands, was a matter of deep shame. Women had to conform to such societal expectations to ensure the fledgling religion was not shamed by their behaviour in the eyes of possible converts. In that respect the early church was certainly not counter-cultural. Or the texts were instructions to particular congregations in which women were misusing their newfound freedom in Christ. Without information about the precise context, it is now impossible to say which interpretation is correct.

What is disturbing is that again and again, Sydney Anglicans refuse to respect alternative viewpoints on the interpretation of key biblical texts about women and ministry. They insist that their interpretation is the only acceptable one, and that to be faithful to Scripture, Christians must accept their interpretation. This was the thrust of all the speeches their representatives made in the 2004 General Synod debate on women bishops, for example. After the defeat of the legislation, Peter Jensen said he was pleased that the Synod had 'stood by the plain teaching of Scripture'. Speaking during the debate, he said Sydney's objections arose from belief in the authority of the Bible. 'The very book that brings liberation is also the same book that says "equal but different"', he said. 'Authority ultimately rests with God's Word.' As if the rest of us do not accept the ultimate authority of God's word! It can so easily make it look as if that is the case, however, and influence uncertain voters into thinking that if they too accept the ultimate authority of the Bible, then they have no option but to vote with Sydney.

The Sydney mantra of 'equal but different' is a classic case of 'doublespeak'. As Julian Burnside QC has defined it, '"doublespeak" uses language to smuggle uncomfortable ideas into comfortable minds'.[40] Older conservative Christian rhetoric spoke of female inferiority or weakness, terminology that would be completely unacceptable for contemporary women. 'Equal but different' sounds plausible, even fashionably post-modern. But whatever it might mean about women's souls and eternal salvation, in earthed reality it means that women *are* inferior by virtue of their biology. They must always submit to a form of male authority, even if they are unmarried. That intelligent, capable women accept and promote such teaching is testimony to the power both of the doublespeak, and

---

[39] See I Corinthians 14:34–5 and 1 Timothy 2:11–15 particularly.

[40] Julian Burnside, 'Perspective', ABC Radio National, 3 March 2005.

the charismatic nature of the male leadership of Sydney Diocese, that together have made them psychologically vulnerable. In fact, they have been rendered submissive by what seems to be a most successful form of brainwashing.

Many of us at the 2004 General Synod were disturbed by a petition that women from 'Equal but Different' produced. The petition was signed by 1300 Australian laywomen, the organizers claimed, and called for General Synod not to pass the legislation for women bishops 'in the light of Biblical teaching and the nature of the Episcopal role'. An analysis of the document, distributed to every synod member, revealed that though the organizers claimed it represented 150 churches from almost every Australian diocese, two thirds of the signatures came from a few Sydney parishes. Of those who had come from dioceses with women priests, almost all of them were from parishes that had not actually experienced the ministry of women clergy. The petition, then, represented a minority position and came almost entirely from women who had either by design or accident, not seen women functioning as clergy. It was noted in the debate that given the size of Sydney Diocese alone, a petition of just 1,300 seemed rather light. Had it been signed by 13,000, let alone 130,000, it might have been worth taking seriously. However, its limited coverage seemed only to suggest that ordinary laywomen even in Sydney were not as strongly opposed to women in ministry as was being claimed. If that is the case, though, their obvious reluctance to refute publicly the claims of their diocese about female submission suggests they too have been intimidated.

It is intriguing that, in common with other fundamentalist and conservative Evangelical groups in both Australia and the United States, Sydney Anglicanism has turned its back on the developments that over the past 80 years have changed the views of mainstream church bodies about the role of women. As I have pointed out, the 1920 Lambeth Conference of bishops maintained that women were inferior. By 1968, the bishops were a long way down the track of revising their views in line with those being propounded by contemporary biblical and theological scholarship. Since then, the bishops have moved to acknowledge, by majority votes if not unanimous support, the acceptability of women as both priests and bishops. The 1998 Lambeth Conference counted 11 women bishops (from the United States, Canada and New Zealand) among its number, and though there had been threats of walkouts, by and large the women bishops were accepted without fuss. By the 2008 Lambeth Conference, 18 women bishops – including two from Australia – were eligible to attend. Again, they were accepted without fuss.

Sydney's swift answer to these changes would be that mainstream Anglicanism, together with other churches such as the Methodist Church in England and the Uniting Church in Australia, have been seduced by the 'spirit of the age'. They have given in to the secular culture of feminism. Proponents of the 'equal but different' argument proudly proclaim that this stance is counter-cultural in a feminist society. What they fail to acknowledge, however, is that earlier versions of female inferiority were scarcely counter-cultural, being the product of the cultures that created them.

Sydney's most trenchant Evangelical critic, Kevin Giles, has pointed out that Sydney and its like-minded friends refuse to accept that the Bible can be, and has been throughout history, read in more than one way 'even on important matters'. The tradition of biblical interpretation on both slavery and women (their status and ministry) should be 'honestly acknowledged and categorically rejected', he has written. That tradition 'reflects a reading of Scripture that was dictated by the world in which the interpreters lived. No other reading was open to them.' It was nothing more, he writes, than the acceptance 'of what everyone in earlier times – Christian and non-Christian alike – believed on these matters'. It was only when 'God's work in history changed cultural values' that a different interpretation became possible.[41]

Giles's comments suggest that, to understand Sydney's intransigence in this area, we perhaps need to understand more fully the particular inner 'world' in which these interpreters live. Possible psychological causes have been noted in passing, as has the ongoing tendency in Sydney religion, for historical reasons, to be separatist and indeed deliberately and even artificially counter-cultural as a means of self-protection. Is there a deep concern about the power of women (and all aspects of the feminine) to erode manliness at work here? Historically, the most successful way to control women has been patriarchal marriage. It ensured male ascendancy, male control, and that seems to be an important subconscious issue here. A comment made by Peter Jensen in a press interview – if it was accurately reported – suggests there may be an underlying concern about masculinity. Until 40 years ago 'everyone' accepted that the husband should be the head of the home, the *Weekend Australian*'s Greg Callaghan quoted Jensen as saying. 'We have now succeeded in turning men into children.'[42] This is telling, suggesting as it does not only a concern with masculine pride and status, but also the corollary – that where men do head the home, *women* are effectively 'children'. The claim that there was no dispute about male headship in the home until 40 years ago is itself questionable, given the lively debates about marriage among Sydney Anglicans in particular in the closing decades of the nineteenth century, a debate that has been carefully documented by a Sydney Anglican priest.[43] The debate in wider society erupted many times throughout the twentieth century.

Callaghan also points out that Jensen blames feminists and homosexuals for the decline of the family since the 1960s, 'the decade when, in his view, society started to go helter-skelter'. The protection of 'family values' is certainly the rallying cry for the new conservatives in our society, and both feminism and homosexuality are frequent scapegoats. The conventional family has become

---

[41] Giles, *The Trinity and Subordinationism*, p. 9.
[42] 'Jensen's Crusade', *Weekend Australian Magazine*, 14–15 May 2005. It should be noted that the article contains several factual errors.
[43] William James Lawton, *The Better Time To Be: Utopian Attitudes to Society Among Sydney Anglicans 1885 to 1914* (Sydney: University of New South Wales Press, 1990), pp. 151–80.

the icon of societal stability, and again there are elements of doublespeak in the rhetoric. To most people, the term 'family' connotes idealistic feelings of warmth, comfort and 'home'. It conjures up cosy scenes of happy domesticity, of harmonious relationships, love, caring and security. That is, it does for those people who have either not experienced the pain of a dysfunctional family, or who do not acknowledge that pain. It brings little comfort to some gay people, for whom the image is one of profound exclusion. But that is the point. Conventional notions of the 'nuclear family' are overwhelmingly excluding, protecting as they do the status of the exclusively heterosexual couple and their children. De facto couples, divorced people, sole parents and gay liaisons are all relegated to a lesser status by this rhetoric, if not rejected outright. Not that most conservatives publicly denounce any but homosexual partnerships, often maintaining a rhetoric of acceptance of less-than-ideal family units. But this acceptance, where it exists, is low-key in comparison to the status accorded the nuclear family.

The nuclear family that many conservative Christians support and eulogize is at heart patriarchal. Though they do not often draw attention to this aspect in general public discussion, for obvious reasons, it lies at the centre of the male headship argument. A detailed presentation of the importance of the patriarchal family is found in a book published by the key Sydney Anglican publishing house, Matthias Media, and warmly commended by Peter Jensen.[44] Kirsten Birkett, who has written a number of books for Matthias Media, claims (disapprovingly) that the frequent description of a family as 'mum, dad and the children' is actually a description of matriarchy. The mother is the one whose presence is assumed to transform a group of individuals into a family. This, she argues, is evidence of our conditioning (presumably by a feminist society), because the Bible's model of family is based on the presence of the father.[45]

Step by step, she builds a picture of the biblical patriarchal family as the ideal family for all cultures, for all time. This model of family is integral to the creation of a stable, positive society: 'the revisionist attempt to deny this needs to be seen for the ideological deception that it is', she writes.[46] More, this model is really the only acceptable model: 'If we want to protect children and enjoy satisfying relationships, we must accept that this requires an absolutist definition of family.'[47] The patriarchal family is the 'creational pattern of life', a means of raising children that is '"meant" to be'.[48] This ideal is rejected by our society because of the 'ideological dominance of feminism', which has 'fought so strongly against

---

[44] Matthias Media, which calls itself a 'reformed Evangelical publishing house', grew out of Phillip Jensen's previous parish, St Matthias', Centennial Park, and now publishes a wide range of books, audio-visual materials and other publications.

[45] Kirsten Birkett, *The Essence of Family* (Sydney: Matthias Media, 2004), p. 20. Peter Jensen commended the book in his 2004 Synod Charge.

[46] Ibid., p. 57.

[47] Ibid., p. 82.

[48] Ibid., p. 109.

marriage' and requires women to have full-time careers, which of necessity puts 'intolerable stresses' on marriage.[49] Independence and power are the goals for a feminist life, she argues, but 'this is a doctrine doomed to failure'.[50]

Birkett's argument is highly selective, failing to take sufficient note of the prevailing pattern of polygamous marriage and concubinage in the Old Testament, which is hardly an ideal model for modern family life. It has been pointed out that there is just one monogamous married couple – the patriarch Isaac and his wife Rebecca – in the entire Old Testament! Birkett also fails to acknowledge the overwhelming evidence of domestic violence, incest and other forms of sexual abuse in conventional families where the father reigns supreme. Nor does she note Jesus' rather critical attitude to marriage and family, the subject of some interesting and confronting theological discussion in recent times.[51] But those considerations aside, the construction of the model patriarchal family, with its concomitant rejection of feminism and homosexual partnerships, is strong evidence of the underlying masculinist philosophy at work in the promotion of 'family'. Of course, this promotion is not limited to Sydney Anglicans. It is unthinkingly resorted to by many other Christian bodies concerned about dysfunction in society, and more deliberately by groups such as the 'Family First' political party.

In the exaltation of family there seems to be a concern for male purity. Conventional marriage is seen as the only real protection for men against the dangers of all forms of sexual licence, including homosexuality. The promotion of personal family status seems to indicate that a man is sexually pure. Anglicans outside Sydney are sometimes surprised at the eagerness with which otherwise austere Sydney Anglican leaders define themselves primarily by their marital and family status. Before they indicate their ministry role or scholarship interests, for example, individual male leaders usually introduce themselves first and foremost as husband, father and even grandfather. They are also more likely to have their wives accompany them to residential church meetings than Anglicans from other dioceses. Some observers sense an unacknowledged emotional dependence, as well as the obvious flag-waving for 'family values'. This is not to deny that their marriages are in the main good, wholesome and happy. Doubtless most of them are, though probably neither more nor less satisfactory than marriages of other Anglican clergy and leaders. It is the public flaunting of them that is so unexpected.

Birkett's book, like other conservative religious polemic, also ignores research that reveals that, despite the rhetoric, Evangelical personal morality is not much better than that found in the rest of society. An article in the respected American Evangelical publication *Christianity Today* commented that 'whether the issue is divorce, materialism, sexual promiscuity, racism, physical abuse in

---

[49] Ibid., pp. 116–17.

[50] Ibid., p. 121.

[51] For example, see Rosemary Radford Ruether, *Christianity and the Making of the Modern Family* (London: SCM Press, 2001), in particular Chapter 1, in which she discusses Jesus' numerous hostile comments about family.

marriage or neglect of a biblical worldview, the polling data point to widespread, blatant disobedience of clear biblical moral demands on the part of people who allegedly are evangelical, born-again Christians'. The article continues: 'The statistics are devastating.' American statistics reveal that the divorce rate among US Evangelicals is the same as the national average, and that rates of premarital sex among Evangelical young people are only marginally lower than among the general population.[52] These revelations are particularly significant coming from the United States, which has a far higher rate of claimed church attendance and conservative Christian values than any other Western country.

The conservative Evangelical attitude to women, characterized by the views promulgated by the Diocese of Sydney, is one that would shock most thinking Australians if they understood its full significance. Though their literature frequently uses pictorial representations of attractive, assured young contemporary women, looking no different from the best of their generation – as a quick glance most days at the Sydney Anglican website will reveal[53] – they actually promote a very different form of womanhood. From their various statements about marriage, family and career options for women – without even mentioning ordination – a composite picture can easily be assembled. The ideal woman in Sydney Anglican rhetoric is a submissive, obedient[54] wife who dedicates herself to her (dominant) husband and their children, and whose personal and working life is restricted to enable that dedication to be fully exercised. In her spare time, she is active in her church, but in a subordinate role of ministry with or to other women and children. Divorce is not an acceptable option. Replace the current graphic representations with nineteenth-century women in bonnets and gloves, and the end result would still be the same. Twenty-first century Sydney Anglican women are in essence no different to the respectable matrons of an earlier age, despite their right to vote, open bank accounts and have an independent legal identity. It goes without saying that Sydney Anglican women must not live in a de facto relationship, and they certainly need to be heterosexual; women who identify as lesbians, and particularly lesbians who seek to have children by in vitro fertilization, are well beyond the pale. (De facto relationships and lesbian partnerships are officially unacceptable in all other Anglican dioceses, but in grassroots parish life in those dioceses, they are often quietly accepted.)

Overall, the Sydney position is a complete rejection of almost all the gains in terms of female choice and autonomy that the various stages of the women's

---

[52] Ronald J. Snider, 'The Scandal of the Evangelical Conscience: Why Don't Christians Live What They Preach?', *Christianity Today*, 11(1), January/February 2005.

[53] http://www.sydneyanglicans.net/.

[54] During the 1995 General Synod debate about *A Prayer Book for Australia*, Sydney representatives tried to add a version of the old vow of obedience for wives in the two forms of the marriage service. This was strongly resisted, but they were successful in having the requirement that wives promise to 'honour' their husbands added to the more conservative version: *A Prayer Book for Australia* (Sydney: Broughton Books, 1995), p. 649.

movement have achieved over the past 150 years. The only real difference between the twenty-first century woman and her nineteenth-century great-grandmother is that the current Sydney Anglican leaders do not want to deny women education, suffrage, or legal and financial equality with men.

The model of conservative womanhood promoted by Sydney is, then, a great deal wider than merely the denial of ordination. This is something that is not readily apparent even to other Australian Anglicans used to Sydney's opposition on the issue of women priests and bishops. The arcane theological rhetoric about male 'headship' seems to imply that this is about internal church order only, but as we have seen, that is far from the case. Sydney's opposition is significantly different to that of traditionalist Anglo-Catholics and Roman Catholics, whose arguments are based on particular interpretations of Jesus' intentions in choosing 12 male apostles, and supposedly sharing his Last Supper with males only.[55] Those arguments are clearly restricted to church practice, and have little if any immediate significance for marriage and family life, let alone female participation in society. This is not to deny that many traditionalists have deeply misogynist views, but they do not promote a cohesive and comprehensive theology of female subordination in the same way that Sydney has.

I need to state clearly here that I am not opposed to marriage and motherhood. Too readily, my concerns about conservative attitudes to women and the family are interpreted as an attack on marriage per se. I have in the past been caricatured as a proponent of sexual licence and promiscuity. The reality is that I am a conventional middle-class homebody who has been happily married (to an Anglican priest) for close to four decades. We have two adult children, and a grandson. Our family life is deeply precious to me, and is in fact of first importance in my life. Nevertheless, I acknowledge that conventional heterosexual marriage is not either available to or suitable for many others, and consequently believe the church should openly support other forms of loving, monogamous committed relationships such as same-sex partnerships.

If the denial of full equality to women in the church is Sydney Diocese's 'great cause', then the full equality of women in church leadership at every level is *my* 'great cause', a Gospel imperative that I believe cannot be denied. As a deeply committed Christian who honours the authority of Scripture every bit as much as Sydney Anglicans do, I believe my views on women's role to be entirely consonant with both the biblical witness and the development of church tradition, as I have argued on many occasions and most fully in an earlier publication.[56] It is a cause to which I have been committed for more than 25 years.

---

[55] See Judi Fisher and Janet Wood (eds), *A Place at the Table: Women at the Last Supper* (Melbourne: Joint Board of Christian Education, 1993) for a discussion of the likelihood that women were present at the Last Supper.

[56] Muriel Porter, *Women in the Church*.

Chapter 7
Current Challenges

The Mission

For almost a decade, Sydney Diocese has been consumed by its grand 'Mission', a project to have at least 10 per cent of Sydney's population worshipping in 'Bible-believing' churches by 2012. The Mission, signalled by Archbishop Peter Jensen almost immediately he became archbishop in 2001 and formally adopted by the Synod the following year, is a telling symbol of what the diocese now stands for, and of its underlying ideology.

The Mission is staggeringly ambitious, given that 10 per cent of Sydneysiders represents about 400,000 people. If the Mission achieved its goal, at least another 300,000 people would have been attracted into church membership in just a few short years, if the most optimistic current membership estimates are correct. In 2002 Peter Jensen estimated that 1.5 per cent of Sydney's population – 60,000 people – were attending Anglican churches at that stage, a rather generous figure given that just a year earlier the National Church Life Survey had put Sydney Anglican attendance at 52,000. He added an estimated 40,000 Sydneysiders already attending other 'Bible-believing' churches to provide an overall attendance of 100,000 at the start of the Mission.[1] An attendance projection carried out in 2004 indicated that the Anglican attendance rate would have to reach 230,000 to fulfil the 10 per cent goal.[2]

However, despite some initial growth in the first years of the Mission project, attendance figures quickly stabilized, showing just 0.5 per cent growth between 2004 and 2007, with the attendance figure hovering just below 57,000 in 2006.[3] In 2010, two years before the deadline set back in 2002, though a growth of 5,000 worshippers between 2001 and 2006 is welcome, there is nothing like the attendance growth so eagerly sought when the Mission was established. In his 2010 Presidential Address to Sydney Synod, Archbishop Jensen claimed that 2009 had seen numerical growth, perhaps of as much as 5 per cent, through the efforts of the most recent of the Mission's programmes, 'Connect 09'. He was cautious about the

---

[1] These figures were quoted by Peter Jensen in his Presidential Address to Sydney Synod, 14 October 2002.

[2] Attendance projection by National Church Life Survey and Anglicare, based on 2001 Census figures, reported in 'The Diocesan Mission – Midpoint Report; Achievements and Challenges in Becoming a Missional Diocese', report presented to Sydney Synod 2008, p. 18.

[3] 'The Diocesan Mission – Midpoint Report' p. 8; National Church Life Survey 2006.

figure, stressing that it 'may be approximate', but nevertheless commenting that 'to grow by anything like that percentage is sensational'. He gave no indication of where the figure came from, though the diocesan newspaper subsequently said the figure came from parish returns. Recommending that the figure should be treated with caution, the newspaper nevertheless suggested that there were now more that 76,000 'regular members'.[4] The final report of the Connect 09 programme, printed in the Synod report from the Sydney Standing Committee,[5] made no such claim. It was much more cautious: there is evidence, it said, 'of new contact being made with churches by members of the wider community, of some people visiting or joining congregations and *even some becoming Christians or church members*. This ... has been on a small scale in most parishes ...' (emphasis added).

According to the most recent census in 2006, Anglicans account for about 19 per cent of the Australian population. That represents a huge erosion of Anglican influence on Australian society. In 1881, 55 per cent of Australians identified themselves as Anglicans. From 1901 until the end of World War II, Anglicans had stabilized at about 40 per cent of the population, a reflection of the predominantly British migration patterns that still prevailed at the time. The Anglican Church – officially called the Church of England in Australia until 1981 – was still the dominant Australian church, as it had been since the beginning of white settlement. Never formally linked to the state in the way its mother Church of England still is in Britain, it nevertheless enjoyed considerable cachet as the sovereign's church, the church of the 'Establishment'. But that is no longer the case. By 1981, when its name changed, the percentage of Anglicans had dropped to a third and by 2001, the proportion was just under 21 per cent. Post-war immigration from Catholic countries was the main cause of this dramatic shift, with the Catholic Church overtaking the Anglican Church as the largest church by the mid-1980s. Today the Catholic Church accounts for almost 26 per cent of the population.[6] (The fastest growing Christian group in Australia are the Pentecostals. They are still only a tiny proportion of the Australian population at just over 1 per cent, but by 2006 they had grown to 220,000 adherents from 160,000 in 2001.) In 2006, 20 per cent of Australian Anglicans lived in Sydney, while 12 per cent of them lived in Melbourne. Secularization has been a bigger factor in reducing church affiliation than competition between Christian churches or even other faiths. Between 1971 and 2006, the proportion of people who stated 'No Religion' on census forms increased from 6.7 per cent of the population to 19 per cent. Most of these people

---

[4] *Southern Cross*, November 2010. Parish returns, which are self-reported, are never as reliable as professional surveys.

[5] 'Connect 09: (A Final Report from the Connect 09 Management Committee)', Supplementary Report of Standing Committee and Other Reports and Papers to Sydney Synod 2010.

[6] Tricia Blombery, *The Anglicans in Australia* (Canberra: Australian Government Publishing Service, 1996) p. 44f.

are from the younger generation. The Anglican Church has an older age profile than the general population, and about two-thirds of worshippers are women.

Religious identification does not translate into significant church attendance. Attendance figures reveal how marginal the institutional churches have become to Australian life. National Church Life Survey statistics for 2001 – the most comprehensive available – showed that just 8 per cent of Australians attended church weekly, half of them Catholics. But the Catholic Church has little cause for celebration – Mass attendance dropped by 13 per cent over the five years from 1996 to 2001. For Anglicans, though, the situation is undeniably serious. Fewer than 5 per cent of those who identified as Anglicans in the national census actually attended church on a weekly basis.

A few decades ago, if nominal Anglicans rarely darkened a church door on a Sunday morning or even for the major festivals of Christmas and Easter, they still had contact through rites of passage. They married in an Anglican church, had their babies baptized there, and made their last earthly journey through an Anglican church door. But that has changed dramatically since the Australian Federal Government licensed private marriage celebrants in 1973. Before then, 86 per cent of Australian marriages were celebrated with some form of religious rite. By 1993, this had fallen to 58 per cent,[7] and by 2007, just 37 per cent of marriages were celebrated in church. Seventy-seven percent of bridal couples had lived together before marriage.[8] About a third of Australians will never marry, however, with most of them choosing to live in de facto relationships. So fewer and fewer nominal Anglicans have even the minimal contact with the church that church weddings provided. And if they do not marry in church, then they are even less likely to bother about baptism for their children; besides, civil celebrants now offer naming ceremonies. Funerals are now the only rite of passage that significant numbers of Australians observe in church, and with funeral parlours and civil celebrants increasingly taking over this area as well, the implications for institutional religion are serious.

With Australia's divorce rate now about 45 per cent, there is far greater fluidity in Australian society than was the case up until the 1970s. Together with the rising rate of long-term female employment, the changes to marriage and cohabitation have resulted in a birth rate that until recently was plummeting.[9] All of this has huge implications for Christian churches that have, ironically, over the past four decades intensified their focus on the nuclear family. Partly in response to changing patterns of family life, but mainly in an ill-considered reaction from

---

[7] http://www.abs.gov.au/AUSSTATS/abs@.nsf/2f762f95845417aeca25706c00834efa/5bc01a9fba727452ca2570ec00787e6f!OpenDocument.

[8] http://www.abs.gov.au/ausstats/abs@.nsf/mf/3306.0.55.001.

[9] These changes have been explored in detail by Hugh Mackay in 'Australia at the Turning Point', an address he gave to the NSW Council of Churches forum in Sydney on 4 June 2002 and in 'Social Disengagement: A Breeding Ground for Fundamentalism', the Annual Manning Clark Lecture, Canberra, 3 March 2005.

more controversial issues of societal change, they have exalted the nuclear family into the pinnacle of religious respectability. This 'secular Australia', where the Anglican Church is no longer the dominant Christian denomination and where religious observance of any kind is an increasingly minority activity, is the context into which Archbishop Jensen launched his ambitious Mission.

The Mission's primary strategy was to 'multiply fellowships', that is, to create as many as a thousand new church congregations of varying sizes and styles to accommodate the hundreds of thousands of Sydneysiders the Mission sought to engage. Halfway through the Mission decade, 136 new congregations had commenced (but up to 30 had closed in that time).[10] To staff these new congregations, it was estimated that additional pastoral workers – 1,000 full-time and up to 10,000 part-time – needed to be trained, with Sydney's Moore Theological College needing to expand so it could eventually train 1,000 students at a time. That would have required the college to more than triple in size, given that it had 305 students enrolled in 2005. But despite an initial growth spurt resulting in the largest enrolment ever in 2006, those figures too have stabilized at 350.[11] Seventy-four of those were ordination candidates in 2010. Probably just as well, as the college's earlier plans for physical expansion seem to have ground to a halt, partly because of the damage done to the diocesan finances during the global financial crisis.

The 'Bible-believing' churches Archbishop Jensen included in the Mission plan did not encompass the other two large mainstream denominations – the Catholic Church and the Uniting Church – or even any of the Orthodox churches, let alone the Pentecostals. Instead, they are smaller, reformed churches of a narrower kind, churches that 'owe their theological structure to the Reformation, and who thus see their fundamental authority in the great "scripture alone" of the Reformation', as Jensen explained.[12] These are churches that trace their lineage from the sixteenth-century break with the Roman Catholic Church, and/or whose theological basis is that the Bible – generally interpreted narrowly – is the only authority to which they are answerable. In other words, they owe no allegiance to church tradition, let alone to the hierarchical authority of a pope or other overarching leader. In practice, this means the churches that belong, with Sydney, to the conservative, Protestant NSW Council of Churches – the Baptist Union of NSW, Churches

---

[10] Connect 09 final report; *Southern Cross*, November 2008.

[11] In 2010, the total student enrolment at Moore College was 350: Judy Adamson, 'Theological Training Flourishes', 18 February 2010, http://www.sydneyanglicans.net/news/stories/theological_training_flourishes/; John Woodhouse, 'Moore College Confronts Turbulent Future', 27 April 2009, http://www.sydneyanglicans.net/ministry/churchlife/moore_college_confronts_turbulent_future/.

[12] Presidential Address 2002.

of Christ, the Christian Reformed Church, the Fellowship of Congregational Churches, the Presbyterian Church[13] and the Salvation Army.[14]

Christianity has always been a missionary religion, committed to spreading the 'Good News' (gospel) of Jesus Christ as required in the writings of the New Testament. St Matthew's Gospel ends by portraying Jesus commanding his disciples to 'Go therefore and make disciples of all nations'.[15] The origin of the term 'Evangelical' – to evangelize – reflects its missionary priority. But this restriction of the Mission's planned converts to a select group of Protestant churches is the key to understanding the purpose of the Mission and provides a powerful indicator of the primary theological motivation behind Sydney's attitudes and behaviour. Put starkly, Sydney Diocese wants to bring 400,000 people into certain Protestant churches because they offer the only kind of Christianity that Sydney Anglicans believe is acceptable, rather than the 'suspect' teachings they would encounter in the Catholic or Uniting churches, for instance. Peter Jensen has said the real goal should be 100 per cent of Sydneysiders,[16] and while he knows this is impossible, the very suggestion is proof that to Jensen and his supporters, anyone who does not accept the Christian Gospel on their very specific terms is not really Christian.

In terms of their theological understanding, there is no uncertainty or humility in the Sydney mindset. They are utterly dogmatic about their religious convictions, and brook no challenge. No mainstream church member would have any problem with a whole-hearted desire and commitment to evangelize the people of Sydney and draw them to the God of love. It is an entirely worthy agenda and one that most Christians would believe is commanded by the Gospel. But the Sydney evangelization plan suggests that people can only be 'real' Christians if they conform to the strict theological principles these acceptable churches espouse. It is also seriously anti-ecumenical, a strange phenomenon in the twenty-first century after more than half a century of intense activity among Christian churches around the world towards greater understanding and mutual respect, if not outright reunion.

---

[13] The Presbyterian Church in Australia is a small, deeply conservative church, comprising those minority Presbyterians who refused to follow the rest of the denomination into partnership with the Methodist and Congregational Churches as the Uniting Church in Australia, formed in 1977.

[14] The NSW Council of Churches should not be confused with the NSW Ecumenical Council, to which all the other NSW Anglican dioceses belong, along with the Catholic Church, the various Orthodox churches, the Quakers and the Uniting Church, reflecting the mainstream spectrum of Christian denominations.

[15] Matthew 28:19 (NRSV).

[16] Peter Jensen, *Christ's Gospel to the Nations: The Heart and Mind of Evangelicalism Past, Present and Future* (London: The Latimer Trust, 2003), p. 43, cited in Chris McGillion, *The Chosen Ones: The Politics of Salvation in the Anglican Church* (Sydney: Allen & Unwin, 2005), p. xii.

Outlining in detail the rationale for the Mission in his 2002 Synod Address, Jensen referred to those outside Bible-believing churches as 'the lost'. They are condemned to a 'miserable' fate, he said, explaining that nothing is more important for them than 'their need to know Christ and be saved from the wrath to come'. That is why the diocese needed to focus on this programme at all costs and above all other priorities, because it was focused on what he proclaimed to be the number one human priority. Other churches which did not accept this priority and the theological position driving it were plainly wrong, according to Jensen.

Four years into the Mission project, Archbishop Jensen had to acknowledge that all was not well. In his 2006 address to the annual meeting of Sydney Synod, he signalled that there was a level of disappointment and fatigue with the Mission, particularly among parish clergy. He said that he was not surprised that the diocese was finding the Mission 'rugged work and sometimes dispiriting'. While the Mission had forced 'positive changes in parishes and organisations', there had also been 'a tendency towards timidity and passivity, sometimes even selfishness and sloth', he said. 'Many of our clergy are tired and some are a little dispirited … The evangelisation of the world, starting with Sydney has proved harder than we imagined!'

Several times in the lengthy address, Dr Jensen returned to the need for better, more energetic leadership, particularly from parish clergy, some of whom were 'still acting as though they are only congregational leaders rather than missional leaders'. But passivity in congregations and a resistance to change was one reason for clergy tiredness, he added.[17] When the 2006 Census figures were released the following year, they revealed a 10.5 per cent drop in the number of nominal Anglicans in Sydney since the 2001 Census. This was more than the 9 per cent drop recorded in Melbourne, where there was no specific mission underway. The cold reality was that the Sydney Mission was having little effect. By the time the diocese released its 'Strategic Directions 2010–2012' document in 2009, the initial concrete goal of at least 10 per cent of the Sydney population in Bible-believing churches in a decade had been softened. It was spoken of as a rhetorical device to 'fix our eyes beyond the church community … into the mission field around us'. The decade time span had become 'an attempt to create a sense of measured urgency which will lead to change'. The report continues: 'The decade as such is less important than the sense that time is passing and the challenges before us remain. Without it we are too inclined to accept the status quo.'[18]

Anecdotal evidence suggests Jensen was right when he spoke about clergy disillusionment in 2006, but perhaps not just because of 'passivity and resistance to change'. Some clergy are tired and disillusioned because of the nature of the Mission itself. One such cleric is Philip Bradford, rector of a Sydney 'stole' parish and currently president of 'Anglicans Together', an association of stole church people and parishes who lobby for a more open, inclusive and welcoming diocese.

---

[17] Peter Jensen, Presidential Address to Synod, 16 October 2006.

[18] 'The Diocesan Mission: Strategic Directions 2010–2012', pp. 15–16.

While praising evangelism in general, Mr Bradford has written that the mission has also had its down side:

> The emphasis on numerical growth has led to considerable discouragement and even depression among some clergy. I have no statistical evidence for this but plenty of anecdotal evidence from conversation with other ministers. Many clergy feel pressured to perform and to keep the statistics favourable. If one's congregation is not growing significantly then the temptation is to feel that you are failing, or not working hard enough.

He recalls leaving a meeting related to the Mission and hearing one minister remark, 'How much more do they expect us to do?' He commented: 'We have forgotten that God calls us to be faithful, but not necessarily successful.' He continued:

> I believe we have become so focused on evangelism that we have neglected the spiritual growth of our congregations and in particular their pastoral needs. We have been so busy planning the next big evangelistic outreach that we have neglected the sick, the lonely and the marginalized in our congregations.[19]

The 'midpoint report' on the Mission presented to Synod in 2008 hints at a lack of real commitment to the Mission priorities as a major reason why not much has been achieved to date. Bishop Peter Tasker, the author of the report, wrote that 'through all this we are praying for the Holy Spirit to lead a mind-change or paradigm-shift in all our members so that many more of us will be filled with a sacrificial compassion for the lost in all the world and become active in mission'.[20] The need for a mind-change is urgent, he insists; 'not enough parishes are planting congregations, particularly new missional congregations'; and while there has been growth in student numbers at Moore College, there is 'significant concern' that 'a relatively low number of students have the special aptitudes and opportunities to be church planters'.[21] Clearly the Mission was not working as hoped.

With the emphasis on clergy activity not producing the kind of results expected, the Mission changed its focus onto the laity, and onto 'missional church planting'; that is, entirely new church plants rather than splitting existing congregations. For the laity, it established the 'Connect 09' programme, to begin in 2009, described by Archbishop Jensen as 'a co-ordinated campaign by all Sydney Anglicans to pray for and personally contact every resident in our Diocese with the word of God, in such a way that that person may connect with us and with the Lord Jesus'.[22] Again, the programme was breathtakingly ambitious in its scope. The mind boggles at the

---

[19] *Anglicans Together* newsletter, no. 41, March 2010.
[20] 'The Diocesan Mission – Midpoint Report', p. 2.
[21] Ibid., pp. 4, 8, 11.
[22] Peter Jensen, Presidential Address to Sydney Synod 2008.

prospect of every worshipping Anglican in Sydney engaging individually in this missionary activity to four and a half million people. Not to mention that 80 per cent of Sydney residents are not Anglicans and many of them would already have other faith commitments, Christian and non-Christian.

Archbishop Jensen explained that Connect 09 was 'a revolutionary campaign, not a program; a spiritual movement rather than a planned event'. It would rely on local people 'wanting to serve Jesus'. It was 'a prayer campaign first and foremost, prayer for the world we live in, prayer for our community', calling people to 'pray street by street, suburb by suburb, people group by people group'. Friendship evangelism and multiplying churches remained integral to the Mission, but Connect 09 'calls on us to drastically expand the circle of our friends and neighbours'. One of the elements of the campaign was to reconnect with the parishes, that is, the geographic communities in which churches were set, because 'the parish is our mission field'. Another was to train lay people for this role: 'there is frustration by church members over a lack of opportunities for leadership by lay Christians'. It was to involve visiting people in their own homes.[23] One of the advantages of this campaign was that, though it required substantial commitment and was expected to have far-reaching effects, it did not require significant central funding.[24] This would be important when the impact of some unwise speculative investments hit the diocese's funding hard in the global financial crisis. For the church-planting initiative, a Sydney assistant bishop was moved out of his region to develop a programme.

Financial Problems

The Mission, particularly in its church-planting strategies, was always going to be expensive. Sufficient clergy and laity had to be trained for their new roles, and that meant a substantial increase in the costs of theological education. Then the church planters and other workers had to be paid, as did the overseers of this vast enterprise. And more buildings would be needed, either to build or lease, to house those tens of thousands of new churchgoers. Sydney Diocese has for decades been wealthy beyond the dreams of other Australian dioceses, mainly because of disciplined stewardship of its significant financial assets, themselves the result of shrewd management in the 1960s of its colonial land grants, as we have seen. But the demands of the Mission required even more income than Sydney had at its disposal through the normal budgetary processes. So in the early years of the twenty-first century when conditions on the stock market looked good, the

---

[23] Presidential Address 2008.

[24] 'The Diocesan Mission: Strategic Directions 2010–2012', p. 10. However, a 2009 estimate was that Connect 09 would cost almost $1 million over the two years 2008–10, with much of that paid by parishes according to a pre-determined formula based on their net operating receipts.

diocese's money managers decided to do what many other entrepreneurs were doing – to borrow money to make more money. And like so many of the secular speculators, the 2008 global financial crisis dealt them a severe blow. They were hit so hard that not only was the projected major expansion no longer possible, but the whole diocesan structure had to be reduced dramatically.

In 2002, the year after Jensen came to office, the decision was made by the Glebe Administration Board, the body that manages the diocese's funds, to borrow money to invest in the share market. According to *The Australian Financial Review*, the Board 'switched from a conservative, debt-free investing policy to an aggressive strategy of leveraging holdings in local and international equities and property securities investments to try to reap bumper returns'.[25] In the early years, while the share market was booming, the new strategy paid off, bringing in greater than average returns. Between 2003 and 2009, the Board was able to distribute $35 million more than if there had been no gearing.[26] By December 2007, the net assets of the Diocesan Endowment stood at $265 million.[27] Income from the fund is apportioned by the Diocesan Synod, usually in accordance with the budget prepared by the all-powerful Sydney Standing Committee. This budget pays for most of the diocese's grants to its regions, its media arm, its grants to theological education and for the training of youth leaders, its financial commitment to the national and international church (when Synod agrees to meet those commitments), grants outside the diocese and a host of other activities. (The core administrative activities are funded out of a separate fund, the Endowment of the See.) But already by 2005, the level of debt for the borrowing was $150 million, owed to two major Australian banks, Westpac and ANZ.[28]

Then came the global financial crisis. By December 2008, the net assets had shrunk to $105 million. The fund had lost $160 million. In November 2008 the Board had sold $100 million of growth assets, and all bank debt was repaid.[29] By that stage the Board had been in breach of bank covenants, but apparently the banks had not demanded repayment of their funds.[30] Rather than renegotiate with the banks, the Board decided to sell at the bottom of the market. It had done something similar nearly 20 years earlier when, in the 1990s recession, it lost more than $100 million when it sold its investments in Sydney property at a low ebb in the market, and transferred what was left into the stock exchange.[31]

---

[25] *The Australian Financial Review*, 15 October 2009.

[26] The Glebe Administration Board annual report 2009, reported in *The Australian Financial Review*, 15 October 2009.

[27] *The Australian Financial Review*, 15 October 2009.

[28] Ibid.

[29] Ibid.

[30] Ibid. and David Marr, 'Anglican Business', *The Monthly*, December 2009–January 2010, p. 10.

[31] *The Australian Financial Review*, 15 October 2009.

The impact on the diocese of the 2008 debacle was huge. Instead of providing the expected $10 million or more per year to the diocese, the Board would now be able to provide only about half that amount. It has meant cutting ministries and programmes funded by the Synod by an average of 50 per cent. However, the impact would be actually much higher, because the second main fund in Sydney Diocese had also been hit. The Endowment of the See funds the stipends, allowances, superannuation, long service leave, housing and office costs of the Archbishop, Assistant Bishops, the Registrar and Archdeacons and the salaries of the registry staff. It has also been funding the stipend, allowances, superannuation, long service leave and housing costs of the Dean, an arrangement currently under review.[32]

This fund, instead of providing between $4 million and $5 million per year, was expected, in 2009, to be providing about half that amount,[33] because presumably it also suffered a heavy loss of assets under the same share sellout decisions undertaken by the Glebe Administration Board. It was hard to know, because this fund is not answerable to Synod. It is overseen by a small committee comprising the Archbishop, three persons appointed by him and three persons appointed by the Standing Committee. If gearing was also used for the Endowment of the See fund, the total losses in 2008 were a good deal higher than $160 million. Some have suggested the total figure was probably closer to $200 million or perhaps even more. As a consequence of the losses sustained by both funds, the diocese had moved from an annual income from investments of about $15 million to about $7.5 million. This meant that the core administrative work of the diocese, as well as its other programmes, faced savage cuts, resulting in a large-scale restructuring programme, about which we will say more. But in late 2010, it became apparent that the situation was far, far worse. The Archbishop told the 2010 Synod that the diocese would have little more than half the expected $7.5 million in future years, because of the worsening situation facing the Endowment of the See fund.

First, a look at the situation in 2009, when $7.5 million a year seemed to be as bad as it would get. This was half of the usual amount for funding the operations of the diocese. With the diocese's budget so directly impacted, such large-scale losses were obviously of concern to Sydney clergy and the lay members of Sydney Synod. The first most of them learnt of the scale of the losses, however, was when the Archbishop wrote to all clergy in June 2009, seven months after the crisis sale. His one and a half page letter was vague, making no mention of the amount of money involved. Nor did he blame the strategy of the Glebe Administration Board for the losses. Instead, it seemed from the letter as if the global financial crisis was the entire reason for the losses. Archbishop Jensen admitted that money had been borrowed for investment, and that this strategy had accentuated losses as the market fell at the end of 2008. 'As a result, our investments have fallen by more

---

[32] From the 2009 Report of the Sydney Synod Standing Committee.
[33] http://www.sds.asn.au/assets/Documents/synod/Synod2009/Synod%202009%20Q%20and%20A.full.separate%20pages.pdf.

than half and the distribution of money from our investments has been cut by 50 per cent', he wrote. There would be pre-synod briefings for Synod members when more detail would be available, he continued, before asking people to 'respond in prayer'.[34]

The pre-synod briefings, however, were not satisfactory to all Synod members. According to one account, those attending were told there was no need to take notes, as detailed material would be sent out later. In the event, it was not. Synod members had to wait until three weeks before the October Synod meeting to receive the financial reports.[35] Anecdotal evidence suggests numerous Synod members were not merely concerned at what they learnt, but angry as well. Only a handful of members, however – mainly from stole parishes – asked public questions and tried (unsuccessfully) to move motions or amendments on the subject during the Synod. The acquiescence of the rest of the Synod in what seemed like a pietistic whitewash of a grave financial situation is testimony to the trust the vast majority of the parishes they represent have placed in their diocesan leaders.

Archbishop Jensen's address to the 2009 Synod was a tour de force. It was a masterpiece of communication strategy, indirectly answering critics and forestalling other criticisms through a persuasive personal and theological reflection. One such early criticism that had emerged was why Synod members and clergy had been kept in the dark for so long. He provided an answer: he himself had not realized what was happening, he suggested. He said: 'It was in November [2008] that I got the first inkling of the magnitude of what had happened to our investments. Each successive month seemed to bring worse news. It has taken a long time to grasp and begin to see the implications of it.' And then, he told Synod, he was cast into emotional turmoil: as the extent of the losses had became apparent, he had progressed through emotions of disbelief, a sense of responsibility, disappointment, doubt, grief and uncertainty. 'My memory is that the full implications were not clear until about May [2009]', he said.

Was the high-risk gearing strategy ethical, given that the Endowment Fund in common with most other churches' investment activities was committed to ethical borrowing? (Churches routinely require their investment arms not to invest in companies linked to alcohol and gambling, for example.) No, it was not ethically dubious, he said, claiming he had 'had to have an argument' with himself to come to that conclusion. But whether he believed the strategy had been unethical or not, it was apparent that the Archbishop had been badly shaken by the losses.

Rather than raise questions about the way the fund had been handled or where blame might be sheeted home, Dr Jensen diverted Synod into a theological discussion – always a good move for a diocese that prides itself on being theologically driven. The question Dr Jensen was interested in was what God might be teaching the diocese through the loss: Was the Lord chastising the Diocese for its sins – the sin of arrogance, or the bishops' attendance at GAFCON

---

[34] Peter Jensen, 'Letter to All Clergy and Curates-in-charge', 4 June 2009.
[35] 'Diocesan Finances Watch', *Anglicans Together Newsletter*, 41, March 2010.

(instead of attending the 2008 Lambeth Conference)? Was God 'seeking to test us'? Was God 'seeking to stop us doing something which is right in itself but not in accordance with his secret will'? Or was God 'challenging our faith, to rely on him more boldly for our finances?' 'Certainly, it is a serious warning to us about what the Scriptures call "the uncertainty of riches"', Dr Jensen said.

Asking where the diocese would be in 50 years' time, he warned that there was the possibility that it would survive only as a 'small but wealthy cult'. Pentecostalism, though attractive to some because of its capacity to 'attract some of the very people who are missing from our churches' was not the answer: 'I judge that its love affair with modern culture will leave it insufficiently tied to historic Christianity'. Only the diocese's 'commitment to conservative theology and to a high view of Scripture' would carry it forward, he said. Maintaining 'purity of doctrine' would be essential. For a diocese historically driven by the zealous pursuit of pure doctrine, this was the trump card.

In tune with the Archbishop's address, the Synod was presented with a lengthy motion couched in theological terms and expressing regret and disappointment rather than outrage or criticism. It began by invoking a curious agrarian, if biblical, metaphor for a diocese in a large, bustling metropolis:

> In light of the global financial crisis and recent large capital losses experienced by the Diocesan Endowment, Synod continues in thankfulness to and dependence on our Almighty God and Loving Heavenly Father, who owns the cattle on a thousand hills, is no man's debtor and knows our needs better than we know ourselves.

When the motion was finally passed, despite a vigorous debate, there were just a few amendments made. One removed the reference to the cattle on a thousand hills; another did at least name the investment strategies of the Glebe Administration Board as being the cause of the losses instead of just the general global financial crisis.

This final resolution was the gentlest of rebukes to those whose strategies had brought the proud diocese to its knees. The Board members had admitted their mistakes and expressed their regret at the losses, and the Synod regretted them as well, the resolution said. This was not the reckoning that media reports had expected,[36] or that a minority of Synod members believed was required. An amendment to censure the members of the Glebe Administration Board was rejected.

Behind the scenes, Board members had already faced a form of censure, however. Synod was told that four members of the Board had retired; the August 2009 meeting of the Standing Committee had reduced the Board size from 12 to eight. When the Standing Committee elected the eight members in December 2009, just four remained from the Board that had made such questionable decisions. The

---

[36] *The Australian Financial Review*, 15 October 2009 and 21 October 2009.

chairman of the Board, Phil Shirriff, a former chairman of ING Bank Australia, was one who left, to be replaced by Bruce Ballantine-Jones, a retired clergyman who is close to the Jensens and a long-term member of the Board. These changes came in response to an external review conducted by Cameron Ralph, an independent ratings agency. According to a progress report on the Board's responses to the review circulated to Synod members in May 2010, the review had recommended changes to the Board's processes in a number of areas – planning for Board renewal, clarifying the roles of Board and management, addressing Board culture, reviewing the format and content of Board papers, strengthening decision-making processes, revisiting the Board's committee structure and driving accountability.[37] Taken together, these suggest that nothing less than a wholesale restructuring of the Board's operation has been advised.

The Standing Committee report notes that, to date, there had been 'substantial implementation' of the various recommendations. It is interesting that one recommendation is yet to be implemented – a policy limiting the tenure of board members to nine years, with 12 for the chairman. The Standing Committee wanted an increased maximum term, and decisions have been deferred until a comprehensive review of tenure on all diocesan boards is completed. It is not hard to see why this matter seems to be proving difficult. A nine-year limitation would remove all four continuing Board members, one of whom has been a member for 20 years. The current chairman has been a member for 17 years.

One problem identified by the review was that the Board operated out of a 'culture of "forgiveness" instead of hard accountability'.[38] This is an intriguing flaw in the light of Sydney Diocese's harsh stance on moral issues and its uncompromising attitudes in so many areas generally. In church circles, Sydney Diocese is widely recognized as taking no prisoners in any of its relationships with the national church, for instance.

The halving of the diocese's investment income and therefore the Synod's income, resulted in an average 50 per cent cut in diocesan spending for the next few years.[39] This has involved a major diocesan restructure. In particular, funding for the five episcopal regions of the dioceses has been halved, with the full-time role of archdeacon removed from each region. Regional bishops have to share secretarial support. The retirement of one regional bishop and the appointment of another to head Evangelism Ministries, a diocesan body reshaped as a church-planting organization, allowed the number of regional bishops to be cut from five to three in the first instance, with a fourth bishop appointed in April 2010. The number of regions remains at five, with executive leadership provided by others in the fifth region. Ministry strategy, formally the responsibility of the regional

---

[37] 'Glebe Administration Board's Investment Management and Governance Processes: (A Progress Report from the Standing Committee to Synod Members)', 6 May 2010.

[38] David Marr, 'Anglican Business', *The Monthly*, December 2009–January 2010.

[39] The diocese also has some income from other trusts.

councils, has been devolved to 20 new mission districts, each headed by a parish rector with some additional financial support from the diocese. The funding to the Sydney Diocesan Secretariat has been significantly reduced.[40]

The biggest cuts in the budget have been to parish grants – cut by $2.9 million – and to Anglican Media, which has been cut by 45 per cent. Funding to Moore Theological College has been cut by 10 per cent. Cuts have also been made to the funding for St Andrew's Cathedral programmes. The funding for the Archbishop's role as honorary secretary of the GAFCON Primates' Council, and for the diocese's membership of the Fellowship of Confessing Anglicans, however, remains untouched. The overall budget line for 'Gospel work outside the Diocese' – which funds a host of interventions in other parts of Australia and the world – has been halved, and is projected to be reduced further.[41]

In developing the restructuring plans, the Standing Committee 'soundly rejected' the option of levying an assessment on parishes to fund diocesan expenditure, the means by which other Australian dioceses fund most of their income. 'The Diocesan Mission's fundamental principle of the parish as "the basic coalface of ... gospel outreach" is to be maintained', according to Peter Kell, the chair of the Mission Board Strategy Committee that developed the restructure plans.[42] (By the close of the 2010 Synod, this stand had had to be modified, with a small temporary assessment on the cards.) Sydney's parishes have a combined annual income of more than $70 million,[43] and they effectively have all that money at their disposal. Their Melbourne counterparts, by contrast, are required to pay an average of 17.5 per cent of their income to the diocese, which relies on parish assessments for almost half its annual budget.

Together with income from other trusts, Sydney Diocese's central budget for 2010 was $7,243,000, according to reports tabled at the 2009 Synod.[44] In future years, it was expected to be almost one million less (even less following the bad financial news revealed at the 2010 Synod). This does not include the income from the Endowment of the See fund, over which Synod has no control. If that fund had produced about $2.5 million as expected, then the overall budget for the diocese in 2010 was close to $10 million – $2.8 million above the budget for Melbourne

---

[40] http://www.sydneyanglicans.net/news/ozanalysis/faq_sydneys_radical_rebuild/; Linda Morris, 'Anglican Church Slashes Staff, Programs', *The Sydney Morning Herald*, 16 October 2009.

[41] Ibid.

[42] *Southern Cross*, September 2009. See also #31 in Synod Appropriations and Allocations Ordinance 2009 explanatory report.

[43] Linda Morris, 'Anglican Church Slashes Staff, Programs', *The Sydney Morning Herald*, 16 October 2009.

[44] 'Synod Appropriations and Allocations Ordinance 2009 Strategic Funding Allocations 2010–2012', Report of Standing Committee and Other Reports and Papers, p. 297.

Diocese.[45] Melbourne suffered some losses because of the drop in returns from the share market during the global financial crisis (not through a borrowing strategy, however), so its income is now almost $2 million less than in 2008. As Melbourne's budget is extremely tight, the comparison shows that Sydney, even before the latest bad news, could no longer be categorized as a hugely wealthy diocese, a major change from its situation in recent decades. And it calls into question its pervasive image as a highly professional operation in contrast to the necessarily amateurish flavour of other cash-strapped Australian dioceses. The evidence of the last two years suggests it was not, and perhaps never had been, as professional as it had seemed.

Worse was to come. Sydney Synod in 2010 was presented with an even more serious financial position. The bad news came during the Archbishop's Presidential Address, the first item on the Synod agenda. Though Archbishop Jensen began his address with a lengthy theological discussion on human nature leading to issues concerning imprisonment, euthanasia and then religious education in state schools, he was forced to devote most of his address to the diocese's worsening financial situation. All the hard work of the previous year's Synod, with its painful cutbacks, had been 'only the beginning', he told Synod. 'We are now seeing all the more clearly and painfully where things have gone wrong and where we need to renew as well as repair', he said. The diocese still had substantial assets, worth almost $200 million, but they were 'lazy assets' that were underperforming.

It was now apparent that even the 50 per cent cut in income that had been adopted the previous year was not enough, he said. Instead of $7.5 million, only about $4 million per year would now be available from the two major funds, the Diocesan Endowment and the Endowment of the See. One of the main reasons he identified for this significant shortfall was the loss of revenue from one of the principal assets of the Endowment of the See fund, St Andrew's House.

St Andrew's House is a 1970s multi-storey office block behind St Andrew's Cathedral. It houses the diocesan offices as well as the St Andrew's Cathedral School, but most of the building is let commercially, providing a revenue stream for the Endowment of the See and the Diocesan Endowment. St Andrew's House Corporation is owned 50 per cent by the Endowment of the See fund and 50 per cent by the Diocesan Endowment, through the Glebe Administration Board. But it seems the building has spelt trouble since its beginnings, when the Endowment of the See fund had to be drawn on to save the project when the builder went bankrupt. That money, meant to be a loan, was never repaid, instead giving the fund its interest in the building.

According to a report to Synod from a commission the Archbishop established to look into the structural and governance problems underlying the financial problems, the Endowment of the See fund had assets worth about $68 million. But

---

[45] Almost 50 per cent of Melbourne's income is from parish assessments. The rest is made up of money from investments – in 2010 just over $1 million – trust funds and various grants. Melbourne's capital base is estimated at about $22 million.

the actual annual cash yield from those assets – largely property – was just 0.4 per cent ($272,000). The St Andrew's House Corporation had been 'over-distributing' its cash flows to the two diocesan funds, the report said. 'As a result of such over-distribution, [St Andrew's House Corporation] does not have the financial means to bear the cost of refurbishment or to renegotiate the reletting of five office floors' that will soon be vacant. 'The only means for [the corporation] to bear these costs will be out of the next three years' rental cash flow', the report said. So neither of the two diocesan funds will receive any money from this asset for three years. The report continued that the costs of the diocesan services apart from the costs of the Archbishop – that is, primarily the costs of the regional bishops – have already been 'aggressively' reduced. The Synod, it suggests, should take responsibility for some of these services.[46]

The answer to an astute question at Synod revealed yet another reason why the Endowment of the See fund is not as strong as it should have been. Ten housing units built as a commercial venture for the fund, on a vacant block of land adjacent to the Archbishop's residence, Bishopscourt, in the premium Sydney suburb of Darling Point, had failed to deliver a hoped-for windfall. A feasibility study had suggested the project would deliver a profit of $7.5 million to the Endowment of the See fund. Instead, the project will result in a loss of $92,000, even if the remaining three unsold units are sold for a satisfactory price.[47] (Currently, two are let, while the third is now the home of a regional bishop.) Reasons given for this monumental loss of expected profit are: higher than expected construction costs, higher sale costs, and poor market conditions when the units were released for sale. A loss of this magnitude on dress circle Sydney real estate is hard to comprehend. The Archbishop's Commission's report recommends that the three unsold units be sold – though that will leave a regional bishop without a home.

Another reason for the loss of expected income was revealed in answer to another question posed during the Synod. The performance of the Australian shares asset class in the Diocesan Endowment's investment portfolio had underperformed the relevant benchmark on a year-to-date basis, the Archbishop said: 'There was a change in the investment manager for the Australian shares asset class in June 2010. The asset class has continued to underperform since that date and this is the subject of ongoing discussions with the new investment manager.'

Even to an untutored eye, it seems apparent that the Endowment of the See fund – for so long virtually a closed book to the Synod – has not been managed as well as it might have been. One speaker at the 2010 Synod claimed that the Fund had been spending more than it had been earning for 17 years. Nor has the Diocesan Endowment been managed too well. Certainly this was the view of the Archbishop

---

[46] 'Progress Report on the Work of the Archbishop's Strategic Commission on Structure, Funding and Governance (A Report from the Standing Committee)', Sydney Synod 2010.

[47] http://www.sds.asn.au/assets/Documents/synod/Synod2010/Questions2010.CombinedPostSynod.pdf.

in his explanation to Synod. The continuing losses had 'uncovered problems with the way in which we conduct our affairs and do our business', he said. In part, this was connected to the diocese's ethos of 'preserving the gospel ... in part at least through the wise governance of our Boards, Council and Institutions'. There was real danger in 'allowing our ministries to be taken over and re-directed by those who do not share this gospel outlook', he said. The Archbishop was not more explicit at this point, but he seemed perhaps to be referring to the ingrained Sydney habit of allowing only the most trusted of insiders to serve on its key committees. His subsequent comments seemed to bear this out:

> It is too easy for us when we put good people in place simply to leave them there for too long a period of time. In some cases, a lengthy period is excellent; it provides wisdom and continuity. But when a Board is old in service together, dangers emerge. Our volunteer status also means that we are sometimes too trusting of one another and not sufficiently acute in seeking accountability.

'Unconsidered and unhelpful relationships and habits' on church governance boards and committees had been allowed to endure, he said. Structures and lines of responsibility and accountability had not been properly worked out; change was now required.

These are extraordinary comments, considering that the boards and committees most responsible for this financial debacle are comprised of the most trusted insiders in the diocese – people trusted for their adherence to its central ideological stance and all part of the Jensen leadership team. Is it possible that the Archbishop was quietly accusing his insiders of letting him down, either by their own mismanagement or their failure to challenge others? Even so, Archbishop Jensen counselled against recrimination. At best it would end in delay and diversion of energy; at worst, it would 'see us tear one another up in an unseemly and ungodly way', he said.

One short-term remedy his commission recommended to the Standing Committee was the sale of Bishopscourt, the 1850s neo-gothic mansion that has been the home of Sydney's archbishops since 1911, now valued at about $24 million. It is a grand house on a large block of land in one of Sydney's most sought-after suburbs, and presumably would be a highly attractive 'trophy' home for a Sydney multi-millionaire. After providing a 'modest' replacement home for the Archbishop for about $8 million and other expenses, a sale would free up capital of about $15 million. This option had been explored on numerous occasions, and before Synod commenced, the sale possibility was mooted on the grounds that such a grand and imposing residence seemed unsuitable for a twenty-first century archbishop. However, Dr Jensen told Synod a sale now would be 'very opportune' given the need of the endowment fund 'for a healthier cash flow'.

The Standing Committee brought the sale proposal to Synod, presumably with the Archbishop's encouragement. His comments on the sale had been sufficiently ambiguous to allow him to save face whatever the Synod decided: he expressed his willingness and readiness to move if Synod wished, but also said that he and his wife had never regretted living there. Its suitability for entertaining, for hospitality, for meetings, and its proximity to the city, had made their tenure 'very fulfilling', he said. But if Synod did not agree to its sale, then it would have to consider 'how our ongoing work will be funded', he said, adding, 'No doubt there are ways, but they may not be as convenient as this'. Nevertheless, whichever way Synod decided, 'you know you have my very good will', he said.

However, although the sale proposal was strongly promoted by a key regional bishop, Robert Forsyth, the Synod decisively rejected the sale by 249 votes to 218 in a secret ballot. The vote came after a vigorous two-hour debate in which numerous speakers voiced concern about governance issues concerning the Endowment of the See fund. The Sydney Diocesan website report of the debate[48] commented that 'those against the sale argued that [Endowment of the See] governance structures are so flawed that they should be fixed before a sale is considered'. A Sydney rector with a background in business strongly argued that the governance problems had to be attended to. 'How can we put another $24 million into that slot?' the Revd Craig Roberts said. The last time the Endowment of the See fund had 'rolled the property dice', the apartment development on part of the Bishopscourt property, the return 'was nothing', he was reported as saying. 'Messing around with property is how the [Endowment of the See fund] got shot in the foot', he said. There were numerous similar speeches, as well as speeches claiming Bishopscourt was an important part of the diocese's mission. It provided a key point of connection with the city's 'movers and shakers', said one speaker. When heads of state and VIPs were invited to Bishopscourt, they came, said Dr Stephen Judd. The problem for the fund was not Bishopscourt, he pointed out, but its interest in St Andrew's House.

It was to the St Andrew's House investment that Synod turned after the sale proposal failed, voting to ask the Endowment of the See fund and the Archbishop's Commission to look into realizing its interest there. If that failed, then parishes would be levied a 1.14 per cent assessment for 2011 only. Subsequent commentary on the diocese's website[49] has revealed a level of dismay at the thought of the assessment, and scepticism that it will be for just the one year, even though at such a low level it is miniscule in comparison with the assessment levied as a matter of course on parishes in other dioceses. But Sydney Diocese has always proudly proclaimed that its parishes' resources are theirs to outlay entirely on their local mission activities, almost as an article of faith. Even a small, temporary assessment is seen as an assault on diocesan ideology.

After the Synod concluded, Archbishop Jensen released a lengthy statement,[50] thanking the Synod for its various decisions in what can only be termed rather florid

---

[48] http://www.sydneyanglicans.net/news/stories/bishopscourt/.

[49] http://www.sydneyanglicans.net/life/daytoday/bishopscourt_sentiment_triumphs_over_sense/.

[50] http://www.sydneyanglicans.net/images/uploads/Synod_Address_Oct_19.pdf.

language. Surprising as it is for an Archbishop to respond at all to one Synod vote, it is more surprising that it is so fulsome. The vote to retain Bishopscourt means that Synod is declaring it is 'in this city for the long haul', he said: 'We wish to remain connected. We recognise the very serious problems we have at this moment; in the long term we are confident we will overcome them.' He concluded: 'For myself, I am not daunted by these challenges. God is still on the throne. But my courage in facing them has been much strengthened by the Synod, its good humour and its good wisdom. I have nothing but thanks to you for your fellowship ....'

This extraordinary statement only makes sense if it is construed as coming from an Archbishop who saw himself as somewhat embattled. He might not have been keen to leave Bishopscourt personally – that view can certainly be read into his remarks in his presidential address – but surely the sale proposal came to Synod with his blessing. It is not feasible that the Standing Committee, which has always supported him, and the commission he himself appointed, would have brought the proposal against his express will. Bishop Robert Forsyth would not have moved the motion against the Archbishop's wishes. His lengthy comments about the sale in his presidential address certainly encouraged Synod to support the sale, though still leaving enough ambiguity to save his face if the proposal was refused. And yet, the Synod said 'no', and said so clearly, decisively and after so many frank speeches from people at the heart of the diocesan establishment. It would be a noteworthy result in any Australian diocesan synod, because synods by and large do not like opposing their archbishops and standing committees. They rarely do. For Sydney Synod to refuse this Archbishop, who has until now been so persuasive a guru, is nothing short of astonishing. Dr Jensen's extraordinary response simply confirms that assessment; it bears all the hallmarks of a leader fearful that he has lost his previously unassailable position.

The diocese's serious financial position must also weaken its influence in the rest of Australia and in the wider Anglican Communion considerably. That influence has been bolstered by Sydney's selective generosity; the answer provided to a Synod question revealed just how extensive that financial influence has been. The diocese has poured hundreds of thousands of dollars in recent years into small rural Australian dioceses that are effectively Sydney satellites; made significant donations to conservative Anglican dioceses overseas (in Mauritius, Nigeria, Uganda and Chile); and made significant donations to conservative international bodies, including $80,795 for the incorporation costs and website construction for GAFCON, $29,941 to the Alexandria School of Theology (a new, conservative college in Egypt), $30,000 to Anglican Mainstream (an international coalition of Anglican conservatives) and an unexplained $103,351 to 'visiting bishops and clergy'.[51] Presumably most of this money – well over one million dollars over five years to explicitly conservative places and causes – was distributed through the aegis of the Standing Committee's sub-committee for 'work outside the

---

[51] http://www.sds.asn.au/assets/Documents/synod/Synod2010/Questions2010.CombinedPostSynod.pdf.

diocese'. Clearly this largesse, which has supported so much of Sydney's local and international influence and furthered hardline conservative causes in the Anglican Communion, will now be well and truly over.

Theological Education

On the surface, all looks to be well with the steady flow of ordinands in Sydney Diocese. In recent years, as part of the Mission strategy, the number of deacons ordained has been significant, to much fanfare in diocesan publicity. In 2010, Sydney saw its largest ever ordination, when 56 were made deacon – 50 of them men. Contrast that with 13 deacons, of whom five were women, ordained in Melbourne in the same month, and the sheer weight of numbers in Sydney is telling. In 2006, 47 male deacons were ordained, in 2007 there were 46 deacons ordained (five women), in 2008 45 deacons (four were women) and in 2009, 33 (four women). This compares with 21 in 2005, 17 in 2004 and 30 in 2003.

The explosion in numbers reflects the significant change to ministry structure in the diocese as a result of the Mission. A permanent diaconate has now been created, designed for a range of different ministries, not just traditional curacies, providing church workers for the anticipated growth of church plants and the like. Parish youth workers are now being ordained, along with school and university chaplains, and the diocese is happy for women to be included in what is effectively a subordinate ministry, despite all the hype to the contrary. The women are, in the main, limited to ministry to other women and to children.

Even with 267 parishes, the Diocese would be hard pressed to find traditional curacy positions for all their deacons and certainly would not be able to provide enough positions as parish rector. So the new structure has severed priesthood from the diaconate. Only 16 men were ordained priest in 2009, for instance. Deacons going on to be 'Senior Ministers', as rectors are usually called in Sydney parlance, are now required to apply and undertake specialist additional training, a process that takes almost two years. They are not ordained priest until the need arises, with the newly-appointed rector of at least one Sydney parish being ordained priest in the same service as his induction to the parish.[52] This change means that parish curates and chaplains are no longer likely to be priests, partially explaining the need to introduce diaconal presidency formally, as happened in Sydney Synod in 2008. Just a few months before Sydney Synod made that momentous decision – explored in Chapter 5 – an article on the diocesan website revealed that a Communion 'drought' was in the offing:

---

[52] For example, the Revd Mike Paget was ordained priest during the same service in which he was inducted as rector of the inner Sydney parish of St Barnabas', Broadway: *Southern Cross*, August 2010.

> Under the new policy ministers will become priest when they are considered ready to take charge of a parish. Only the senior minister will be a priest/presbyter. The problem is that deacons can't 'do' Holy Communion. One church plant went a few years without the Lord's Supper as they had no priest/presbyter. Parishes with more than one site and simultaneous services will have real problems organizing Communion.[53]

The Diocese was 'on the horns of a dilemma' and needed 'to find a way to give deacons the power to do Communion' or go back to priesting clergy not in charge of parishes, the article said. The article also explains why priests in Sydney are now referred to as 'presbyters' and why terminology such as 'rector' has been replaced by 'minister', 'senior minister' and 'pastor'. The old titles have vanished in everyday use 'partly out of discomfort with the title "priest" which sort of implies that Jesus gets sacrificed again and also because the terms sound a bit antiquarian', it says. In fact, the word 'priest' has not simply vanished from everyday use; it has been deliberately replaced in Sydney Diocesan legislation and ordination services by the term 'presbyter' in response to a 2004 Synod resolution concerned that 'priest' in modern usage means 'a person who mediates between man and God'.[54] Another factor in separating priesthood from presidency at the Eucharist is doubtless to underscore the Sydney view that 'presbyters' are parish leaders first and foremost, rather than principally presiders over sacraments.

But though the ordination numbers look good, all is not plain sailing. The diocese's central training institute, Moore Theological College, the college that has been the powerhouse for creating the Sydney model, is under pressure and not just from its constrained inner-city site and reduced funding. As its principal himself has pointed out, it is facing difficulties from a range of external influences. In an address to students in 2009,[55] Dr John Woodhouse identified some of these problems, from the expectations of Generation Y students to the high academic standards Moore imposes. The 'changing expectations of the Christian life and visions for Christian ministry' of Generation Y students had brought pressure for changes that was 'unprecedented', Dr Woodhouse said. The 20-to-30-year-olds who should be considering coming to Moore believed the college was too hard, too academic. There were alarming reports that some were saying that 'to learn to preach you do not go to Moore College' and there was an 'equally disturbing assertion ... that Moore College will not prepare you for mission'. To scotch these specific criticisms, the college was reviewing its academic programme and trying

---

[53] John Sandeman, 'A Drought is Coming ... of Holy Communion', 7 July 2008, http://www.sydneyanglicans.net/archive/indepth/a_drought_is_coming/.

[54] Sydney Synod resolution 35/04; 'Use of the Word "Priest": (A Report from the Standing Committee)', 18 August 2006.

[55] Woodhouse, 'Moore College Confronts Turbulent Future'. This article was an abridged version of Dr Woodhouse's address to students on 20 March 2009.

to increase the college's presence in the church community, particularly among young people, he said.

Some of the criticisms of Moore College are no doubt coming from the pool of potential permanent deacons. As Phillip Jensen has explained (in his role as head of the diocese's Ministry Training and Development programme), permanent deacons 'may have lower levels of education, or a narrower range of gifts than are necessary to be a presbyter. They may be more specialized in their ministry and in their training.'[56] In other words, this new breed of deacons, who will become by far the largest number of ordained clergy in the diocese, no longer need the comprehensive, high-level academic training traditionally offered by Moore College.

The Influence of the New Calvinism

Perhaps the most disturbing factor facing the college (and probably the cause of some of the specific criticisms), was what Dr Woodhouse described as the influence of the 'new and powerful Christian movement from America ... sweeping the evangelical scene in this country – or so it seems'. 'Like many similar movements before it, it promises a great deal, is backed by massive enthusiasm and led by attractive and hugely gifted leaders', Dr Woodhouse said. 'This time, however, it involves definite views about theological education ... [and] quite definite ideas' about how we should be serving the cause of Christ. Presumably Dr Woodhouse was referring to the neo-Calvinism movement, which has had significant influence in Sydney Diocese.[57]

Evangelicals in Sydney and elsewhere have always looked to the sixteenth-century Geneva reformer John Calvin as a key inspirer. Now they are imbibing from the United States a hard-edged bombastic and ultra-conservative neo-Calvinism that could yet threaten Sydney's cohesion. A key proponent of the new thinking, Mark Driscoll, pastor of the Mars Hill Church, Seattle, is the central neo-Calvinist influence in Sydney through his powerful internet presence and his visit to the Diocese in 2008. On that visit Driscoll was described in *The Sydney Morning Herald* as 'God's motormouth', a Generation Y preacher 'spreading a testosterone-fuelled Christianity aimed squarely as a young, hip audience, mainly blokes'.[58] He is on record as deploring the 'chickification of the church' through the dominance of women.[59] The new Calvinism promotes a harsh theology, based

---

[56] 'Understanding Our Ordination Strategy', 16 March 2009, http://www.sydneyanglicans.net/news/stories/understanding_our_ordination_strategy.

[57] Woodhouse, 'Moore College Confronts Turbulent Future'.

[58] *The Sydney Morning Herald*, 23 August 2008.

[59] Brandon O'Brien, 'A Jesus for Real Men: What the New Masculinity Movement Gets Right and Wrong', *Christianity Today*, April 2008.

on a narrow interpretation of the doctrines of pre-destination and the sovereignty of God, unmediated by the other central teachings of classical Calvinism.

Neo-Calvinism's teaching is summarized in the acronym TULIP: T for total human depravity; U for unconditional election (that is, those predestined for eternal life by God were chosen arbitrarily, with no consideration of their own behaviour); L for limited atonement, limited to those predestined; I for irresistible grace (the Holy Spirit overcomes all human resistance in the elect); and P for perseverance of the saints (the elect remain faithful). This extremely limited overview of Christian teaching is based on a twentieth-century summary of a document originating in a Dutch Reformed Church controversy of the seventeenth century. Critics have claimed that TULIP is not a fair representation of the original: it misunderstands the doctrine of predestination and ignores key elements of the Reformed tradition (that Sydney claims to uphold). American theologian J. Todd Billings has written that the new Calvinists 'tend to obscure the fact that the Reformed tradition has a deeply catholic heritage, a Christ-centred sacramental practice and a wide-lens, kingdom vision for the Christian's vocation in the world'.[60] R. Scott Clark has claimed that if Driscoll presented himself for membership in Calvin's church in Geneva, he would be rejected because 'he doesn't believe the faith confessed by the church'.[61]

On his visit to Sydney in 2008, Driscoll gave a lecture, sponsored by the Diocese's Ministry Training and Development programme, to a packed St Andrew's Cathedral. He offered the 800 clergy and church workers who attended some harsh criticisms of the Australian church.[62] Australian Christian men were immature, lacking in entrepreneurial skills, and churches were not giving eager young men the opportunity to plant churches, he said. There were too many 'No. 2' guys in 'No. 1 slots', there was a tall poppy syndrome at work, and there was no great sense of urgency to create new services and new churches. The parish system was making church planting very difficult. Too many were so fearful of Pentecostalism they did not have a 'robust' theology of the Holy Spirit. The criticisms went on and on, but most of the problems he identified were claimed to be restricting talented young men from growing the church. Reading the report of the lecture, it seems as if it was all about young men. At a Sydney press conference he had said that evangelizing 'young men in cities' was where his heart was. No wonder young Sydney Anglican clergy have become devoted disciples of Driscoll.

---

[60] J. Todd Billings, 'Calvin's Comeback? The Irresistible Reformer', *The Christian Century*, 1 December 2009. See also R. Scott Clark, 'Calvinism Old and "New"', http://heidelblog.wordpress.com/2009/03/15/calvinism-old-and-new/.

[61] Scott Clark, 'Calvinism Old and "New"'.

[62] Natasha Percy, 'Driscoll: 18 "Obstacles to Effective Evangelism"', 4 September 2008, http://www.sydneyanglicans.net/news/insight/driscoll_18_obstacles_to_effective_evangelism/.

So much so that apparently 300 people told him they were keen to plant churches but were not being given the opportunity.[63]

Clearly Driscoll's visit and his stinging critique caused controversy among a number of Sydney Anglicans, so much so that the Sydney Anglican website canvassed a range of views on the subject. While each of the clergymen approached was complimentary about Driscoll, there was evidence of real concern behind the scenes.[64] Martin Morgan, from Rouse Hill Anglican Churches, perhaps signalled where some of the concerns originate when he commented that what he really valued about Driscoll's presentation was that 'he put church planting at the core of ministry'. While there is substantial lip service paid to church planting by the diocesan hierarchy, the reality is that church planting has potential risks for the diocese if it is not tightly controlled. If planted churches really take off, the fact that they are outside the parish structure means that they can easily become independent churches, in direct competition with the diocesan parishes in which they are planted. Worse, the plants could easily become affiliated with Driscoll's enterprise or even be planted by his outriders. This became apparent in an article in the diocesan newspaper *Southern Cross* which began: 'Sydney Anglicans' love affair with Mark Driscoll may cool after his mega-church in Seattle took a step towards becoming a worldwide denomination with the launch of Mars Hill Global ....'[65] Mars Hill Global is a worldwide church-planting strategy using media technology to create 'video campuses'. With so many keen young men in Sydney hanging on every Driscoll word, any Driscoll plant into Sydney via the internet would be direct competition for Sydney Anglicans.

Perhaps these concerns helped spur official Sydney involvement in the creation of a national church-planting network.[66] One of Sydney's assistant bishops, Al Stewart, briefly the regional bishop in Wollongong, is one of the key organizers of the network, called 'The Geneva Push' after Calvin's Geneva. This role is aligned to his formal diocesan role as head of the Diocese's Evangelism Ministries department, where his main duties are to encourage 'evangelistic church planting' across the diocese. He had served only three years as bishop in Wollongong before stepping aside to take up what seems primarily to be a church-planting role.

The Geneva Push claims to be non-denominational. Nevertheless, two of its three leaders have close Sydney links: Bishop Stewart, and Andrew Heard, the former Sydney clergyman now running a controversial Sydney-affiliated independent church in the neighbouring Diocese of Newcastle. The third, Mikey Lynch, is from the Australian Fellowship of Evangelical Students, which we have

---

[63] Joseph Smith, 'Driscoll's 300 Give West Sydney a Miss', 24 October 2008, http://www.sydneyanglicans.net/news/stories/300_avoid_driscolls_challenge/.

[64] Jeremy Halcrow, 'Driscoll's 18-point Critique: Sydney Responds', 29 September 2008, http://www.sydneyanglicans.net/news/stories/driscolls_18_point_critique_sydney_responds/.

[65] 'Driscoll's TV Churches Go Global', *Southern Cross*, June 2009.

[66] 'Big Planting Push Launched', *Southern Cross*, September 2009.

already noted is closely affiliated with Sydney Diocese. The network aims to 'to raise up a new generation of church planters dedicated to evangelising churches into existence across this great nation', according to its website,[67] and its activities include assessing and coaching potential church planters, as Driscoll's church-planting network does. Both Stewart and Lynch have attended a boot camp in Seattle run by 'Acts 29', Driscoll's network, which is apparently supporting The Geneva Push. Perhaps this local initiative will forestall any direct church planting in Sydney from the Driscoll operation, but the Driscoll influence could well yet undermine loyalty to the Sydney hierarchy on the part of keen young male clergy in the diocese. After all, didn't Driscoll have so many criticisms of the way Sydney goes about its operations?

The Succession Problem

The biggest challenge the diocese now faces is: who will be its leader when Peter Jensen retires in 2013? When Jensen, on the eve of his 58th birthday, was elected Archbishop in 2001, the retirement age for Sydney archbishops was 65, meaning he would have to step down in 2009. In 2003, the Sydney Standing Committee extended his appointment until he turned 70, bringing his retirement age into line with that of his predecessors and other Australian archbishops. The Standing Committee's annual report noted that 'we recognized the historical significance of the recently adopted Diocesan Mission and the critical importance of Archbishop Jensen's leadership to the Mission'. The report continued that 'the Diocesan Secretary informed parishes that our decision was taken without the Archbishop being present and without any request from him that this action be taken'.[68] In 2009 the diocese gave him even more leeway, making provision for an extension of up to six months should his retirement clash with the General Synod meeting expected round about that time. Even so, Archbishop Jensen will have to retire sometime in the second half of 2013.

It seems the succession is wide open. The key lay people and clergy who worked so hard for so long to see a Jensen elected to Sydney will be either the same age as the retiring archbishop, or older. They secured the Jensen ascendancy, but seem to have failed to secure the next stage. Any possible candidates among the ruling elite will also be of a similar age. As one senior Sydney layman told me, 'the party does not have a candidate'.

Unlike other Australian dioceses, which tend to elect leaders from outside, Sydney Diocese vastly prefers to elect from among its own. Its last 'outside' appointment, Hugh Gough was, from the perspective of the Sydney heartland, a disappointment. The main possibilities on the horizon at present are one of the Sydney regional bishops, Glenn Davies, who has taken a leading role in many

---

[67] http://www.thegenevapush.com/about/who_we_are.
[68] 2003 Report of the Standing Committee.

synodical and national debates, and a former Sydney priest, David Short. Glenn Davies will turn 63 in 2013, so that does not make him an immediately attractive prospect. David Short, son of a former Sydney regional bishop Ken Short, has earned great praise in his home diocese for the stand he has taken as rector of a major conservative Evangelical parish in the Diocese of New Westminster, Canada. His confrontation with his bishop over the issue of the blessing of same-sex relationships has made him something of a hero in Sydney Diocese, but the outcome of the Canadian struggle has left him deposed from holy orders. That would seem to rule him out of any ordained position in Australia, let alone as an archbishop. Sydney lawyers have already sought ways of overcoming that problem, but so far without success.

The *Australian Church Record*, an online publication chaired and edited by Moore College lecturers,[69] has begun promoting discussion of who might become Sydney's next archbishop. In articles written by its executive editor Peter Bolt,[70] it insists that Jensen's successor must be someone already within the diocese (that would cut out David Short), and must be no more than 57 at the time of his election (eliminating Glenn Davies). This might seem an arbitrary age, but it is the age Jensen was when elected, though only just, as he turned 58 the following month. A case is made for the need to have someone from a younger generation, who can give a decent period of service to the diocese. Anyone suspicious that there might be a political motive behind this stipulation would think that the editor is not very keen to see any of the long stayers in the current leadership take the top job. Bishop Glenn Davies would be out of the picture, as would assistant bishops Robert Forsyth (64 in 2013) and Ivan Lee (59 in 2013). Bishop Al Stewart, who stepped aside from Wollongong region to head up the church-planting enterprise, may be a contender at 54, but church planting seems to be viewed with some misgivings by the author of the articles. Stewart's successor as a regional bishop, Peter Hayward, is a possibility as he will be 54 in 2013. The article names just four possible contenders, none of whom are bishops. They are all lecturers at Moore College, each of whom will be close to or in their early 50s when the election happens.[71]

Whoever become the serious contenders to succeed Peter Jensen, they will not have the same cachet with the ruling elite of the diocese that made the Jensen ascendancy so inevitable. But then the powerbrokers themselves will be on the

---

[69] The *Australian Church Record* began in Sydney as an independent church newspaper in the nineteenth century. It had a reputation as a polemical vehicle to promote Sydney-style Evangelicalism. It had been defunct for some years when it was revived in 2004 as an online publication, closely aligned to Moore College.

[70] *Australian Church Record*, June and October 2010, http://www.australianchurchrecord.net/.

[71] Those named are Dr Bill Salier, Vice-Principal of Moore College; Archie Poulos, Head of the Ministry Department; Dr Andrew Shead, Head of the Old Testament Department; and Dr Mark Thompson, Head of Theology, Philosophy and Ethics.

way out, and their successors are yet to emerge. Nor will any contender have the same aura of entitlement that came ready-made with Peter Jensen, having been principal of Moore College for such a long and influential stint. Two of Jensen's three immediate predecessors came from the college's heartland. In a diocese where virtually all the clergy are the products of the one college, a long-term college principal will always have a strong following. The current principal, Jensen's successor and appointee John Woodhouse, will turn 64 in 2013, so he seems to be out of the question, at least as far as the *Australian Church Record* is concerned. The diocese's future leadership, then, is a grey area, where whoever succeeds Jensen inevitably will not be so well known as Jensen was, nor so readily have a diocese happy to eat out of his hand.

Conclusion
The End of the Experiment?

In my earlier critique of Sydney Diocese, published just a few years ago,[1] I commented that the diocese was on a roll, unified under the charismatic leadership of Peter Jensen and supremely confident in the company of its new-found international friends. Jensen's election as archbishop had symbolized the triumph of the radical conservative teaching of Broughton Knox, and its key elements were being swiftly and zealously implemented. The aborted sixteenth-century Puritan reformation was being reborn, this time as a lusty infant rapidly growing to full-strength Calvinism. The ambitious Mission to Sydney was up and running, and surely would deliver substantial growth, if not quite 10 per cent of the population in Bible-believing churches within the decade. Lay and diaconal presidency was high on the agenda, while women priests were as far off it as ever. A new strategy for clergy training and ordination was in hand. St Andrew's Cathedral was in the hands of an even more radical Jensen. The strategy to increase dramatically the diocese's already substantial financial resources was paying off. Sydney was being seen by elated conservative Evangelicals around the world as an alternative Canterbury. With the General Synod thwarted by the increasing Sydney representation and moderate voices all but silenced both in Sydney and in the national church, there seemed to be no real threat anywhere on the horizon. It must have seemed little short of the Second Coming, vindicating the years of plotting and planning by those who had worked for Jensen's election.

But in just a few years, the dream has begun to unravel, quite dramatically. I am told that there is a growing sense of disillusionment in Sydney. The Mission is struggling to make inroads into the wider community. The huge financial losses have devastated the grandiose plans for the future, together with the capacity to influence other Australian dioceses and the Anglican Communion. The credibility of the diocese's leaders responsible for the financial disaster, most of them key leaders in other areas as well, has been tarnished. And with Jensen's retirement looming in 2013, there is no clear candidate to succeed him. The Knox experiment is facing failure.

The national church might have survived intact, but only just. The wash up of decades of radicalism has left a trail of damage in the Anglican Church of Australia. The 23 dioceses no longer share a prayer book, ministry patterns, or genuinely shared financial responsibilities. 'Independent' churches affiliated with Sydney Diocese have intruded into other dioceses, compromising diocesan autonomy.

---

[1] Muriel Porter, *The New Puritans: The Rise of Fundamentalism in the Anglican Church* (Melbourne: Melbourne University Press, 2006).

The most serious threat to national unity, however, is Sydney Synod's decision to reject the decision of the Appellate Tribunal on lay and diaconal presidency. This is unprecedented, and calls into question the whole constitutional arrangement. Though as yet neither the Primate, nor the House of Bishops, nor the General Synod Standing Committee seem to know how to respond, this could prove to be the straw that breaks the camel's back. On the other hand, if they fail to exert at the very least significant moral pressure on Sydney to ensure the church's constitution is upheld, then their own credibility is at stake.

The next little while will be difficult, but I am hopeful that in time the traditional Anglican penchant for moderation will prevail in Sydney. Hardline young clergy keen to plant new churches and save the world, beginning with Sydney, might be eager to usher in the Puritan reformation of the Knox teaching, but many Sydney parishes are still populated by people who just want to be Anglicans. And moderation is a central attribute of Anglican DNA; extremism is not. When they travel interstate and experience the ministry of women priests or more traditional prayer book worship, these ordinary parishioners are often delighted and relieved. Extremism such as currently characterizes Sydney Diocese cannot last for very long in a mainstream church in a culture such as Australia's. Even in the Synod, the 'loyal opposition' is growing a little. The recent financial debates showed that, where once just one or two voices might speak up to challenge the hierarchy, now a few more are prepared to ask hard questions publicly. The growing awareness that the Second Coming has in fact not yet arrived may embolden them further. The Knox legacy will take time to peter out; there will be no overnight change. But in time a more reasonable, generous, kindly form of Anglicanism may re-emerge in Sydney. It will still be conservative in character and low-church in worship style, but hopefully it will be respectful of other Anglican traditions and points of view. And respectful of the national church whose good name and reputation it enjoys. It might even, one day, be more willing to embrace the leadership of women. That would be a great day for Anglicans in Sydney, in Australia, and around the world.

Select Bibliography

Books

Bates, Stephen, *A Church at War: Anglicans and Homosexuality* (London: I.B. Tauris, 2004).
Behnke, Donna A., *Religious Issues in Nineteenth Century Feminism* (New York: Whitston Publishing, 1982).
Bendroth, Margaret Lamberts, *Fundamentalism and Gender: 1875 to the Present* (New Haven, CT and London: Yale University Press, 1993).
Birkett, Kirsten, *The Essence of Family* (Kingsford NSW: Matthias Media, 2004).
Blombery, 'Tricia, *The Anglicans in Australia* (Canberra: Australian Government Publishing Service, 1996).
Bolt, Peter, Thompson, Mark and Tong, Robert (eds), *The Lord's Supper in Human Hands: Epilogue* (Sydney: Australian Church Record and Anglican Church League, 2010).
Cameron, Marcia, *An Enigmatic Life: David Broughton Knox, Father of Contemporary Sydney Anglicanism* (Brunswick East: Acorn Press, 2006).
Carnley, Peter, *Reflections in Glass: Trends and Tensions in the Contemporary Anglican Church* (Sydney: HarperCollins, 2004).
Clark, Elizabeth and Richardson, Herbert (eds), *Women and Religion: A Feminist Sourcebook of Christian Thought* (New York: Harper & Row, 1977).
Coleman, Peter, *Christian Attitudes to Homosexuality* (London: SPCK, 1980).
Collinson, Patrick, *The Elizabethan Puritan Movement* (London: Jonathan Cape, 1967).
——, *The Reformation* (London: Weidenfeld & Nicolson, 2003).
Cowdell, Scott and Porter, Muriel (eds), *Lost in Translation? Anglicans, Controversy and the Bible, Perspectives from the Doctrine Commission of the Anglican Church of Australia* (Melbourne: Desbooks, 2004).
Cross, F.L. and Livingstone, E.A. (eds), *The Oxford Dictionary of the Christian Church*, third edition (Oxford: Oxford University Press, 1997).
Davis, John, *Australian Anglicans and their Constitution* (Melbourne: Acorn Press, 1993).
DeBerg, Betty A., *Ungodly Women: Gender and the First Wave of American Fundamentalism* (Minneapolis, MN: Fortress Press, 1990).
Edwards, Ruth B., *The Case for Women's Ministry* (London: SPCK, 1989).
Fisher, Judi and Wood, Janet (eds), *A Place at the Table: Women at the Last Supper* (Melbourne: Joint Board of Christian Education, 1993).
Giles, Kevin, *Women and Their Ministry: A Case for Equal Ministries in the Church Today* (Melbourne: Dove, 1977).

———, *Created Woman: A Fresh Study of the Biblical Teaching* (Canberra: Acorn Press, 1985).
———, *The Trinity and Subordinationism: The Doctrine of God and the Contemporary Gender Debate* (Downers Grove, IL: InterVarsity Press, 2002).
Grocott, Allan M., *Convicts, Clergymen and Churches: Attitudes of Convicts and Ex-Convicts towards the Churches and Clergy in New South Wales from 1788 to 1851* (Sydney: Sydney University Press, 1980).
Harris, Harriet A., *Fundamentalism and Evangelicals* (Oxford: Clarendon, 1998).
Heeney, Brian, *The Women's Movement in the Church of England 1850–1930* (Oxford: Clarendon, 1988).
Hogan, Michael, *The Sectarian Strand: Religion in Australian History* (Ringwood: Penguin 1987).
Hole, Judith and Levine, Ellen, *Rebirth of Feminism* (New York: Quadrangle Books, 1971).
Jensen, Peter, *The Revelation of God: Contours in Christian Theology* (Leicester: InterVarsity Press, 2002).
Judd, Stephen and Cable, Kenneth, *Sydney Anglicans: A History of the Diocese* (Sydney: Anglican Information Office, 2000).
Lawton, William James, *The Better Time To Be: Utopian Attitudes to Society among Sydney Anglicans 1885 to 1914* (Sydney: University of New South Wales Press, 1990).
Marshall, Colin, *Passing the Baton: A Handbook for Ministry Apprenticeship* (Kingsford NSW: Matthias Media, 2007).
McGillion, Chris, *The Chosen Ones: The Politics of Salvation in the Anglican Church* (Sydney: Allen & Unwin, 2004).
Millikan, David, *Imperfect Company: Power and Control in an Australian Christian Cult* (Melbourne: William Heinemann Australia and ABC Books, 1991).
Morris, Leon, Gaden, John and Thiering, Barbara, *A Woman's Place: Anglican Doctrine Commission Papers on the Role of Women in the Church* (Sydney: Anglican Information Office, 1976).
New Revised Standard Version of the Bible, by the Division of Christian Education of the National Council of Churches in the USA (1989, 1995).
Nichols, Alan (ed.), *The Bible and Women's Ministry: An Australian Dialogue* (Canberra: Acorn Press, 1990).
Nicolson, Adam, *God's Secretaries* (New York: HarperCollins, 2003).
Piggin, Stuart, *Evangelical Christianity in Australia: Spirit, Word and World* (Melbourne: Oxford University Press, 1996).
Porter, Muriel, *Women in the Church: The Great Ordination Debate in Australia* (Ringwood: Penguin, 1989).
———, *Sex, Marriage and the Church: Patterns of Change* (North Blackburn: Dove, 1996).
———, *Sex, Power and the Clergy* (Melbourne: Hardie Grant Books, 2003).

——, *The New Puritans: The Rise of Fundamentalism in the Anglican Church* (Melbourne: Melbourne University Publishing, 2006).

Reid, J.R., *Marcus L. Loane: A Biography* (Melbourne: Acorn Press, 2004).

Ruether, Rosemary Radford, *Christianity and the Making of the Modern Family* (London: SCM Press, 2001).

Summers, Anne, *Damned Whores and God's Police: The Colonization of Women in Australia* (Ringwood: Penguin, 1975).

The Doctrine Panel of the Anglican Church of Australia, *Faithfulness in Fellowship: Reflections on Homosexuality and the Church* (Melbourne: John Garratt Publishing, 2001).

Journal Articles, Book Chapters and Conference Papers

Golding, Douglas, 'Endangered Species? "Mainstream" Anglicans in the Diocese of Sydney', paper delivered at the conference *From Augustine to Anglicanism: Anglicans in Australia and beyond*, St Francis College, Brisbane, 14 February 2010.

Hilliard, David, 'Sydney Anglicans and Homosexuality', *Journal of Homosexuality*, 33(2) (1997), 101–23.

——, 'Gender Roles, Homosexuality, and the Anglican Church in Sydney', *Gender and Christian Religion*, Studies in Church History, 34 (Suffolk: Ecclesiastical History Society, 1998), 509–23.

Mason, Keith, 'Believers in Court: Sydney Anglicans Going to Law', The Cable Lecture 2005, delivered at St James' Church, King Street, Sydney, 9 September 2005.

Methuen, Charlotte, 'Vidua – Presbytera – Episcopa: Women with Oversight in the Early Church', *Theology*, May/June (2005), 163–77.

Porter, Muriel, 'The End of the "Great Debate": The 1992 General Synod Decision on Women Priests', in Mark Hutchinson and Edmund Campion (eds), *Long Patient Conflict: Essays on Women and Gender in Australian Christianity* (Sydney: Centre for the Study of Australian Christianity, 1994).

——, 'Women in Purple: Women Bishops in Australia', *Voices: Quarterly Essays on Religion in Australia*, 1(2) (2008).

——, 'Paying the Price: An Australian Perspective', in Peter Francis (ed.), *Rebuilding Communion: Who Pays the Price? From the Lambeth Conference 1998 to the Lambeth Conference 2008 and Beyond* (Hawarden: Monad Press, 2008).

Reid, Duncan, 'Anglican Diversity and Conflict: A Case Study on God, Gender and Authority', in Bruce Kaye (ed.), *'Wonderful and Confessedly Strange': Australian Essays in Anglican Ecclesiology* (Adelaide: ATF Press, 2006).

Robinson, Donald W.B., 'David Broughton Knox: An Appreciation', in Peter T. O'Brien and David G. Peterson (eds), *God Who is Rich in Mercy: Essays Presented to Dr D.B. Knox* (Sydney: Lancer Books, 1986).

Sherlock, Peter, '"Leave it to the Women": The Exclusion of Women from Anglican Church Government in Australia', *Australian Historical Studies*, 39(3) (2008), 288–304.

Smart, Judith, 'The Evangelist as Star: The Billy Graham Crusade in Australia, 1959', *Journal of Popular Culture*, 33(1) (Summer 1999), 165–75.

Thompson, Mark D., 'The Church of God and the Anglican Church of Australia', in Bruce Kaye (ed.), *'Wonderful and Confessedly Strange': Australian Essays in Anglican Ecclesiology* (Adelaide: ATF Press, 2006).

Index

A Prayer Book for Australia 1995 9, 10, 77, 133n
Adam, Canon Dr Peter 116
Adelaide, Diocese of 91
Agnew, Del 50
Agnew, Nancy 50
Agnew, Vera 50
An Australian Prayer Book 1978 10, 105
Andrews, Deaconess Mary 113
'AngGays' 67
Anglican Church League 4n, 36-38, 41
Anglican Church of Australia xiii, 1, 6-9, 28, 46, 63, 68, 69, 82, 83, 123, 163
Anglican Church of Canada 2, 3, 6, 7, 53, 55, 58, 62, 99, 123, 129, 160
Anglican Church of North America 3
Anglican Church of Southern Africa 61
Anglican Communion xiii, xiv, xv, 1, 2, 3, 6, 7, 8, 9, 17, 41, 52, 53, 54, 56-61, 63, 64, 74, 78, 79, 89, 98, 99, 103, 107, 120, 153, 154, 163
Anglican Consultative Council 3, 78, 79
Anglican Covenant 59
'Anglicans Together' 140
Appellate Tribunal xiii, 6, 7, 82, 83-86, 89, 91-98, 102, 103, 106-109, 111, 164
Armidale, Diocese of 4, 81
Aspinall, Archbishop Phillip 51, 52, 61, 92, 103, 106
Assemblies of God 27
Association for the Apostolic Ministry 86-87
Australian Fellowship of Evangelical Students (AFES) 5, 158

Ballantine-Jones, the Revd Bruce 44, 147
Ballarat, Diocese of 81
Baptist Union of NSW 138
Barry, Bishop Alfred 35, 36
Bates, Stephen 54-55, 57, 75

Beal, Bishop Robert 88
'Better Gatherings' 9, 10
Bishopscourt, Sydney 150-153
Bleby, Justice David 89
Boleyn, Anne 25
Bolt, the Revd Dr Peter 160
Book of Common Prayer 1662 9, 10, 11, 33, 39, 105, 109
Bradford, the Revd Philip 140-141
Brain, Bishop Peter 92, 95n, 105
Brown, Antoinette Louisa 120
Bryson, Dr A.M. 71
Burke, Kelly 11n, 22

Cable, Dr Ken 35-37, 39
Cameron, Neil 82n, 95n
Canon Concerning Services 1992 102
Canonical Fitness 6, 91-96
Carnley, Archbishop Peter 22, 23, 42, 51, 67, 82, 84-85, 87, 88, 114, 116, 117, 123
Catherine of Aragon 25
Catholic Church 1, 21, 136-138
Census 1, 135n, 136, 137 140
Chin, Richard 5
Chiswell, Bishop Peter 88
Christ Church St Laurence, Railway Square, Sydney 11, 36
Christian Reformed Church 139
Chukwuma, Bishop Emmanuel 55
Church of England 3, 17, 23, 25, 26, 29, 30, 33, 36, 39, 46, 53, 55, 57, 58, 65, 66, 89, 90, 91, 92, 93, 94, 109, 113, 120, 136
Church of England Canon Law 46, 92-94
Church of England in South Africa 61
Church planting 4, 5, 11, 141, 142, 147, 157, 158, 159, 160
Churches of Christ 138
Collinson, Dr Patrick 25

Cox, Mr Justice 84
Cranmer, Archbishop Thomas 25

Darling, Bishop Barbara 5n, 96
Davies, Bishop Glenn 16, 56, 102-107, 159, 160
Dawani, Bishop Suheil 62
Diaconal presidency xiii, xv, 6, 7, 12, 77, 94, 97-111, 154-155, 163-164
Divorce 74-75, 97, 133, 137
Donatism 110
Dowling, Bishop Owen 39, 84-87
Driscoll, Mark 156-159

Edward VI 23-25
Elizabeth I 23, 25, 26
'Equal But Different' 115, 125, 129
Evangelism Ministries 147, 158

Fellowship of Confessing Anglicans (FCA) 2, 62-64, 148
Fellowship of Congregational Churches 139
Fisher, Archbishop Geoffrey 46
Forsyth, Bishop Robert 9n, 21, 152, 153, 160
Forty-two Articles of Religion 23, 25
Full-time Paid Ministry in the Diocese of Sydney 102
Fundamentalism 12-20, 34, 114, 120
Furlong, Monica 113

Gaden, the Revd Dr John 123
GAFCON (Global Anglican Future conference) 2, 3, 7, 53, 60, 62-64, 145, 153
GAFCON Primates' Council 62, 148
General Synod Canon/Church Law Commission 88, 89, 93
General Synod Doctrine Commission 67, 68, 71, 80, 82
General Synod Standing Committee 69, 78, 82, 88, 90n, 94, 96, 164
General Synod, Australia 24n, 36, 45-48, 78-79, 80, 84, 91, 96, 98, 102, 103, 104, 107, 121, 159, 163
1950 46
1955 47

1966 96
1977 10, 123
1985 81-83
1987 81, 83, 114
1989 81, 83, 92-94
1992 81, 85-89
1995 9, 10, 133n
1998 89
2001 90
2004 51, 68, 90, 101, 110, 128-129
2007 52, 69, 95
2010 59, 64, 96, 111
Geneva Push, The 158-159
George, Archbishop Ian 85, 88
Giles, the Revd Dr Kevin 13, 16n, 72, 115-116, 130
Glasspool, Bishop Mary 59
Glebe Administration Board 45, 143-144, 146-147, 149
Global South 60, 62, 99, 100
Golding, Douglas, Dr 11n
Goldsworthy, Bishop Kay 96
Goodhew, Archbishop Harry 10, 11n, 17-19, 22, 53, 55, 81, 94, 98, 99, 100, 122
Gough, Archbishop Hugh 39-40, 44, 159
Graham, Billy 40, 43-44, 122
Grindrod, Archbishop Sir John 123
Grubb, George G. 36

Hammond, T.C. 37-40, 47, 49, 52, 116-117
Hayward, Peter 160
Hazlewood, Bishop John 88
Heard, Andrew 158
Hearn, Bishop George 84-85
Henry VIII 25
Herft, Archbishop Roger 92
Hilliard, Dr David 67, 71
Hillsong Church, Sydney 27
Hobson, Theo 63
Holland, Bishop Alf 84-85
Homosexuality xv, 7, 20, 31, 32, 53-58, 59n, 61, 64-71, 73, 75, 97, 110, 130, 132
Hong Kong, Diocese of 113, 123
Horsburgh, Professor Michael 27
Hunter, Bishop Barry 88

Irish Church Missions, Dublin 37

Jarrett, Archdeacon Narelle 108
Jensen, Mrs Christine 125
Jensen, Mrs Helen 125
Jensen, the Revd Dr Michael 12n, 14n, 110n
Jensen, Archbishop Peter xiv, xv, xvi, 1n, 2, 3, 7, 8, 10n, 12, 13, 14, 15, 17, 18, 19, 20, 21, 31, 32, 41, 42, 44, 50n, 51, 52, 53, 55, 56, 58, 59, 60, 61, 62, 63, 64, 65n, 67, 71n, 79, 81, 95n, 98, 99, 100, 101, 102, 103, 107, 108, 109n, 110, 111, 117, 122, 125, 128, 130, 131, 135, 138, 139, 140, 141, 142, 143, 144, 145, 146, 149, 150, 151, 152, 153, 159, 160, 161, 163
Jensen, Dean Phillip 3, 4, 5, 10, 21, 22, 23, 44, 57, 106, 107, 125, 131n, 156, 163
Jerusalem Declaration 63
John, Dean Jeffrey 55-58
Johnson, the Revd Richard 30, 34
Judd, Dr Stephen 35, 36, 37, 39, 152

Kell, Peter 148
Kingston, Margo 87
Knox, the Revd Dr Broughton 7, 14n, 40-43, 46, 47, 49, 50, 66, 67, 71, 77, 78, 80, 81, 98, 100, 108, 109, 123, 124, 163, 164

Lambeth Conference 3, 79
  1888 74
  1920 118, 120, 129
  1958 54
  1968 129
  1988 54
  1998 2, 53-55, 57, 68, 99, 129
  2008 60, 61, 62, 129, 146
Lay Assistants at Holy Communion Canon 1973 102, 104, 106
Lay presidency xv, 6, 7, 51, 77, 88, 94, 97-111, 163, 164
Lee, Bishop Ivan 160
Li, the Revd Tim Oi 113, 123

Loane, Archbishop Sir Marcus 24, 31, 35n, 40-41, 49, 50
Lynch, Mikey 158-159

Marriage celebrants 137
Mars Hill Church, Seattle 156, 158
Marsden, the Revd Samuel 30, 34
Marshall, Colin 3
Mary I 25
Mason, Justice Keith xiii, 80, 82n, 97
Matthias Media 5, 131
McGillion, Chris 8n, 17, 44
McGowan, Canon Dr Andrew 101
Melbourne Diocese 1, 4, 66, 91, 108, 148, 149, 154
Melbourne Synod 66, 72, 83, 96
'Memorial', The 38
Methodist Church 32, 33, 122, 129, 139n
Millikan, David 49
Ministry Training Strategy (MTS) 3-5, 121
Ministry, Training and Development 4, 156-157
Mission (the Diocese of Sydney's) 7, 19-21, 32, 100, 135-142, 154, 159, 163
Mission Board Strategy Committee 148

Moore Theological College xv, xvi, 2, 3, 5, 7, 9, 35, 37, 38, 39, 40, 41, 44, 47, 52, 67, 72, 77, 78, 81, 98, 100, 108, 115, 116, 121, 138, 141, 148, 155, 156, 160, 161
Morris, the Revd Dr Leon 71-72, 123
Mowll, Archbishop Howard 5, 37-40, 42, 47

National Church Life Survey 1, 135, 137
National Council of Churches 78-79
Neo-Calvinism 156-157
New Westminster, Diocese of (Canada) 58, 160
Newcastle, Diocese of 104
Newell, Bishop Phillip 85
Nicols, Canon Alan 72
Nicolson, Adam 26, 27n
North West Australia, Diocese of 45, 81
NSW Council of Churches 138

O'Reilly, Canon Dr Colleen 81
Order of Perpetual Indulgence 68
Ordination Service for Deacons Canon 1985 102, 105-107
Orombi, Archbishop Henry 63

Pell, Cardinal George 31, 32
Penman, Archbishop David 72, 82-83
Pentecostalists 27, 136, 138, 146, 157
Perth, Diocese of 81, 84-85
Pfahlert, Ben 3
Phillimore, Robert 93
Phillip, Governor Arthur 30
Piggin, Dr Stuart 35, 49-50, 70
Polygamy 54, 56
Pope John Paul II 31
Pope Paul VI 31
Poulos, the Revd Archie 160
Presbyterian Church 32, 33, 97, 110, 122, 139
Primmer, the Revd Dalba 86
Propositional revelation 14, 41-42, 44, 49
Puritans, Puritanism xiv, 13, 17, 20, 25-27, 109, 111, 163, 164

Rayner, Archbishop Keith 84-87, 88n, 98, 123
'Red Book', the 38-39
'Reform' 57-58
Reformation, the 17, 24-27, 38, 46, 47, 66n, 93, 98, 109, 111, 138, 163, 164
Reid, the Revd Dr Duncan 14, 41-43
Ridley (College), Melbourne 4, 72
Robarts, the Revd David 86
Roberts, the Revd Craig 152
Robinson, Archbishop Donald 10, 40, 41, 47, 49, 50, 78, 80, 81, 86, 87n, 88, 94, 95n, 98
Robinson, Bishop Gene 58-61, 65, 75

Salier, the Revd Dr Bill 160n
Salvation Army, the 120, 139
Saumarez Smith, Bishop William 36
Scandrett, Dr Laurence 86
Seymour, Jane 25
Shand, Michael QC 103

Shead, the Revd Dr Andrew 160n
Sherlock, the Revd Dr Charles 24, 72
Shirriff, Phil 147
Short, David 3, 58, 160
'Sinless perfection' 34, 49, 111
Slavery 15-16, 117, 119, 120, 130
Smart, Dr Judith 43
Spong, Bishop Jack 9
Spry, Dr Ian 86, 88
St Andrew's Cathedral 3, 10, 11, 23, 36, 148, 149, 157, 163
St Andrew's House 149-151
St James' Church, King Street, Sydney 11
St John's Church, Shaughnessy, Diocese of New Westminster 58
St Matthias' Church, Centennial Park, Sydney 5, 23, 122
Stewart, Bishop Al 158, 159, 160
Subordinationism 115-117, 124
Summers, Anne 29
Sydney Diocese, Doctrine Commission 98, 116
Sydney Diocese, Ethics and Social Questions Committee 66
Sydney Diocese, financial crisis 8, 142-154
Sydney Synod xiii, xvi, 1n, 2, 6, 8, 10, 17, 18, 19, 37, 41, 44, 47, 53, 57, 63-64, 67, 68, 79, 80-81, 82, 87, 94, 95, 97, 98, 99, 100, 101, 102, 103, 104, 106, 107, 108, 131n, 135, 136, 140, 141, 143, 144, 145, 146, 147, 148, 149, 150, 151, 152, 153, 154, 155, 164
Sydney Synod Standing Committee 59, 60, 61, 67, 79, 80, 86, 87, 92, 94, 136, 143, 144, 146, 147, 148, 151, 153, 159

Tasker, Bishop Peter 99, 100, 141
The Episcopal Church (TEC) 2, 6, 53, 54, 55, 58, 59, 60, 99
The Murray, Diocese of 81
Thirty-nine Articles of Religion 23-24, 33, 110
Thomas, Bishop Max 123
Thompson, the Revd Dr Mark 78, 160
'Tinker Tailor' 49, 114

Tong, Robert 95n
Tutu, Archbishop Desmond 55

Uniting Church in Australia 97, 122, 129, 138, 139

Walden, Bishop Graham 88
Wangaratta, Diocese of 81
Watson, Archbishop Peter 91
Wesley, Charles 33
Wesley, John 16, 33
Whitefield, George 33
Wilberforce, William 16, 33
Williams, Archbishop Rowan 6, 56, 57, 60, 61, 63, 64, 103
Wilson, Bishop Bruce 84-85
Wilson, Bishop John 72

Windsor Report 59, 100
Women, bishops xv, 6, 8, 48, 51, 72, 83, 89-96, 102, 108, 114, 128, 129
Women, ordination of 5, 7, 8, 20, 31, 32, 39, 43, 47, 48, 50, 65, 66, 70, 71, 72, 77, 80-89, 93, 94, 96, 97, 98, 99, 107, 108, 110, 111, 113-134, 163, 164
Women, role 8, 13, 16, 65, 70, 71, 75, 113-134
Woodhouse, Canon Dr John 155-156, 161
Woods, Archbishop Sir Frank 123
World Council of Churches 78-79
Wright, Bishop Tom 64
Wylde, Bishop Arnold 38-39

Young, Justice Peter 95